Paul Mosher: Psychoanalytic Citizen and Visionary

Paul Mosher: Psychoanalytic Citizen and Visionary

Judith S. Schachter, Editor

IPBOOKS.net
International Psychoanalytic Books

International Psychoanalytic Books (IPBooks)
New York • http://www.IPBooks.net

Paul Mosher: Psychoanalytic Citizen and Visionary

Published by IPBooks, Queens, NY
Online at: www.IPBooks.net

Front cover photo by Paul W. Mosher
Front cover layout by Kathy Kovacic, Blackthorn Studio
Interior layout and design by Noel S. Morado

ISBN: 978-1-956864-23-6

Contents

The Work

The Impact

Editor's Note

The announcement of Paul Mosher's unanticipated death on September 14, 2021, unleashed a torrent of emotionally rich personal memories from grieving friends and colleagues. As editor of this memorial volume I have read, contained, and ordered a selection of spontaneous responses and selected a few substantive contributions to highlight the range of his genius and enable us to appreciate and be thankful for all he gave us.

New to us is the unfinished autobiography he'd embarked on as his health was failing, meant for his five grandchildren. Stimulated by an "immersive" dream, diverting to a discussion of Penfield, we then are introduced to the graphic details and sequelae of his traumatic childhood struggles with Legg-Perthes disease. The draft material is reproduced with minimal editing. The Personal Statement, although written years earlier to describe his lifelong immersion in the digital world, touches glancingly on the intervening years. With it we include a working document that allows us access to Paul's careful decision making.

Personal disclosures emphasized that through his physician father, he was privy to the well-known corruption of the Albany police department, predisposing him to forge a clear ethical code and a fine nose for corruption. A favorite cartoon showed businessmen seated at a table, one stating, "let's draw a clear ethical line and then see how close we can get to it." Jeffrey Berman's description of their work together on "Confidentiality" and their two subsequent books about psychiatric transgressions, indicates how central to his identity was his moral core. In addition we can find in that essay Paul's moving discussion of what retirement felt like to him

Paul's childhood hospitalizations led to a more isolated life, with scrupulous exercising, and careful financial planning due to a doctor's warning that he'd be a cripple in his 50's. Jonah Schein delineates how the APsaA Finance Committee benefitted from his interests and skills. Paul was proud both of his investment strategies and his graphic skills, and was pleased that, after many years, his fact based research was incorporated into APsaA's investment strategies and governance. While Harvard and medical school are only alluded to in the autobiographies, he was proud of his frequently still referenced cardiology paper which we include, of his licensed stint on the radio station and of his home for four years, Dunster House. All remained close to his heart. The LSD record of his personal experiment, suggested by Tom Bartlett, is an example of his grasp of opportunities to learn and expand his understanding. Overall, we discern Paul's drive to pursue each interest to the highest expertise and proficiency in the significant achievements of a radio license, his professional computing/programming skills, legal research, and parliamentary concerns. All exhibit that trait, as do his papers written with carefully selected and respected partners who enhanced his range and mastery.

The transition to psychoanalytic education was not smooth; his formidable aunt by marriage, Henriette Klein, warned him that his relentless questioning of received wisdom made a comfortable career in New York unlikely. He, then married to Paula, returned to Albany, and a successful psychoanalytic practice in a charming small private office near the medical center and the state law library. He raised his family in a secluded house far from the city and there, from Apple II days on, began to create and sell programs, as both Neils describe, and he continued to study and embrace new computer languages. A copy of a personal, early experiment with computerized design, a mash-up celebrating the 1996 APsaA meeting that is a playful example of the centrality of organizational psychoanalysis in his life and his visions for its future is reproduced on the inside back cover of this book. A later, beautiful photograph of the Taiwan 101 skyscraper on the book's cover is Paul's unique view of that country's tallest (1,671 feet) innovative, earthquake resistant building, itself a symbol that combines aspiration, creativity, and stability.

The hierarchical rigidities visible at psychoanalytic meetings and the chaos he observed in organizational functioning led him to frequent the adjacent NY State Law Library to research Not for Profit Corporation law and join with others who were committed to creating change in APsaA governance. Despite his planned retreat from psychoanalytic battles, he became the intellectual engine of this struggle through his "Civics Lessons," published online, that enabled him to reach and inform a newly activated membership and enrich and undergird organizational change. At the time of these initiatives, Leon Hoffman further articulated the bicameral organizational concept inimical to Paul's historical and legal interpretations as he contended against Paul's view which you can read in Civics Lessons 3, 4, and 5 in chapter 15. Paul's reliance on Robert's Rules became an "in" joke that Bob Galatzer-Levy describes. It, characteristically, led Paul to participate in a parliamentarians' study group to improve his skills.

Paul's generous contribution of his self-conceived and published *Jourlit* invited and supported his colleagues' pleasures in research and prepared the membership for investment in the creation of PEP. The Members List as well as private email lists followed. Student members, as Tom Bartlett describes, benefitted worldwide from his mentoring of those who sought the ability to reach outside isolated consulting rooms to find likeminded others. Paul, unappreciated as a candidate, surely realized that his critiques of the status quo, especially certification, while empowering of others and moving them from precarious positions, might again stimulate his own marginalization, subsequently demonstrated by a shameful lack of recognition by the Sigourney Trust.

One of the pleasures of collecting the essays for this volume was my introduction to Paul's carefully chosen work partners. I have been impressed anew with his range of talents and interests and the intensity with which they were pursued, his stable rationality, and his sense of humor. It has highlighted many aspects of this brilliant, creative man who was a kind, loving and significant mentor to those less endowed. He befriended me as an elected officer and was a responsive, consistent, thoughtful, often acerbic friend. A generative partner to many, he enhanced and encompassed us all.

Judith S. Schachter

Personal Note:
Sigourney Award Nomination Letter

Though diminutive in stature, Paul Mosher was a giant in American psychoanalysis. His contributions had a profound effect on the course of APsaA's history in many, many ways. Paul's intelligence was formidable, and he was a great teacher. I learned more from him about more things than from any teacher I ever had. He was the big brother that I never had.

The best way to inform you of his accomplishments is to provide the letter (below) that I wrote in 2018, recommending him for a Sigourney Award. Why he didn't receive a Sigourney rests on many things, but not on Paul. He later won a Sigourney Award as a part of the PEP team.

You will read of Paul's many accomplishments in this letter and in this book, but I want to share some personal experience of Paul that will reveal just how incredibly broad and deep were his interests and his breadth of knowledge. For several years, Paul hosted a monthly study group about the formative years of psychoanalysis. Our small group first read Frederick Crews's book, *The Making of an Illusion,* marveling at the cynicism, venom and implacability in Crews's systematic attack on Freud, and how hypocritically, or possibly without awareness, Crews used his own psychodynamic speculations to discredit Freud's psychodynamic speculations about others and to disparage Freud's theory building. In many ways, however, the book raised our curiosity about some of Crews's assertions. Paul discovered and supplied us with one reference after another so that we could study Freud and this formative period in psychoanalytic history from many angles. These included many papers on hysteria, Freud's patients, Freud's relationship with his disciples and with family members, his neuroses and experiences with cocaine, his dreams, his aspirations, his proprietary feelings about psychoanalysis that were based on these aspirations, the consequences for psychoanalysis as a science, and so on. What a course our syllabus would make! The breadth and depth of our reading were based on Paul's ongoing discoveries of new subjects to consider.

Paul's broad and deep interests also included artificial intelligence, the evidence base for the efficacy of psychoanalysis and psychotherapy and the relationship between the two. He became interested in memory and could not understand why new findings about memory did not interest and inspire discussion among us listserv subscribers after he posted about it, along with references, to the Members List. He was fascinated also by the findings of Ramachandran on phantom limb and mirror neurons, and many more topics. See the books he wrote with Jeffrey Berman to see the range and depth of his mind at work.

Paul researched and wrote about things as if he were an eyewitness, because he went to the sources. His understandings of APsaA's history, the not-for-profit corporation law and the Jaffee-Redmond case are examples. APsaA's Regional Association designation is another example. After we looked into it together, we discovered how it evolved, and what autonomy it gave to APsaA in the area of educational standards. I then was able to share our findings with the APsaA Executive Committee, on which I served as Secretary, during the development of the APsaA Six Point Plan. I will never forget how one of the BOPS leaders expressed outright disbelief at our assertions. At this, I had an inner reaction of outrage mixed with glee, because I was confident that we were right. A search of the IPA website and a letter from the IPA Executive Director proved us correct, and paved the way for the development of the evolution of APsaA and its Standards that continues today.

To close this introduction, I want to comment on Paul's excellent self-esteem and humility, a combination that you don't see that often. It is what made him a great teacher, because he never condescended to others. In fact, he assumed that others were on his plane, and he often asked people for their opinions about his own writing. He sent drafts of his chapters to several of his friends and was grateful for our suggestions, questions, and proofreading and always acknowledged our contributions. It's hard to believe that Paul is gone, because he had an aura of permanence and constancy as if he always had been here and always would be.

Sigourney Award Nomination Letter (2018)

It gives me great pleasure to nominate my colleague, Paul Mosher MD, for the Sigourney Award. Dr. Mosher has practiced psychoanalysis for the past 45 years in Albany, New York where he is also a Clinical Professor of Psychiatry at Albany Medical College. As a result of his genius, his vision and his particular combination of talents, he has made several profoundly important, unique and on-going contributions to psychoanalysis that have transformed it in fundamental ways over the last half-century.

SCHOLARSHIP

In the last several years, Dr. Mosher, along with Jeffrey Berman, has turned to scholarly work and published a fascinating book entitled *Confidentiality and Its Discontents: Dilemmas of Privacy in Psychotherapy*. New York: Fordham 2015. It received the 2016 "Courage to Dream Book Award" from the American Psychoanalytic Association. It is a virtual casebook for the practicing psychoanalyst and psychotherapist, as well as the interested public. We know that Freud promised his patients absolute confidentiality, but legal developments in the last half-century have often put psychotherapists in the role of "double agents" with dual and often conflicting allegiances to patient and society. This book explores the human stories arising from the loss of confidentiality and addresses different types of psychotherapy breaches, beginning with the story of the novelist Philip Roth, examining the duty to protect, the landmark Jaffe v Redmond case, the murder case of Robert Bierenbaum and the harassment story of former N.Y. State Chief Judge, Sol Wachtler. All of these cases confirm that the fear of the loss of confidentiality may prevent a person from seeking treatment with disastrous results and affirm the importance of the psychotherapist-patient privilege.

He and Berman are currently well along on a two volume work concerned with boundary violations and other serious ethical transgressions in psychoanalysis and allied fields. It will be of great use to students, scholars and historians of our field. The most important point of this effort, and one that makes Dr. Mosher worthy of the Sigourney Award, is that this is a difficult area for psychoanalysts to confront, and Dr. Mosher possesses the courage and equanimity to research, describe and analyze this history, in order to educate us to the dangers and seductions inherent in the powerful position that we occupy as psychoanalysts and psychotherapists.

Licensure Activities

Dr. Mosher represents the highest standards of psychoanalysis as a member of the New York State Board for Mental Health Practitioners, which works with the New York State Department of Education in the regulation of the training and practice of licensed psychoanalysts and certain other mental health practitioners in that state. These regulations often serve as models for other regulatory bodies.

Reimbursement for Psychoanalytic Treatment

Dr. Mosher played the lead role in the 2011 initiative to make the case for an increase in the Medicare reimbursement (the RVU) for psychoanalysis, relative to other psychotherapy codes. This change in reimbursement has been incorporated in the regulations. For the first time, individual sessions of psychoanalysis are compensated at a higher rate than other psychotherapy sessions of comparable length within this major government program. This change could have significant long-term implications for the recognition of psychoanalysis as a procedure, and for the enhancement of psychoanalytic practice.

Two lifelong interests have resulted in even more significant contributions. These are:

1. The spread of knowledge and the opening of the psychoanalytic literature to an international audience through computerization of the psychoanalytic literature.
2. A refined view and deep understanding of the legal issues involved in the needs and limits of confidentiality in the practice of psychoanalysis and the associated psychotherapies.

Dissemination of the Psychoanalytic Literature Through Computerization

An early computer adopter in the 1970's, Paul Mosher began to index the psychoanalytic literature as a member of the APsaA Committee on Indexing. In the 1980's, he began the *Jourlit* project. On his own and at his own expense, he created and printed the camera-ready copy for the *Title Key and Author Index to Psychoanalytic Journals*, a bound reference volume which went through two editions and sold over 2,000 copies. He DONATED it to APsaA. It was the first practical consolidated index to the psychoanalytic journal literature across a number of journals, and at the time it bridged a gap that eventually closed when personal computers became more widely available.

In its time, it introduced scholars and educational institutions to a unique resource, which they relied upon for the better part of a decade, before the development of the Internet.

Eventually it became clear to Dr. Mosher that technology had developed sufficiently that a CD ROM could be produced to contain searchable full texts and he turned his attention to that endeavor. The product of that initiative, the PEP (Psychoanalytic Electronic Publishing) enterprise, of which Dr. Mosher remains a founding Board member, is a not-for-profit entity funded jointly by the American Psychoanalytic Association and the British institute of Psychoanalysis. It has now grown into PEP Web, an Internet database containing the entire significant psychoanalytic literature, including all of the significant psychoanalytic journals, the Standard Edition of Freud's work and other essential texts. PEP Web is now available on computers in the homes and offices of psychoanalysts worldwide, as well as to students of psychoanalysis and countless scholars who are now able to access our literature in university libraries. Analytic groups in countries such as China, where interest in psychoanalysis is newly developing, but where library-based psychoanalytic literature resources have never existed, can now rely on PEP Web for access to the psychoanalytic literature. The development of PEP may be the single most important contribution in the history of psychoanalysis to the fostering of psychoanalytic scholarship and research.

CONFIDENTIALITY OF THE PSYCHOTHERAPEUTIC RELATIONSHIP

Another of Paul Mosher's profoundly important contributions has been his concern about the confidentiality of therapist-patient communication, which is of fundamental importance to the integrity of psychoanalysis. His interest and dedication spawned and sustained a number of very important initiatives. Dr. Mosher recognized the importance of the Jaffee v. Redmond case that was accepted by the Supreme Court in 1996 and he initiated the involvement of APsaA. Working with the chosen lawyer, he coordinated the funding and production of an amicus brief before the U.S. Supreme Court. Thus, he helped to shape the case for a therapist-patient privilege in the Federal courts, which was explicitly established in the majority opinion itself. The write-up is available in Wikipedia and on the Jaffee v. Redmond website, http://jaffee-redmond.org, which Dr. Mosher maintains. It remains a resource for all clinicians, and legal professionals.

Dr. Mosher co-chaired with Dr. Drew Clemens for many years, a Discussion Group at each APsaA meeting where current important figures in law and politics who have shaped confidentiality and privacy regulations were invited to discuss these issues with attending psychoanalysts. He, through this venue, played an important role in the creation of the HIPAA Privacy Rule provision for psychotherapy notes, by presenting the history of the Jaffee privilege to the Chief Privacy Officer of HHS, John Fanning, while the rules were being written. He later co-authored an article with the overall head of Privacy in the Clinton administration on the subject.

In addition to these significant national and international efforts that have impacted psychoanalysis, Dr. Mosher has used his computer expertise to improve the functioning of APsaA in a myriad of ways, starting with his 1990's initiative to computerize its administrative and bookkeeping activities, to establish email lists for its members, officers and committees. He thus enabled engagement and discussions that have transformed the participation of the membership and served as models of democratic and inclusive services that are copied widely.

ESTABLISHMENT OF THE APsaA LISTSERVS AND EDUCATION OF THE MEMBERS ABOUT GOVERNANCE

It was Paul Mosher whose research, conducted with his characteristic meticulousness and integrity, during his twenty-three years as an APsaA Executive Councilor, alerted and focused the Executive Council, the APsaA governing board, about the importance of understanding and following its Bylaws, the New York State Not for Profit Corporation Law, and Robert's Rules, so that APsaA's governance could be accomplished by the Councilors, in full and clear understanding of their fiduciary responsibilities, and with the comprehension of the members who elect them. The main vehicle he used to accomplish this was his authoritative series of essays, collected under the title of "Civics Lessons" that he published on the APsaA Members List, one of a series of APsaA list serves that he originated. This list serve has been a valuable medium for discussions, not only of governance issues, but also of a wide variety of topics of great importance to psychoanalysts. By virtue of its inclusiveness, and through Dr. Mosher's exemplary participation, the Members List and other list serves have transformed and invigorated discussion within the APsaA in a profoundly more knowledgeable, democratic and inclusive direction.

ROLE IN ENDING POLITICAL CONFLICT WITHIN THE AMERICAN PSYCHOANALYTIC ASSOCIATION

Additional organizational roles include his service, along with Donald Rosenblitt, M.D., as Co-Chair of the APsaA Task Force on Externalization, which broke new ground as a result of his genius, patience, and firm but gentle guiding hand. This Task Force was the first to make extensive use of the web for its work. It developed rules of transparency and inclusivity between the participants, enabled interested APsaA members to provide input, and developed a non-adversarial procedure for the inclusion of all points of view in its deliberations and final report on a proposal designed to end forty years of conflict within the American Psychoanalytic Association. It remains a model of conflict resolution through respectful discussion and accommodation. The Task Force report put forth concepts that formed the basis of the 6 Point Plan that has brought about the reorganization of the American Psychoanalytic Association, the creation of the American Board of Psychoanalysis, and the external accrediting organization, the American Association of Psychoanalytic Education (AAPE).

I hope that the above highlights the particular accomplishments that make Paul Mosher MD eligible under the criteria established for the award and singularly worthy of being honored by the Sigourney Trust. His personal characteristics include tremendous integrity, profound dedication to psychoanalysis and to the American Psychoanalytic Association, originality, genius, a capacity for the hard work necessary to see a project through to its completion, a generative, educational and personally modest approach to all of his collegial interactions, and the widest and deepest breadth of knowledge and interests of anyone whom I have ever had the pleasure to know.

Ralph Fishkin

In His Own Hand

CHAPTER 1

Catastrophe Strikes! (Working Version)

I've been thinking about writing something on this topic for several months but because of obvious ambivalence about proceeding have done nothing concrete other than "thinking" about it. What I am describing is a childhood experience of a somewhat uncommon illness, which had such a profound effect on the rest of my life that there is almost no aspect of my following years that has not been touched.

What seems to have gotten me started on this project today is a dream I had last night. It was one of those very immersive dreams in which a person, in this case me, lives through a more or less cohesive narrative which brings with it a very clear sense, during the dream, that one is actually living through something "real" and that the accompanying feeling of anxiety, sometimes verging on panic, is clearly justified by such an experience.

As a result of his work with patients undergoing brain surgery in the 1930s through the 1950s, the Canadian neurosurgeon Wilder Penfield hypothesized that there is a second set of memories locked away in the brains of most people and which constitute a kind of videotape of a person's entire life. He thought that during the operations in which he was able to activate such forgotten events through electrical stimulation of the brain that he was "playing back" such memories. The patients, in describing this phenomenon, referred to the peculiarly "immersive" quality that characterizes these recollections and reminds me of the similar feeling that people, including me, experience during so-called nightmares[1], that is, anxiety dreams that seem real at the time one is dreaming them. I have had numerous such dreams, but not for several years until last night, as I was thinking about writing down this story. I have often wondered if such dreams, with their immersive quality might be tapping into memories recorded in that second memory storage system described by Penfield and hinted at more recently by discovery in 2001 of the phenomenon of hyperthymesia, a phenomenon which has been documented in at least 60 individuals who actually have complete access to what appears to be a literal recording of all the events in their lives since about age 11. Such memories, as they are being accessed, are characterized by an "immersive" quality reminiscent of that described by Penfield's patients.

In my dream,
I was my present age, and had an appointment to see a dentist, endodontist, Dr. F, to whose office I have gone at least twice yearly for many years for routine monitoring of what had appeared years earlier to be some gum problems. I have had very few actual problems of that nature but in the past year I had a tooth that ended up in hopeless condition and required an extraction and an implant, which Dr. F also performed. In the dream, I became aware that Dr. F. had moved his office to Manhattan and so I was required to take a train to New York, stay overnight in a hotel on the East Side near Grand Central

---

1   https://www.mayoclinic.org/diseases-conditions/nightmare-disorder/symptoms-causes/syc-20353515
A nightmare may involve these features: Your dream seems vivid and real and is very upsetting, often becoming more disturbing as the dream unfolds. Your dream storyline is usually related to threats to safety or survival, but it can have other disturbing themes. Your dream awakens you. You feel scared, anxious, angry, sad or disgusted as a result of your dream. You feel sweaty or have a pounding heartbeat while in bed. You can think clearly upon awakening and can recall details of your dream. Your dream causes distress that keeps you from falling back to sleep easily.

Station, and then visit Dr. F's office the next day. When I woke up and started to head for Dr. F's office I realized that I had forgotten the office location, had no cell phone or computer to look up the address, and so I started walking on streets among Manhattan's tall buildings, in search of the office. I was getting quite worried. As time went by and my aimless wandering didn't seem to be getting me any closer to the office, I finally realized that I would miss the appointment and instead decided to head for Penn Station to take the train home. However, I was also unable to find my way to Penn Station and with ever mounting anxiety continued to wander in a westward direction. I thought of taking a cab but none appeared. All of this wandering was accompanied by a very strong feeling of fright at being hopelessly lost. As the feeling of panic at being lost reached a crescendo, I awoke with a start and after a few confused seconds realized that what I had dreamt was not "real" and that I was safely at home in my bed and that it was morning.

Only a few minutes thought brought me to connect this dream, and many earlier dreams about being lost which I have had over the years, with a traumatic incident at around age 10 connected to my childhood illness and my relationship with my father. All those dreams contained similar elements of being lost or at least disoriented, often in tall buildings with elaborate elevators.

The event, which seems to have been represented in some concrete ways took place when I was nine years old. At that time I had been treated without much success for a serious disability for more than the past two years, beginning when I was 7 years old. I will describe that life-changing illness and disability in a bit but suffice it to say at this point that it must have been a tremendous physical and emotional burden on my parents to have their only child so seriously disabled. So in desperation, my parents decided to take me for a consultation with a prominent orthopedic surgeon in Philadelphia. This surgeon, Dr. A. Bruce Gill, was famous for having refined a surgical treatment for the condition from which I suffered, and he was considered one of the world's experts on the illness. From the point of view of a child, however, the idea of being subjected to an operation was terrifying and I can recall vaguely my apprehension about what this doctor was going to recommend.

So, in September 1946, when I was nine years old, my father and I set out for Philadelphia for a consultation with the famed Dr. Gill. I have no memory of the trip to Philadelphia, and only a vague recollection of Dr. Gill. Like most orthopedic surgeons I encountered in that era, he appeared to me to be a distinguished older gentleman who wore a long white coat, had a gentle manner, and like his colleagues spoke in a jargon-filled mumble heavily loaded with impressive but incomprehensible technical terms. With the consultation over in a matter of a few minutes my father and I set out to return to Albany. I think I caught the idea that Dr. Gill had suggested that, at least on a trial basis, I should be treated conservatively but in a different way than previously, and that surgery would be the final resort if the conservative treatment didn't work out. So I was relieved of my fright, at least temporarily. I do not know, however, how my father felt about this outcome because the treatment that Dr. Gill recommended was itself going to be a challenge to carry out.

Travelling from Albany to Philadelphia by train in those days required a change of both trains and a transit between two different train stations in New York City. Albany trains arrived and departed for Grand Central Station on Manhattan's East Side, whereas trains from New York to Philadelphia arrived and departed from Penn Station on the West Side.

We must have begun the return trip from Philadelphia to Albany in the early or midafternoon and arrived in New York at perhaps four or five PM. I assume we then took a taxi from Penn Station to Grand Central, found the train to Albany, which was sitting at the platform, went on board and took our seats. The train wasn't due to leave for perhaps fifteen or twenty minutes. It was quite warm and I remember that my father took off his suit jacket, which had our tickets in the inside breast pocket. With nothing to do but wait, my father said he'd like a newspaper to read on the train and stood up to leave the train to find a newsstand. He handed me his jacket and asked me to watch it.

After perhaps ten minutes I started to feel a bit anxious since my father had not returned. A few minutes later the conductor shouted, "All aboard!" and it was evident that the train was about to leave. I then became very concerned with no idea what to do. After a few more minutes, I decided that I shouldn't stay on the train by myself, and dragging our single suitcase and my father's jacket, decided to get off the train. The conductor, seeing my struggle, (with my full leg brace, crutches, and strange built up shoe on the other foot I must have looked like a poster boy for the March of Dimes) helped me to get down to the platform. I expected my father to come along at any moment, so I simply sat down on the suitcase and waited. I can still remember the frightened, sinking feeling I had watching the train pulling out of the station. Suddenly, I felt terribly lost, helpless and alone. I had no idea what to do and started crying. I must have been a pathetic sight.

Before long a woman came up to me and started to speak in what I imagine she believed was a comforting way. As I recall she said something like "Oooh, is wittle snookums lost?" — clearly trying to convey sympathy and at the same time betraying little or no experience with children. I was in no mood to be trifled with and immediately, without standing up, kicked her in the ankle – hard. Why did I kick her? Obviously I was angry with someone, but I didn't feel anger toward anyone except her, and my feeling is that it only made my situation worse and made me feel humiliated, to be spoken to in that tone of voice – like I was some kind of cry baby! But was I actually, unknowingly, angry with my father for seemingly abandoning me?

At this point, she backed off and went to summon station personnel. In a few minutes, a person in some sort of uniform came along, asked me to follow him, and picked up my suitcase. I continued to cling to my father's coat and followed him. Eventually we came to an office with a sign saying "Travellers Aid" and he took me inside and asked me to sit on a bench. I was still crying. In addition, it was nearing supper time and I was starting to feel a bit hungry.

I have a recollection, a kind of "snapshot memory," of that office. It was a very bland public sector looking room, with oak furniture, austere decor, and a very large clock on the wall with Roman numerals and two large hands. A woman in the office brought me something to eat. Eventually two men in suits came along, introduced themselves as New York police detectives, and asked me what I was doing there. Pulling myself together, I answered their questions as best I could, gave my name and address and told them my story of getting on the train with my father, of my father leaving to get a paper, of seeing that the train was about to leave, and not seeing my father, of deciding to disembark. They left, saying they'd be back in a while. No one else spoke to me.

After perhaps an hour, the two detectives returned and began to question me about my father. Did he drink? Did he gamble? Did he know anyone in New York, particularly women? Did he leave me alone many times before? (No, no, don't know, no, etc.). All these questions seemed to imply that they believed I had been intentionally abandoned, which I remember feeling a sort of disconnect between their line of thought and my actual situation because in my mind my father's intentionally abandoning me seemed unthinkable. They left again, but returned with more questions, perhaps at hourly intervals. It started to get later and later and I have a vivid memory of watching the hands on the clock creep through the evening, hour by hour. A woman staffing the office kept watching me, and every once in a while, asked me if she could bring me anything else to eat or drink. I was obviously very frightened and confused, having no idea what happened, or if I would ever see my parents or home again. It was getting quite late, later than I had ever been up, and this in itself contributed to my feelings of unreality about the whole situation.

Around midnight, the two detectives reappeared and informed me that they had located my father – in Albany! What had happened, they said, was that he had gotten back onto the train with his paper but got on the wrong car. The train left for Albany with him aboard. He obviously hadn't seen me on the platform. The plan, as they explained it to me, is that they would put me on the next train to Albany and my parents would meet me when the train arrived. So, placed in the charge of a kindly conductor, I was taken to a seat on a train bound for Albany. I was still pretty frightened and stayed wide awake and on guard during the entire trip which seemed to take forever.

Finally, the train pulled into the Albany train station (the now repurposed classic Union Station on Broadway in downtown Albany) and, as promised, my parents were anxiously waiting for me on the platform. Our reunion on the platform wasn't tearful, was somewhat joyous in a muted sort of way, and now makes me think of the end of a sitcom. It was about two AM.

This entire episode, with its theme of abandonment, took place about two thirds of the way through a three year period in my childhood, which I will now describe in more detail. That period had started about two years earlier, when I was seven years old, with a single event which forever changed my life. It presaged a later and even more dramatic episode of abandonment, which I believe left in its wake a permanent alteration of my personality…

The Original Catastrophe, or How Fate Changed a Cheerful, Outgoing little Boy Into a Case of "Acquired Asperger's."

For this part of the story we have to go back in time an additional two years. Up until I was seven years old my family lived in an apartment in what was then a middle class apartment house on Morton Avenue in downtown Albany. That building, and its twin building next door were directly across the street from Lincoln Park and were a distinct step up for immigrant Jewish families who had previously occupied older housing in an even older part of the city. The little neighborhood where this somewhat more modern housing stood, and the park across the street, was my entire (non-summertime) world at that time. I had a number of friends essentially my own age whose middle class Jewish families lived in some of the 30 or so apartments. We formed an inseparable group. As best as I recall I was a cheerful outgoing child. There was always someone to play with, either in the small yard behind the apartments or on the back porches which were on the side of the building facing away from the street. I began school at Public School #25, a few blocks further up Morton Avenue and most of the time we walked to school as a group. For a child, this was a wonderful safe environment with a group of culturally and ethnically compatible friends, friends I had known "forever," in a safe neighborhood, with ice skating and sledding right across the street.

However, in 1943, right in the midst of World War II, my parents decided that it was time to move to a "better" neighborhood, and so they purchased a house in an "uptown" neighborhood, which I had never seen before, and on a block that probably deserved of being called "elegant." Our new home, 692 Madison Avenue, was located on what at the time was probably one of the finest blocks in the city. For me, the move to the new house was a tremendous shock, although I do not remember protesting in any way.

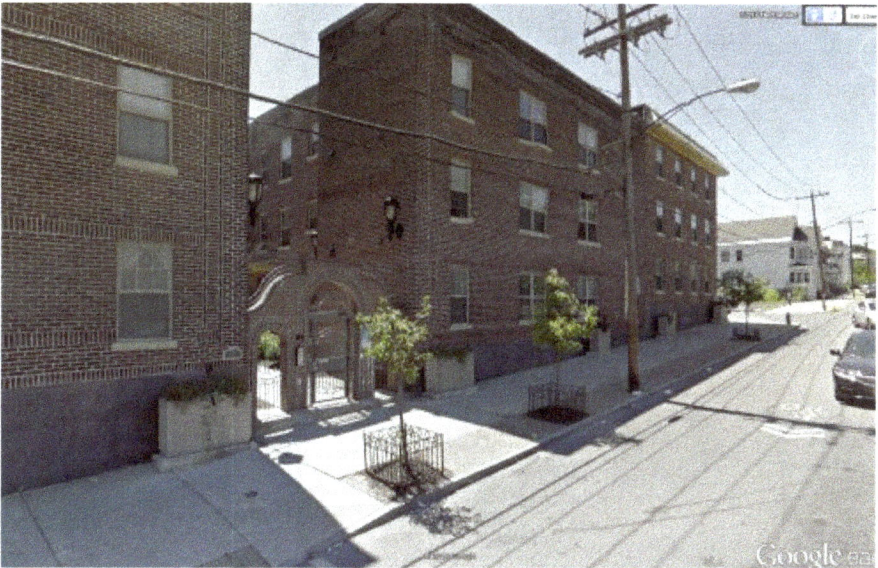

We lived in this Morton Street apartment house until I was seven years old.

This city block on the south side of Madison Avenue between Robin Street and Lake Avenue was very beautiful. Not only did the houses face Washington Park, directly across the street, but the street itself was lined by a row on each side of immense Elm trees, which in the summer months formed a cooling canopy over the street, as the branches from the two sides of the street met overhead. Many of the houses on the block, especially on the east end of the block, were what would have been considered then to be mansions, large single family homes with spacious front lawns, large backyards, many three stories high.

Albany, N.Y., Madison Ave. near Lake Ave.

Looking West on Madison Avenue in the 1920s from very near our house. (We moved there in the 1940s)

At our end of the block, the Lake Avenue end, the houses were a bit more modest. The house my parents purchased (I believe for about $8,000) was not exactly a mansion but was unusual in another way: Although the houses on the block were fairly close together, and the lots were narrow with barely a driveway's width between them, the lots were quite deep, for the most part, backing onto lots of much more modest homes on the next street to the south, Morris Street. Our house was different, however. Our new property went almost all the way through the block to Morris Street, so that behind our house was another house on the same property. In addition, when the lot reached the depth of other lots on the block, our property also extended to take up the space between the back of our next door neighbor's house, so that the back part of our lot had a second building, which housed a two car garage, as well as an apartment above the garages. This "mini-estate" thus gave us room for a garden, a garage, and most importantly two tenants. The apartment above the garage was rented to a family who served as caretakers for the property. All of these buildings were serviced by a single driveway, which ran along the east side of our house, and broadened out as it reached the back to give access to the garages.

692 Madison Avenue as it appears today. The driveway broadened out to the left behind the yard of the building next door.

All of this is to say that the new environment in which I suddenly found myself was completely different from the setting of my cozy, friend-filled seven first years in the Morton Street apartment house. And, of course, I had to transfer to a new school. I had been attending the second grade at

Public School #25, a quaint red brick building on Morton Avenue, about three blocks from our Eagle Apartments. As I recall, all of us, the whole gang, typically had walked to school together. Now I was enrolled in Public School #4, a much larger, more imposing, and more modern building (now demolished) on Madison Avenue at the corner of Ontario Street, about two blocks west from our new home. Since I knew no one in that neighborhood, I typically walked to school and back home alone.

I cannot recall at what point in the school year I actually started in my new school but I can recall the feeling of strangeness in trying to adapt to a completely different school, a new group of classmates, and a new teacher. I made the acquaintance of one new friend, Chris Stahler, who was the son of one of my father's medical school classmates. The Stahlers lived in a brownstone about one block further east on Madison Avenue, between Robin Street and New Scotland Avenue, which meant that Chris would pass our home on his way to school. However, the Stahlers were integrated into the Albany Protestant community (the entire city was socially segregated by ethnic groups and, more particularly, religions at that time) so my fit with Chris and his family was not comfortable. Those people ate *ham*, went to *church* on Sunday, and did many other unfamiliar things I had never known about or seen before.

One day in early June toward the end of the second grade, I was walking home by myself in the middle of the afternoon when I suddenly began to experience a distinctly painful feeling in my left knee. I took no more than two or three additional steps, when the pain became almost impossible to bear. This was the beginning of a prolonged illness and I have another "flashbulb memory" of the exact moment, and exactly where I was on the sidewalk approaching the Lake Avenue corner of Madison Avenue. I limped across the street, and made my way past the five houses, which separated our house from the corner. Little did I realize that my life had suddenly taken a dramatic turn.

Because of the continuing pain in my leg, which made me almost unable to walk, I was taken to see an orthopedist in the next day or so. From my understanding, an x-ray immediately confirmed that I was suffering from the acute onset of an illness called Legg-Perthes Disease, a serious affliction of the hip joint which occurs in boys of that age and leads to a virtual collapse of the head of the femur, the large thigh bone of my left leg at the point where it forms a joint at the top of the leg.

Within a day or two I then found myself in a hospital bed in the pediatric ward of Albany Medical Center under the care of a Dr. Ghormley, the head of Orthopedics (and, I might add, the person who, through an offhand remark, inadvertently played the greatest role in motivating me to become a psychoanalyst). Within another day or so I was placed in an immense plaster cast reaching from my waist down my left leg to below my left knee. I remained in this situation, with occasional replacements of the cast and repeat x-rays until sometime in September, when I was finally sent home, but *with the cast.* This meant, of course, that I was unable to sit in an ordinary chair, use an ordinary toilet, or walk without the use of crutches, bearing all my weight, and the weight of the cast, on my right leg. A kind of throne-like high chair made of sturdy plywood had to be constructed so that I could sit with my left leg (and cast) extended through a cutout in the seat.

My parents both worked. My father was a general practitioner with his own practice in Albany, and my mother was a third grade public school teacher, so neither of my parents was home during the day, five days a week. Since I was unable to start the third grade and had to stay home, my parents hired an older middle-aged woman by the name of "Miss Minogue" to stay home with me all day.

I had no significant contact with anyone except my parents and Miss Minogue for many months, although I did receive an occasional visit from a "home schooling" teacher provided by the city for shut-ins. As I recall, I had very little schoolwork to do, so a substantial part of the third grade was actually missing from my formal schooling. By coincidence, the third grade was the grade my mother taught, so I believe she made up for some of the lost lessons. I can recall long lonely days at home, listening to the radio, occasionally wandering out for a walk in the neighborhood on my crutches, even walking around the corner to visit with my mother's sister, my Aunt Fanny, who was home all day and always welcomed me to sit with her in her kitchen. Miss Minogue, while a very caring person, was utterly incapable of providing anything other than meals and housekeeping, certainly no companionship or mental stimulation, so much of my time was spent waiting for my father to come home for his lunch break, or my mother's return from school in the late afternoon. I had no contact with other children and I believe my social development, at least as it involves peer relationships, came to an abrupt halt.

At some point in the school year, the spika cast was removed for good and replaced by a full left leg length brace, with knee locks, configured so that when standing or walking my weight was born on my right leg and through the left leg brace transferred to a padded ring above my left hip. When seated, the brace's knee locks could be released so I could sit normally. I was allowed to return to school – but with restrictions.

These restrictions were imposed by the school system, presumably for my protection, but had the effect of isolating me from other children. I was not allowed to enter or leave the school at the same time as the other children, but instead had to arrive and leave ten minutes early. I was told this precaution was so that I would not get "knocked over" by the rush of kids entering or leaving the building. In addition, of course, I was not allowed to attend gym classes or engage in any school activities, which were similarly physical.

[describe what I can recall about that year and a half at school as
the "crippled kid"]

Shipped Away

So how did it happen that in 1991, almost 30 years ago, I put forward the proposal to create an archive of the fully digitized psychoanalytic journal literature, the proposal, which ultimately led to the creation of Psychoanalytic Electronic Publishing (PEP)? To answer this question you might as well ask questions like these:

How did I end up as a college sophomore spending an entire summer of nights (12AM to 8AM) alone in a large metal industrial building in the middle of a deserted field somewhere between Albany and Schenectady, N.Y., babysitting the country's most powerful radio broadcasting transmitter, which had been entrusted to my nightly care by one of the world's most powerful corporations? Or, you could ask how it happened that while other students were enjoying their non-study time at college, I spent an entire semester's "free time" wandering through an immense underground labyrinth of hidden steam tunnels, which connect most of the buildings of Harvard University like an academic recreation of Phantom of the Opera? Or, how did my completely senseless choice of courses at a leading liberal arts college, like "Alternating Current Circuits" lead to my publishing, as a medical student, what is now described as a "classic" article in coronary artery physiology? Or how a college experience writing an English thesis, which I could do because it required a knowledge of electronic instrumentation, lead me to publish one of the first personal descriptions of an LSD trip? Or, how as an intern at a Seattle hospital, I found myself in the hospital lobby being interviewed by an agent of the FBI about my attempted recruitment by a Russian KGB Colonel who had been acting as a spy for the Soviet government in Manhattan? Or, why as an early career psychiatrist I spent an entire weekend, 48 continuous hours to the point of exhaustion, operating a shortwave radio station from what was then the primitive Caribbean island of Anguilla?

This zany red thread of technology which has run through most of my life, including the PEP proposal, seems to me to have been born of a major psychological trauma that I suffered when I was nine years old, showing, I think, that an emotionally devastating trauma can shape a person's life in ways that are entirely unforeseeable, and not of necessity, entirely negative.

On November 6, 1946, just a few days shy of my tenth birthday, my parents packed me into the family Chevy, and drove 120 miles south from Albany, on what was then a narrow two lane highway, to the New York State Reconstruction Home in Haverstraw, New York, a state supported institution for children with orthopedic disabilities — mostly in those days for survivors of polio. As I recall, no one said very much to me about why we were going there, except that it was "another hospital" and I would need to stay there for "a while." I cannot recall what must have been a tearful goodbye, but I do vividly recall the mixture of terror and sadness that overtook me when my parents left me in this strange new place, so far from home and where I knew absolutely no one.

This unexpected, and seemingly sudden, separation from my parents was made worse by the fact that for the previous two years I had been significantly disabled, more or less isolated from other children, and probably even more attached to, and dependent on my parents, than most kids of that age. Six months of homeschooling, starting when I was seven, followed by a year and a half of attending school wearing an elaborate leg long weight bearing brace, had made me an object of ridicule, scorn and pity. All this was the result of my having developed a serious orthopedic problem, Legg-Perthes Disease, which results in painful collapse of a hip joint, typically in pre-pubertal boys.

My recollections of the first few days in "Haverstraw" are of shock and sadness. I seem to recall crying continuously for days, before reaching a state of silent depressed resignation. I had found myself amid strangers, and with no visitors, confined to a bed in a ward housing a total of 22 boys. The ward itself was arranged so that there were five pairs of beds, plus one extra, along each side with movable curtains hung from overhead pipes so that it was possible to provide some privacy by sliding the curtains, which were almost never moved to that position. Many of the boys had serious residual symptoms of polio, such as permanently paralyzed arms or legs. Nearest the nurses' station at one end of the ward were two boys confined continuously to iron lungs. I was told gently but firmly I was not allowed to get out of bed for any reason. No one spoke to me about what was to happen next.

A day or so after my admission to the hospital, without any warning, I was placed in traction. The traction consisted of a rope connected to a small piece of wood below my left foot and which in turn was taped to my left leg by adhesive tape which reached almost to my knee. The rope passed at the foot of the bed through a large pulley and held a weight hanging at the foot of the bed so that continual traction was applied to my left leg. This arrangement made it impossible to move very far in the bed other than to roll a bit to one side or the other.

Next to the bed, a small table held all the possessions I was allowed to have with me: a small radio, a few books, a toothbrush. There was, of course, no telephone. Having been significantly disabled in the midst of an attentive and indulgent family, I had come from a room packed with all kinds of toys and materials for various activities, so this was a startling change.

Life on the ward was a blur of days going by, seemingly without end, paced by a daily cycle of meals delivered like clockwork. Occasionally, as I recall weekly, a group of doctors made rounds, moving as a group from bed to bed, standing in a semicircle at the foot of each bed in succession, while one of them spoke too quickly and in language too technical for a child to comprehend. The point of the exercise seemed to be to make a decision as to which of the patients was to have surgery that week. We all lived in fear of being chosen in this weekly ritual. No one ever told me that surgery was not even under consideration in my case, but for many of the polio survivors the only option to resume anything like a normal life would be the transplantation of muscles to try to compensate for the ravages of polio. I had nightmares for years involving groups of men in white coats standing at the foot of my bed staring at me and speaking unintelligibly.

The ward was suffused by a kind of grim resignation. Occasionally, some of the patients would sing this little ditty:

Mama, Mama take me home
From the Reconstruction Home
I've been here a year or two,
Now I want to go home with you.

Boredom was the biggest enemy we all faced. The hospital staff were kindly, considerate, and in reasonably good humor most of the time. A small crew of occupational therapists attempted to provide some diversion, but this consisted mostly of absurd activities like stitching together useless wallets from kits, weaving belts from loops of leather-like material, or braiding bracelets from plastic cord.

This "situation" continued (for me) with little interruption for about eight months. Periodic interruptions consisted of trips every few days to a "sunroom" where six of us at a time were placed inside a large booth on a series of cots arranged in a circle, daisy-petal like, under an immense ultraviolet light, our eyes covered with dark goggles. I suppose this was an attempt to compensate for the fact that we were barred from any outdoor activities or natural sunshine.

Additionally, each week we were obliged to attend religious services of our (required) choice. Until that time in my life I had never attended a religious service except for holiday services at a strictly orthodox synagogue at which my grandfather had been the rabbi. My memory of those services, which I never understood, was of a warm family environment where our family occupied seats of honor in the front row; my father and my mother's brothers seemed to know what was going on, but I myself understood nothing and no one made any attempt to explain anything to me even though the entire service was conducted in Hebrew.

But the "services" at the hospital were completely different. They must have been conservative or reform services, involved audience participation, much singing, etc. All the other Jewish kids seemed to be familiar with this kind of service, but for me it might have been in a different foreign language and I felt completely out of place, like a kind of imposter, and suddenly realized that I didn't belong in such a place. The discomfort of that situation has stayed with me all my life and I avoid all religious services as much as I can (Not to mention that I am a confirmed agnostic!).

But I guess, even for agnostics miracles can happen, and one happened to me that made the entire hospital experience more than tolerable, in some sense fun, and, I believe, ultimately life changing. That miracle came in the form of a kindly, elderly hospital volunteer named "Mr. Rose."

Mr. Rose appeared on the ward one day with no fanfare or prior notice. He carried with him a large box filled with somewhat unfamiliar looking objects and several rolls of wire. He explained to some of us that he was a retired Western Union telegrapher and that the equipment he had brought with him was telegraph equipment. Each hardware item was neatly mounted on a wooden board and basically there were two types of items, keys and sounders. Mr. Rose and one of the hospital orderlies then proceeded to run wires all over the ward, using the divider curtain supports to hold the wires. He then connected all the equipment to a battery and it all came to life. Each boy who participated, and there were probably about ten of us, had a key and a sounder and when any of us pressed the key, all the sounders at the other bedsides made a "click". The click was caused by the electricity flowing through the wires, energizing the electromagnets in the "sounders" which then pulled a small metal rod toward the magnet, which it struck with a loud "click." When the key was released the current stopped and the rod was pulled back into its initial position by a spring, making another "click." So pressing and releasing the key quickly resulted in a rapid "click..click" at the sounder. Pressing the key, holding it in place for a short interval and then releasing it also resulted in two clicks but they were further apart in time: "click....click."

Key

Sounder

We learned that "click..click" meant a "dot" and "click....click" meant a "dash." This was the Morse Code in its earliest practical form! We were each given a sheet of paper with the different dot-dash combinations for each letter of the alphabet and all ten digits. Given that we had time on our hands, we learned quickly and within a few days, and numerous visits by Mr. Rose, who left the equipment in the ward for several weeks, several of us were sending messages all over the ward using our newly discovered ability.

About 8 ½ months after I was admitted to the hospital, I was told that my hip had healed to the point where I no longer required traction or bed rest and so I was "mobilized" in preparation for discharge. By that point, after all that time in bed, my legs had weakened considerably and I was dismayed to find that I could neither stand nor walk. However, after a couple weeks of physical therapy, mostly walking with the aid of parallel bars, I was able to stand and walk on my own, and finally after what seemed like years away was able to go home. In addition, I was relieved to hear that there were no restrictions on my activity and that the only residual effect of the whole years long episode was that my left leg was now almost an inch shorter than my right, which required me to wear a left shoe with a specially built up heel. However, I never regained the ability to run with any confidence, so that even though I could walk, running was a rare event in my life ever after.

So there I was, four months short of my eleventh birthday, physically "healed" enough to resume more or less regular activities and about to enter the sixth grade in a school I had attended in the past but in which everything had changed. During that long period of social near isolation, children of my same age had been experiencing the usual range of social interactions and sorting out. I, on the other hand, was almost completely lacking in whatever social and other skills one might have. Nonetheless, I reentered school that September and began the sixth grade as if I was just like everyone else.

I wasn't of course. I had no friends, very few age-appropriate social skills, and absolutely no guidance of any sort. Probably, in today's world a great deal of attention would have been given to a kid's adjustment and social development during such a period of transition, but in the 1940s and 1950s, very little attention was paid to such matters, so it was a kind of psychological "sink or swim" situation!

The one thing I did have going for me was that I found school extremely easy, suddenly found myself deeply attracted to certain subject areas, began to read widely in science, mathematics, and science fiction. I wonder if the outgoing little kid who years earlier had entered this long course of illness hadn't emerged with what might be called a case of "Acquired Asperger's."

Jobs, After School and In the Summer

As my interest in amateur radio deepened, and as I was able to upgrade my license status from "Novice" to "General Class" and eventually to "Extra

Class" (the highest level attainable) I found myself more and more attracted to the beautiful radio equipment shown in magazine ads, compared to the clunky and marginally functional versions I could build for myself. Typical receivers of the day, such as the Hallicrafters S-40, which I had, were relatively inexpensive but very hard to use. For some reason, my heart got set on a 1951 National Radio HRO-50, a very capable and technically innovative receiver, which was the culmination of a line of receivers that had played an important role in World War II.

This receiver had been sold new for $383 (about $4,000 in current dollars) plus an additional $16 for an external matching loudspeaker. The external power supply was included. The current model, the HRO-60, was obviously out of my reach ($484!) but the model I was interested in was being sold used for much less, two or three years after it was superseded.

So, hopefully, and without any idea what to expect, I approached my father, explained my need for the receiver and asked him if he'd help me pay for it. I'm not sure why, because ordinarily my father had been very generous when it came to things, I "needed." But for some reason, he saw my interest in electronics as a useless distraction, and therefore told me that if I really wanted such a thing, I should "get a job and pay for it" myself. I recall a mixture of hurt, anger, disappointment, and a cold recognition that not everything that interested me had value in his eyes. But, whatever the mixture of feelings involved, I did exactly what he said: I got a job and bought the radio myself. This experience became a defining moment for me because ever after that, I was always determined to get what I wanted by *working for it, not asking for it.*

[Telegraph boy, Filing Clerk, Flour Sifter, Assistant to Truck Driver, Studio Floor Audio Technician, Shading Desk Operator, Transmitter Engineer (WGY, VOA, WCRB)]

Chronology Footnote

Chronology (just for reference while I am writing this)

June 1944 - First symptoms (Age 7)

June - September 1944 - Hospitalized AMCH with bed rest and cast (Age 7)

September1944 - School with cast and crutches (Age 7-8)

December 1944 - November 1946 Ischial weight bearing brace, no crutches (Age 8-10) September 1946 - Consultation with Dr. Gill (Age 9) November 5, 1946 - Admitted to Haverstraw.

November 10, 1946 - Strict bed rest with traction

November 20, 1946 - Tenth birthday

July 23, 1947 - Discharged from Haverstraw (Age 10, after 8 months in hospital)

A.Bruce Gill,M.D.   C o p y.
1930 Chestnut Street
Philadelphia,3

September 28,1946.

Dear Doctor Ghormley,

          Thank you for the privilege of examining Paul Mosher
and for your history of the case. The following is a copy of my notes of
the examination.

There is a history of trauma. In June of 1944 he began to limp in his
left leg. He complained of pain about the left hip and left knee. He was
hospitalized untill September. He never had extension on his legs but was
put up in plaster casts and was sent home in September to go to school
with a cast on. One cast came to above the knee and another cast which
was applied came to below the knee. He walked on crutches and there was
some question in the history as to whether he had a high shoe from the
beginning but later on he did wear a high shoe. In December of 1944 he
had an extension brace put on with a high shoe. He did not use crutches
after having the brace applied.

The series of X-rays shows that in the first one made 7.5.44 there was a
very definite Legg-Perthes disease of the left hip. The one made 6.19.45
showed projection of the upper end of the femur from the upper end of the
acetabulum, protically complete crushing of the outer half of the head,
increased density of the remaining portion of the head with areas of rarefaction. The last X-ray made 6.25.46 shows almost complete disappearance
and crushing of the head and projection of the outer margin of the head
at least ¼" beyond the margin of the acetabulum, thickening and broadening of the neck, and areas of rarefaction persisting in the upper portion
of the neck.

This is a condition of Legg-Perthes disease which has progressed to almost complete destruction of the head of the femur, with deformity and
subluxation and broadening and shortening of the neck of the femur. There
is some evidence of recalcification of the remaining portion of the head
but this recalcification is not yet complete.

I advise that this boy be put to bed with Buck's extension, and kept
there until there is evidence of fairly complete regeneration of the portion of the head which remains. The end result will be a marked deformity
of the hip with flattening of the head and projection of the head beyond
the margin of the acetabulum. There is almost complete absence of abduction and external rotation of the femur. Abduction is markedly limited.
It may be necessary later on to do a shelf or buttress operation on the
hip to provide sufficient acetabulum to cover the entire head of the
femur and give adequate support for it.

If the father so desires I could probably secure the child's admission to
the Childrin's Seashore House in Atlantic City for the period during the
remainder of his convalescence. He would be kept ther in bed with extension on his leg until X-ray examination shows that the head has regenera-
ted.

                    Sincerely yours
                   (Signed) A.Bruce Gill.

CHAPTER 2

Control of Coronary Blood Flow by an Autoregulatory Mechanism

by Paul Mosher, B.A., John Ross, Jr., M.D., Patricia, Ann McFate, M.A., & Robert F. Shaw, M.D.

[*Circulation Research,* Vol 14: March 1964. From the Biomedical Engineering Laboratory, Electronics Research Laboratories, School of Engineering and Applied Science, and the Department of Surgery, College of Physicians and Surgeons, Columbia University, New York, New York. Supported by National Aeronautics and Space Administration Research Grant NSC 112 and U.S. Public Health Service Research Grant H 5032. Received for publication August 30, 1963.]

The relative importance of the several determinants of coronary blood flow remains an area of controversy. It is generally agreed that coronary flow results from the interplay of coronary perfusion pressure, ventricular contraction, and coronary vascular tone. But the extent to which each of these factors regulates flow and the extent to which their influence is modified by regulatory mechanisms has not been determined.

Some investigators have supported the view that the hydraulic relationship between the mechanical forces of aortic pressure and ventricular contraction regulates coronary flow; others have suggested that while these physical forces determine the metabolic needs of the heart, the regulation of coronary flow to meet these needs is effected by variations in coronary vasomotor tone. If this latter hypothesis is correct, it should be possible to vary coronary perfusion pressure while cardiac function is held constant and observe no change in coronary flow. Conversely, it should be possible to change cardiac effort and observe a directionally similar alteration in coronary blood flow while coronary perfusion pressure remains constant.

Although it has been shown that active changes in the tone of the coronary blood vessels can occur in response to alterations in perfusion pressure, this response has not been characterized quantitatively in the *in situ* heart. The present study examines mechanisms which are brought into play when, during a period of constant cardiac function, coronary flow rates are suddenly increased or decreased by the imposition of sudden changes in coronary perfusion pressure. A pressure-independent autoregulatory mechanism was observed. The transient characteristics of this mechanism, the pressure range over which it operates, the effects of alterations in cardiac function, and the instantaneous pressure-flow relationships at various levels of coronary vascular tone were examined and are the subject of the present report. These studies have been reported previously in preliminary form.

Methods

Studies were conducted on 22 mongrel dogs weighing between 14 kg and 34 kg. After induction of anesthesia (see below), the animals were intubated and respired with intermittent positive pressure from a Harvard respiratory pump. A left thoracotomy was performed, the heart was suspended in a pericardial cradle, and the circumflex coronary artery was dissected free close to its origin. Heparin (10 mg/kg) was administered and the dose repeated every half hour during the experiment. The vessels were then cannulated and a complete exchange transfusion with mixed donor blood was performed.

The extracorporeal circuit used to permit variation of coronary perfusion pressure independent of aortic pressure is shown in figure 1. The coronary artery was perfused either from the femoral artery or, by turning a stopcock, from a reservoir from which nonphasic perfusions were carried out for periods up to thirty minutes. No difference in the rate of coronary blood flow was noted when sequential perfusions from the femoral artery and from the bottle were performed at identical mean pressures. The reservoir was attached to a compressed air system; a 20-liter buffer bottle prevented decay of pressure during perfusion.

The reservoir was filled between runs from one femoral artery while mixed donor venous blood was simultaneously transfused at a matched rate.

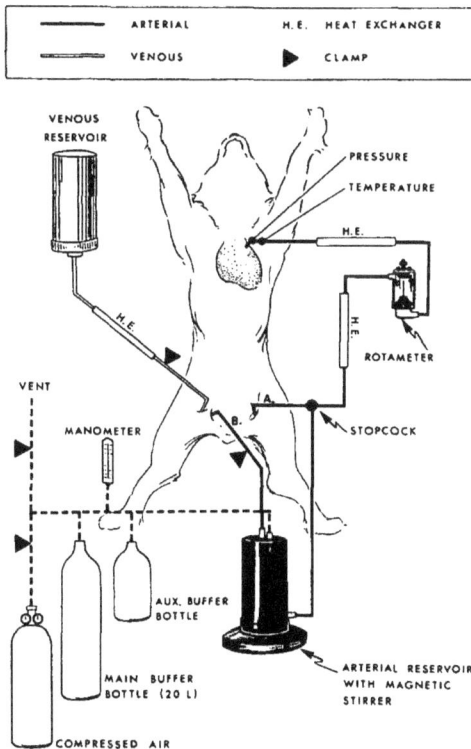

Figure 1: *Schematic representation of extracorporeal circuit employed for study of autoregulation of coronary blood flow. Perfusion of coronary artery was carried out either from left femoral artery (line A), or from arterial reservoir bottle. The bottle was filled intermittently from right femoral artery (line B). Perfusion pressure was measured proximal to coronary cannula.*

Whenever the coronary artery was perfused from the reservoir, precisely matched bleeding from the femoral vein maintained the animal's blood volume constant.

Blood loss during the experiment was replaced with donor blood and with 6% dextran solution. The quantity of dextran solution administered never exceeded 10% of the total pool of blood and had a negligible effect on hematocrit. During any run, hematocrit levels drawn from the perfusion circuit did not vary more than 4%. In two experiments, digitalis preparations[2] were administered because of signs of cardiac failure. The results of these experiments did not differ from the others.

Countercurrent heat exchangers in the arterial line were regulated from a thermistor probe placed in the perfusion line near the coronary cannula. A thermistor in the vena cava regulated heating pads beneath the animal. A heat exchanger was also employed in the line to the venous reservoir.

The compliance and resistance of this perfusion circuit were measured. A pressure step of 100 mm Hg applied to the circuit with the cannula occluded resulted in negligible flow; blood flow of 100 ml/min produced a pressure drop of less than 5 mm Hg between the reservoir and coronary cannula.

Four parameters were continuously recorded on a multi-channel photographic oscillograph[3]. Coronary flow was measured with a Shipley-Wilson rotameter, either directly or through a damping circuit with a filter-time constant of 0.5 sec. Coronary perfusion pressure was obtained through a side arm of the perfusion cannula; aortic pressure through a catheter inserted into the aortic arch by way of the left carotid artery and left ventricular pressure through a catheter passed by way of a segmental pulmonary vein. All pressures were measured with Statham pressure transducers.

---

2   Digoxin (expt. 21) and Cedalanid-D (expt. 22), 0.06 mg/kg.

3   Electronics for Medicine, White Plains, NY.

The ventricular pressure signal was fed to an integrating circuit which was balanced to accumulate voltage only during systole. An external switch driven by a synchronous motor discharged the integrator every 10 sec. This technique provided a simple, convenient method of continuously computing the total pressure generated by ventricular contraction over 10-sec intervals, and will be referred to as the ventricular pressure integral (VPI). In the absence of significant variations in ventricular volume, VPI is a function of the tension developed by the shortening of myocardial fibers, and, is thus an index of the level of myocardial performance. It is similar to the "tension-time index" of Sarnoff et al. and the "cardiac effort index" of Cerola et al.[4] present study, the VPI was used as one measure of the constancy of cardiac performance.

Because a relatively steady cardiovascular state during the course of each experimental run was essential, several different anesthetic systems were assayed and employed in the experiments. The anesthetics employed were: sodium pentobarbital (30 mg/kg), (expt. 1–3); morphine-Dial-urethane-pentobarbital, (expt. 5, 10); halothane (0.5 to 1.0%) and nitrous oxide (60%) and oxygen (40%), (expt. 6–9); nitrous oxide (60%) and oxygen (40%) and succinylcholine (0.05 mg/kg/min), (expt. 4, 11); nitrous oxide (60%) and oxygen (40%) and succinylcholine (0.05 mg/kg/ min) and morphine sulfate, (expt. 12–14). A steady cardiovascular state could be obtained for varying periods with each of these techniques. Periodic administration of barbiturates and urethane produced an undulating anesthetic level. The inhalation agents provided a more stable anesthetic state; however, halothane (0.5 to 1%) sufficiently depressed myocardial reserve to prohibit elevation of ventricular function by aortic constriction or transfusion. With nitrous oxide and oxygen and succinylcholine, tachycardia and arrhythmias were

---

4 In addition, however, the VPI eliminates the sustained diastolic pressure in the aorta as well as the passively developed diastolic pressure in the left ventricle. It also takes into account the time course of development of ventricular pressure and irregularities of heart rhythm.

frequent; this problem was largely circumvented by the addition of morphine and this combination of agents provided the most stable as well as the most reactive experimental preparations.

STEADY STATE PRESSURE FLOW CURVES

Two experimental protocols were employed. In the first the arterial reservoir was pressurized to a given level while the coronary artery was perfused from the femoral arterial line. By changing the position of the stopcock, perfusion was rapidly changed to the reservoir. The change in coronary flow in response to the alteration in perfusion pressure was recorded until stabilization had occurred (from 30 seconds to 2 minutes), and perfusion via the femoral artery was then re-established. After coronary flow had again stabilized at the control level, the cycle was repeated with a different pressure in the reservoir. Following perfusion at low pressure levels, reactive hyperemia necessitated perfusion at arterial pressure for periods of 3 to 5 minutes to regain control flow levels. The response of coronary flow to sudden changes in perfusion pressure for a series of pressure steps from 0 to 300 mm Hg were studied in this manner. With the second protocol, the coronary bed was perfused continuously from the reservoir during an entire run; pressure levels within the reservoir were changed, following stabilization of flow, by temporarily occluding the compressed air line between the manometer and the auxiliary buffer bottle. This method permitted any pattern of sequential variation in perfusion pressure to be employed.

In five animals, upon completion of a series of pressure steps at a constant level of cardiac function, the level of function was changed by bleeding, transfusion or aortic constriction. A series of pressure steps was then imposed at this new stable level.

INSTANTANEOUS PRESSURE-FLOW CURVES

In five animals the perfusion technique was modified to determine the pressure-flow characteristics of the vascular bed at a particular level of vascular tone and constant cardiac work, exclusive of compensatory or regulatory changes. To accomplish this, the coronary artery was perfused at a chosen pressure until flow became stable, at which time the perfusion pressure was abruptly changed to a different pressure. F 10''' was determined 1 to 2 sec after the pressure change, i.e., before any active compensation occurred. Perfusion pressure was then returned to the initial value and flow was allowed to restabilize at its initial value. This procedure was repeated until rapid changes from the same initial pressure to a number of other pressures had been made. The reference pressure was then changed to a new level, and a new series was recorded. During this part of the experiment, the rotameter signal was recorded without electrical damping.

In two experiments, in order to test the degree of coronary dilatation during perfusion at low pressures, 325 μg of nitroglycerin were rapidly injected into the coronary cannula during perfusion at 40 mm Hg. Control injections of identical amounts were also made during perfusion at approximately 100 mm Hg.

At the completion of each experiment, methylene blue was injected into the coronary cannula during perfusion. The heart was then excised, weighed, and the dyed area dissected out and weighed separately. Staining by this technique permitted coronary flow to be reported in ml/100 g heart muscle/min in 11 experiments.

An experimental run was considered satisfactory when a sufficient number of pressure steps was obtained without obvious signs of alteration in cardiac state. Stability of cardiac state was judged on the basis of lack of variation of the VPI, aortic pressure, and heart rate. Points on runs were discarded if any of these parameters appeared to be unstable. If progressive failure, evidenced by increasing left ventricular end diastolic pressure, developed during a high work run, the run was discarded since it was observed that elevation of left ventricular diastolic pressure was accompanied by significant diminution in coronary flow at constant perfusion pressure. Although myocardial function frequently declined if perfusion pressures below 60 to 70 mm Hg were sustained, these data were not discarded since the coronary bed was considered to be fully dilated at perfusion pressures below this level, for reasons described below. The results reported are from 14 technically satisfactory experiments out of a total series of 22.

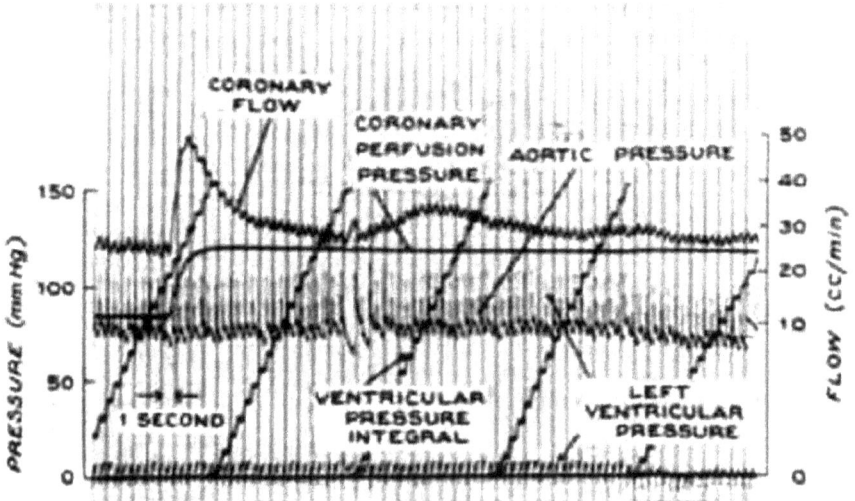

Figure 2: *Recording of coronary blood flow, coronary perfusion pressure, aortic pressure (full pulse and mean), left ventricular pressure, and ventricular pressure integral, demonstrating transient flow response to a sudden increment in coronary perfusion pressure.*

RESULTS

TRANSIENT PRESSURE-FLOW RESPONSES

The response of the coronary bed to a sudden change in perfusion pressure was similar in all experiments, A sudden change in perfusion pressure was accompanied by an initial abrupt change in flow in the same direction. Almost immediately, however, coronary flow began to return toward its former value while perfusion pressure remained at the new level. In figure 2 a recording of a sudden increase in perfusion pressure from 82 to 110 mm Hg is reproduced. In addition to the rapid return of flow toward its previous value during a period of approximately 10 sec, oscillation of flow with a period of about 15 sec was noted. The stabilized flow was very close to the original flow despite the considerable difference in perfusion pressure.

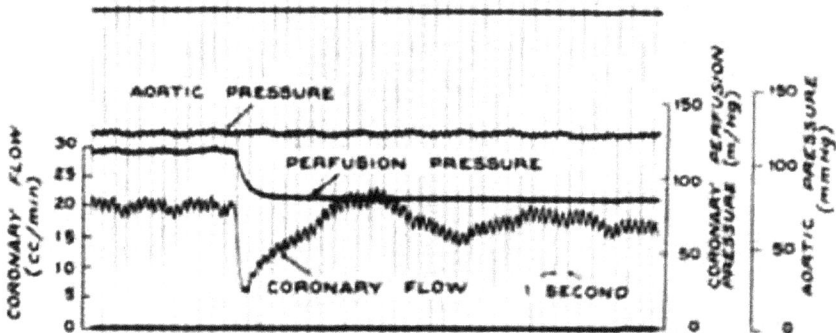

Figure 3: *Recording of coronary blood flow, mean aortic pressure, and mean coronary perfusion pressure, demonstrating transient flow response to a sudden decrement in perfusion pressure.*

In response to a sudden decrease in perfusion pressure (from 120 to 85 mm Hg, fig. 3), the same type of flow change in the opposite direction was seen, and, again, oscillations occurred.

Two exceptions to this type of transient behavior were observed. Following periods of perfusion at pressures below approximately 70 mm Hg, a sudden increase in perfusion pressure to values over 70 mm Hg caused the usual abrupt increase in coronary flow, but flow failed to return rapidly toward control values and, instead, slowly drifted downward for periods as long as five minutes before restabilizing. This type of reactive hyperemia has been described following temporary occlusion of a coronary artery. The second exception to the usual type of transient behavior was noted when perfusion pressure was changed from a pressure below 70 mm Hg to another pressure below 70 mm Hg. In this case no compensatory change in flow was noted; coronary flow passively followed perfusion pressure.

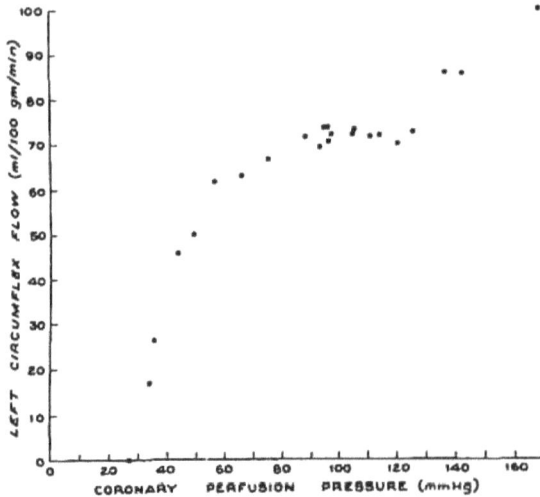

Figure 4: *Steady-state pressure-flow curve (expt. 10) obtained in a single experimental animal during constant cardiac function.*

STEADY-STATE PRESSURE-FLOW CURVES

The postcompensation, stabilized flow values observed following each pressure step were plotted against the corresponding perfusion pressures. A "steady-state" pressure-flow curve was thus obtained. A typical curve is reproduced in figure 4 and exhibits a range of pressures, from 70 to 130 mm Hg, in which coronary flow was independent of perfusion pressure. In each of the 14 experiments in which a sufficient number of pressure steps could be imposed (10 to 20) while the indices of cardiac function remained unchanged, a curve of similar shape was obtained (table 1). The average pressure at the lower end of the range over which flow was independent of pressure (A) was 70 mm Hg; the average for the upper end of this pressure range (B) was 144 mm Hg. The smallest range of pressure over which flow was independent of pressure was in experiment 5 (62 to 120 mm Hg) and the widest was in experiment 12 (70 to 225 mm Hg). For each experiment, one-half of the difference between the highest and the lowest flows at the extremes of these pressure ranges was expressed as percentage of the average flow in that range (table 1, % Δ CBF A-B). The average maximum deviation of flow over these wide pressure ranges was ± 7%. In the 11 experiments in which the perfused myocardial segment was weighed, the average coronary flow at pressures between 70 and 140 mm Hg (124 points) was 64.6 ml/min/100 g, and ranged from 45.0 to 103.9 ml/min/100 g. The average absolute flow rate in all experiments at pressures between 70 and 80 mm Hg was 59.8 ± 5.5 ml/min/100 g, and at pressures between 130 and 140, 72.6 ± 7.0 ml/min/100 g.

At pressures lower than 60 to 70 mm Hg, coronary flow was directly related to perfusion pressure, and in five experiments in which zero flow was obtained, flow ceased at an average pressure of 23 mm Hg.

In most experiments, postcompensation stabilized flows were directly related to perfusion pressure at pressures greater than 140 mm Hg, but the pressure at which this dependence began was variable. In three dogs in which light anesthesia was employed (expt. 12–14), minimal changes in stabilized blood flow rates were observed with high perfusion pressures, ranging up to 225 mm Hg.

TABLE 1

Steady-State Pressure-Flow Relationships in Coronary Vascular Bed

Expt. no.	Cor. perf. pr. mm Hg A	B	Avg CBF ml/min/100 g * A-B	%Δ CBF A-B	Avg MABP (range) mm Hg A-B	Avg H.R. (range) beats/min A-B	%Δ VPI A-B
1	68	148	(18.8)°	± 15	98(93 — 102)	167(164 — 170)	—
2	76	165	(20.2)°	± 15	121(118 — 123)	116(110 — 121)	—
3	60	120	48.4	± 7	116(109 — 130)	126(119 — 129)	—
4	73	136	103.9	± 8	126(105 — 146)	205(186 — 219)	—
5	62	120	64.9	± 2.5	85(68 — 94)	189(180 — 195)	± 15%
6	80	140	69.9	± 5	112(107 — 121)	163(136 — 168)	± 9%
7	85	147	53.5	± 8	107(101 — 114)	126(123 — 132)	—
8	60	120	49.1	± 11	106(98 — 111)	154(150 — 156)	± 9%
9	70	155	54.0	± 14	112(108 — 117)	143(136 — 147)	± 4%
10	70	130	71.5	± 2	104(103 — 106)	205(198 — 216)	± 1%
11	68	145	90.8	± 16	123(119 — 128)	114(102 — 120)	± 3%
12	70	225	59.3	± 8	136(126 — 145)	114(102 — 120)	± 3%
13	70	140	45.0	± 2.5	97(90 — 101)	166(162 — 174)	± 5%
14	68	135	(28.5)°	± 4	96(98 — 102)	158(156 — 162)	± 2%

Cor. perf. pr. = coronary perfusion pressure. A = lowest perfusion pressure at which autoregulation was observed. B = highest perfusion pressure at which autoregulation was observed. Avg CBF A—B = average coronary blood flow at pressures between A and B. %Δ CBF A—B = deviation of most widely separated flows observed between pressures A and B expressed as per cent of average flow between pressures A and B. Avg MABP (range) A—B = average and range of mean systemic arterial blood pressure between A and B. Avg H.R. (range) A—B = average and range of heart rate between A and B. %Δ VPI A—B = maximum per cent change in ventricular pressure integral between A and B.

° Weight of perfused myocardium not obtained; flows expressed in ml/min.

CORONARY AUTOREGULATION

TABLE 2

Steady-State Pressure-Flow Relationships in Coronary Vascular Bed During Control Period and Following Alteration in Cardiac Performance

Expt. no.	Avg MABP (range) mm Hg A-B	Cor. perf. pr. mm Hg A	B	Avg CBF ml/min/100 g * A-B	% △ CBF A-B	Avg H.R. (range) beats/min A-B	% △ VPI A-B
9	112(108 — 117)	70	155	54.0	± 14	143(136 — 147)	± 4%
	71(69 — 74)	55	155	36.9	± 12	122(120 — 125)	± 8%
11	123(119 — 128)	68	145	90.8	± 16	114(102 — 120)	± 3%
	72(67 — 80)	58	135	64.8	± 13	120(114 — 126)	± 3%
13	136(126 — 145)	70	225	59.3	± 8	114(102 — 120)	± 3%
	140(133 — 148)	72	160	78.9	± 7	120(114 — 126)	± 3%
13	97(90 — 101)	70	140	45.0	± 2.5	166(162 — 174)	± 5%
	171/4 (LVP)	110	200	74.0	± 9	170(126 — 198)	± 14%
14	96(89 — 102)	68	135	28.5	± 4	158(156 — 159)	± 2%
	141/7 (LVP)	80	170	41.1	± 11	166(156 — 180)	± 7%

Captions are identical to those in table 1. In this table, the column showing induced alterations in systemic arterial pressure (Avg MABP (range) mm Hg A — B) has been moved to the left.

° Weight of perfused myocardium not obtained; flows expressed in ml/min.

Captions are identical to those in table 1. In this table, the column showing induced alterations in systemic arterial pressure (Avg MABP (range) mm Hg- A—B) has been moved to the left .

*Weight of perfused myocardium not obtained; flows expressed in ml/min.

EFFECT OF ALTERATION IN CARDIAC PERFORMANCE

In five experiments, alterations in cardiac function were induced. The results are summarized in table 2. In two experiments, a decrease in cardiac effort resulted in a reduction of coronary blood flow; nevertheless, flow was regulated and remained independent of perfusion pressure (fig. 6). In three experiments, cardiac function was increased. In each instance, coronary blood flow increased and was regulated at the higher level of flow.

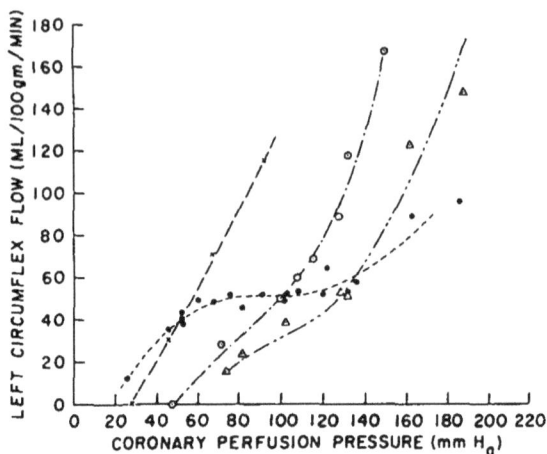

Figure 5: *Steady-state pressure-flow curve has been drawn through solid circles. Instantaneous pressure-flow curves, drawn through the cross marks, open circles, and triangles were obtained from initial perfusion pressures of 45, 97, and 125 mm Hg respectively.*

INSTANTANEOUS PRESSURE-FLOW CURVES

Peak instantaneous flow changes following several pressure steps from a single initial pressure are illustrated in figures 5 and 6. Similar curves were obtained in the five experiments of this type. In figure 5, the steady-state pressure-flow curve is shown, and instantaneous pressure-flow curves from initial pressures of 45 mm Hg, 97 mm Hg, and 125 mm Hg are plotted. At higher initial pressure levels, the slope of the curves decreases and the pressure at which zero flow was observed was higher. In figure 6, the immediate flow responses to various pressure steps from 40 mm Hg are plotted. In this, as in the other four experiments, the lower portion of this curve coincided with the lower portion of the steady-state pressure-flow curves.

40

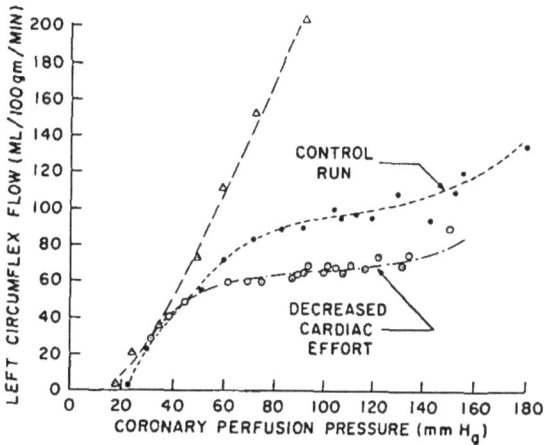

FIGURE 6

Figure 6: *Steady-state pressure-flow curves at a control level (solid circles) and at a decreased level of cardiac performance (open circles). The instantaneous pressure-flow curve from a perfusion pressure of 40 mm Hg has been drawn through triangles.*

A rapid injection of nitroglycerin into the coronary cannula at low perfusion pressure was carried out in two experiments. In one experiment, at a perfusion pressure of 40 mm Hg, flow increased from 32 to 40 ml/min. At a pressure of 11.5 mm Hg, nitroglycerin increased flow from 50 to 120 ml/ min. In the second experiment, injection of nitroglycerin at a perfusion pressure of 38 mm Hg increased flow from 10 to 1.3 ml/min. At perfusion pressure of 100 mm Hg, a similar injection caused flow to increase from 27.4 ml/min to 51 ml/min.

DISCUSSION

Indirect evidence that coronary blood flow is not primarily pressure dependent has been reported by Alella et al., who calculated that changes in coronary blood flow over a wide range of cardiac activity could be fully accounted for on the basis of changes in myocardial oxygen utilization. The steady-state pressure-flow curves obtained in the present studies demonstrate directly that in the physiologic range of arterial blood pressure, coronary perfusion pressure is not a major determinant of coronary blood flow. In addition, the transient flow responses demonstrate an active mechanism that rapidly alters the coronary vascular resistance. Although previous studies have suggested that the coronary circulation can exhibit autoregulation, completeness of the response observed in the present experiments and the wide range of pressure over which it operated were striking. The similarity of transient and steady-state autoregulatory responses in the myocardium to those recently observed in skeletal muscle is also noteworthy.

Below the flat central portions of the pressure-flow curves, coronary flow was directly related to perfusion pressure. The lower inflection in the steady-state curve thus represents the lowest pressure at which vasomotor mechanisms can compensate for decrements in perfusion pressure; at this point vasodilation is complete or near-complete. The shape of the lower limb of the pressure-flow curve, the absence of transient responses to pressure steps, the minimal response to nitroglycerin, and the reproducibility of this portion of the curve in various runs in a single animal, and among different animals, lend support to this concept of near-complete vasodilation at low perfusion pressure.

The upper limb of the steady-state pressure-flow curve is more difficult to interpret. Here, again, it would appear that the inflection may represent the point at which vasoconstriction can no longer completely regulate flow in the face of increasing perfusion pressure. It is also possible that at high pressures a larger area of myocardium was perfused. It was noted that the upper limb exhibited considerable variability from animal to animal, was influenced by the anesthetic agent, and could not be readily reproduced in the same animal.

The mechanism of autoregulation is unclear at present. The myogenic response of vascular smooth muscle to stretch offers a possible explanation although it is difficult to reconcile this mechanism with the increase in resistance and actual diminution in vessel caliber observed following pressure increases. Theories to explain this apparent paradox have recently been proposed, however. It has been postulated that stretch of an elastic element that is coupled in series to the muscle element may result in contraction of the muscle and an overall decrease in vessel wall circumference. Others have suggested that stretch may increase the rate of contraction of individual muscle cells, thereby allowing less time for the relaxation phase.

Another possible explanation for autoregulation is a change in the rate of washout or in the rate of production of a vasoactive metabolite. It has been suggested that this factor may be dependent upon myocardial oxygen tension, or that oxygen tension itself may be operative. Although the transient flow responses described above are consistent with the operation of a feedback control system capable of sensing a flow-dependent variable, the experiments do not provide definitive information concerning the etiology of the autoregulation.

Although the present studies include only indices of cardiac performance, previous studies have demonstrated that the rate of coronary blood flow is closely related to and possibly dependent upon the rate of oxygen utilization by the myocardium. The data presented here support this concept; since after a change in cardiac function, coronary flow changed in the same direction to a new level where flow was again regulated independent of perfusion pressure. It is of interest that Stainsby has recently demonstrated in skeletal muscle that autoregulation persists when the level of blood flow is altered by changing the activity of the muscle.

Since the coronary bed responds to changes in perfusion pressure by rapidly altering its resistance, it is difficult to define the pressure-flow characteristics of the bed at a given state of vasomotor tone. In an attempt to approach this problem, the instantaneous pressure-flow curves were derived. With the reservation that the response time of the rotameter prohibits actual measurement of "instantaneous" flow changes, these curves appear to represent adequately this relationship. Measurements of the pressure-volume characteristics of the coronary arterial tree suggest that the compliance of the coronary arteries does not introduce a significant error. The decreased slopes of the instantaneous pressure-flow curves obtained from higher initial pressure values (fig. 5) appear to reflect increasing resistance of the bed. In addition, flow reached zero at higher pressures as the resistance of the bed increased. These observations are in agreement with the concept of increasing critical closing pressure with increasing vasomotor tone. The pressure level of 20 mm Hg at which cessation of flow into the fully dilated bed occurred is similar to the value for peripheral coronary pressure obtained in animals with negligible collateral circulation. The coincidence of the instantaneous pressure-flow curve obtained in the dilated bed with the lower limb of the steady-state pressure-flow curves at different work levels is apparent (fig. 6). Since this instantaneous pressure-flow curve has a definite although steep slope, the lowest perfusion pressure at which regulation of flow failed was higher when cardiac effort was increased (fig. 6).

These studies offer a possible explanation for some of the conflicting results concerning the regulation of coronary flow. If maximal coronary vasodilation is induced, the autoregulatory mechanism is no longer operative and mechanical factors primarily determine flow. If adequate coronary perfusion follows a period of inadequate perfusion, autoregulation of flow will become apparent only after a period of reactive hyperemia. The activity of the regulatory mechanism may also be impaired by such factors as hemolysis, damage to the myocardium, or decreased arterial oxygen tension. These factors may play a role in the apparently close relationship between coronary perfusion pressure and flow described in some experiments.

Time-dependent properties of the control system are also of importance in considering the relation of coronary blood flow to perfusion pressure. If, for example, regulation occurred more slowly than an imposed continuous pressure change, a curve similar to the "instantaneous" pressure-flow curve would be obtained. In addition, the use of continuously changing pressure may give data which is difficult to interpret, since the tracking error of a control system may be large and appears inaccessible to analysis by conventional techniques. In the present experiments, by allowing stabilization between pressure changes, a steady-state curve nearly equivalent to that which would result from an infinitely slow rate of pressure change was obtained.

Certain limitations in the present experiments are apparent. It is recognized that the use of anesthesia, open chest techniques, an extracorporeal circuit, cannulation of the coronary artery, and the partial use of nonphasic perfusion pressures necessitates caution in extrapolation of the data to intact animals. Despite these limitations, a sensitive autoregulatory mechanism has been demonstrated.

SUMMARY

Control of the coronary circulation has been investigated in an experimental preparation in which coronary flow was suddenly increased or decreased by the imposition of sudden changes in coronary perfusion pressure during periods of constant cardiac performance.

The transient response to these changes in coronary perfusion pressure was an initial abrupt change in flow in the same direction, followed by a prompt return of flow toward the previous level. The response was completed in 10 to 15 sec, and was followed by a few cycles of damped oscillation having a period of 10 to 12 sec.

Steady-state pressure-flow curves demonstrated a range of perfusion pressures over which coronary blood flow was relatively independent of pressure. Below this pressure range the coronary bed appeared to be fully dilated, and the blood flow was directly dependent upon perfusion pressure.

Elevation of the level of cardiac function resulted in autoregulation of coronary flow at a higher level of flow, and decreasing the level of cardiac function resulted in regulation of coronary flow at a lower flow rate.

Instantaneous pressure-flow characteristics of the coronary bed, exclusive of compensatory influences, were also determined.

The experiments demonstrated an intrinsic mechanism that regulated blood flow to the myocardium. In the physiologic range of arterial pressure, coronary perfusion pressure did not appear to be a major determinant of coronary blood flow. Coronary flow appeared to be autoregulated at a level related to myocardial effort.

REFERENCES

Alella, A., Williams, F L., Bolene-Williams, C, & Katz, L.N. (1955). Interrelation between cardiac oxygen consumption and coronary blood flow. *Am. J. Physiol.* 183:570.

Anhep, G.V., & Hausler, H.D. (1928). Coronary circulation: I. Effect of changes of the blood pressure and of output of heart. *J. Physiol.* 65:357.

Bayliss, V.M. (1902). On the local changes of the arterial wall to changes of internal pressure. *J. Physiol.* 28:220.

Berne, R.M. (1961). Nucleotide degration in the hypoxic heart and its possible relation to regulation of coronary blood flow. *Federation Proc.* 20:101.

Braunwald, E., Sarnoff, S.J., Case, R.B., Stainsby, W.N., & Welch, G.H., Jr. (1958). Hemodynamic determinants of coronary flow; effect of changes in aortic pressure and cardiac output on the relationship between myocardial oxygen consumption and coronary flow. *Am. J. Physiol.* 192:157.

Burton, A.C. (1954). Relation of structure to function of tissues of wall of blood vessels. *Physiol. Rev.* 34:619.

Cerola, A., Feinberg, H., & Katz, L.N. (1959). Role of eatecholamines on energetics of the heart and its blood supply. *Am. J. Physiol.* 196:394.

Chambliss, J.R., Demminc, J., Wells, K., Cline, W. W., & Eckstein, R.W. (1950). Effect of hemolized blood on coronary blood flow. *Am. J. Physiol.* 163: 545.

Ckuz, R. (1958), Hemodynamic determinants of oxygen consumption of the heart with special reference to the tension-time index. *Am. J. Physiol.* 192:48.

Coffman, J.D., & Gregg, D.E. (1960). Blood flow and oxygen debt from coronary artery occlusion. *Clin. Res.* 8:179.

Cregg, D.E., & Shipley, R.E. (1944). Augmentation of left coronary inflow with elevation of left ventricular pressure and observations on the mechanism for increased coronary inflow with increased cardiac load. *Am. J. Physiol.* 142:44.

Cross, C.E., Rieben, P.A., & Salisbury, P.F. (1961). Coronary driving pressure and vasomotortonus as determinants of coronary blood flow. *Circulation Res.* 9:589.

Eckel, R., Eckstein, R.W., Stroud, M., & Pritchard, W. (1949). Effects of over and under perfusion upon coronary arterial blood flow. *Federation Proc.* 8: 38.

Eckenhoff, J.E., Hafkeuschiel, J.H., L & Messer, C.M., & Harmel, M. (1947). Cardiac oxygen metabolism and control of coronary circulation. *Am. J. Physiol.* 149: 634.

Eckstein, R.W., Gregg, D.E., & Pritchard, W.H. (1941). Magnitude and time of development of collateral circulation in occluded femoral, carotid, and coronary arteries. *Am. J. Physiol.*132:351.

——— Stroud, M., Ill, Dowlinc, C.V., & Pritchard, W.H. (1950). Factors influencing changes in coronary flow following sympathetic nerve stimulation. *Am. J. Physiol.*162:266.

Fishback, M.E., Burnett, L., & Scher, A.M. (1959). Autoregulation of coronary blood flow in the dog heart. *Clin. Res.* 7:60.

Folkow, B., & Öberg, B. (1961). Autoregulation and basal tone in consecutive vascular sections of the skeletal muscles in reserpine-treated cats. *Acta Physiol. Scand.* 53:105,

Foltz, E.L., Page, R.G., Sheldon, W.F. Wong, S.K., Tuddenham, W.J., & Weiss, A.J. (1950). Factors in variation and regulation of coronary blood flow in intact anesthetized dogs. *Am. J. Physiol.* 162:521.

Gregg, D.E., Green, H.D., & Wiggehs, C.J. (1935). Phasic variations in peripheral coronary resistance and their determinants. *Am. J. Physiol.* 112:362.

Green, H D., & Wechia, R. (1942). Effects of asphyxia, anoxia and myocardial ischemia on coronary blood flow. *Am. J. Physiol.* 135:271,

Hilton, R., & Eichholtz, I. (1925). The influence of chemical factors on the coronary circulation. *J. Physiol.* 59: 413,

Mosher, P.W., Ross, J., Jr., Mcfate, P. A.,& Shaw, R. F. (1962). The regulation of coronary blood flow, (abstr.) *Bull. N. Y. Acad. Med.*38:838,

Osheb, W.J. (1953). Pressure-flow relationship of the coronary system. *Am. J. Physiol.* 172: 403.

Rein, H. (1951). Ober die Drosselungstoleranz und diekritische Drosselungsgrenze der Herz-Coronargefasse.Arch. *Ges. Physiol.* 253:205.

Rosenblueth, A., Alanis, J., Rub1o, R., & Pilar, G. (1961). Relations between coronary flow and work of the heart. *Am. J. Physiol.* 200:243.

Ross, J., Jr., Mosher, P.W., & Shaw, R.F. (1960). Autoregulation of coronary blood flow. (abstr.) *Circulation* 22:728.

Sarnoff, S.J., Braunwald, E., Welch, G.H. ,Jr., Case, R.B., Stainsby, W.N., & Mar (1964). *Circulation Research, Volume XIV, March.*

Shipley, R.E., & Wilson, C (1951). An improved recording rotameter. *Proc. Soc. Exptl. Biol .Med.* 78: 724.

Sparks, H.V., Jr., & Bohr, D.F. (1962). Effect of stretch on passive tension and contractility of isolated vascular smooth muscle. *Am. J. Physiol.* 202:835.

Stainsby, V.N. (1962). Autoregulation of blood flow in skeletal muscle during increased metabolic activity. *Am. J. Physiol.* 202:273.

——— & Renkin, E.M. (1961). Autoregulation of blood flow in resting skeletal muscle. *Am. J. Physiol.* 201:117.

CHAPTER 3

LSD[5]

By Paul Mosher

LSD-25 is the laboratory designation of a synthetic hallucinogen more powerful than any other known. Its full name is d-lysergic acid diethylamide tartrate. The substance, lysergic acid, is derived from a fungus called ergot that on occasion develops in the place ordinarily occupied by the seed of rye and other grasses. Evidencing value in therapy, and but one of the hundreds of new psychopharmaceutical drugs—a large percentage of which are other than hallucinogens—the influence of LSD-25 on the typical and atypical individual continues to be studied. The research of a medical student and the deliberations of a medical seminar with regard to LSD-25 follow.

> *"And then I glanced at the clock again.*
> *This time it read 12:28, which led me to exclaim:*
> *'My God, so much has happened in the last three minutes.'"*
>
> —Paul Mosher

In some drug-experiences, there is the report of what seems to be a notable increase in the rate of thinking. Seconds seem forever,

---

5   From the Chapter "LSD," pp. 353–367 in: The Drug Experience: First-person Accounts of Addicts, Writers, Scientists, and Others. David Elbin, Editor. ©1961 by David Elbin on Orion Press; Evergreen Black Cat edition, 1965.

Returned to the ordinary everyday, the thinking made earlier seems to be out of reach. What, then, was the character of the thinking performed during the drug-experience? Is it, perhaps, that what is called euphoria is new work performed or old work relinquished, or something in between? Would those whose place it is to help the mentally ill be helped if they themselves experienced the change brought about by a psychomimetic drug?

Paul Mosher, a medical student concerned with the last question in particular, made up his mind to use the recently developed synthetic hallucinogen LSD-25, and possibly ascertain the answer for himself. His experiment, which took place in 1960, was written up at the request of the Editor and is published here for the first time.

My friends are inclined to raise their eyebrows when they hear that I took LSD; it seems that in doing so, I stepped slightly but distinctly out of character.

At the time I was a medical student with an awakening interest in psychiatry. Literally ninety percent of my training had been in the natural sciences, chiefly physics and biochemistry. I had been taught that trying a drug for yourself was not necessarily the way to learn its effects; the approved method was to observe other people trying it.

And here was something to unsettle my faith and undermine the wisdom of my teachers: the more I learned, objectively, about hallucinogenic drugs, the larger grew the suspicion that I knew nothing at all. And this disturbed me; among other things, it cast a shadow across the well-known aphorism that a good obstetrician need not be himself pregnant. Why, I would ask myself, must I actually *take* a hallucinogenic drug in order to satisfy my curiosity?

No one could say that I hadn't tried. I had been working with hallucino-genic drugs for several years, generally giving them to animals and watching the animals become insane in a rather uninformative way. But that was to be expected of animals, who cannot talk; people would be different. And so I joined a research project headed by a group of psychiatrists. There I saw large doses of hallucinogens administered to human volunteers, who were able to communicate only slightly more information than the animals.

Meanwhile, I had reached the saturation point with regard to the literature. After having read every kind of description I could find of the hallucinogenic state, I was left with my curiosity stimulated, but if anything, less satisfied than before.

What, then, would I do? An answer towards which I was being gently conducted was this: I would try a hallucinogen myself. A rather odd decision for me to make: I had been taught to question the subjective experience, just as I had been taught to reject hearsay evidence, to laugh at superstition, to avoid unfounded assumptions. In surrendering my status as an unbiased observer, I imagined myself to be taking the least scientific view possible.

And yet the assumption of this position seemed not without merit. All the subjects had been so terribly uninformative; one could only conclude that the things which happened to them under hallucinogens were only in the smallest part available to an observer. Then records we took, the brain waves, the behavioral changes, the physiological disturbances, all of these were of little interest to me compared to the experiences which I assumed the subjects to be having. And so I too, would have these amazing experiences. I would wipe out the one overriding obstacle: the crippling lack of communication between subject and investigator. No longer would subject and investigator be separated by a hopeless gulf; l, in a magnificent experiment, would be both.

I rapidly arranged the event. As companion-observer for the "experiment," I decided upon H—, for many years a close friend of mine. As a pharmacology student he would contribute his own interest in hallucinogenic drugs, and would be relatively qualified, among other things, to keep me out of trouble.

Which of the several hallucinogens to try was not open to question: I had only one available. Somewhere in the course of my research I had ended up with a single vial of LSD-25, most potent of the hallucinogens. It had been destined for the last of my experimental frogs, upon whose untimely death I had inherited the chemical. The vial contained one cubic centimeter of water in which was dissolved one ten-thousandth of a gram of lysergic acid diethylamide tartrate.

On the morning of the appointed day, I arrived at the home of H—, a single furnished room, with the vial in my coat pocket. I had remembered not to eat breakfast, as the drug is absorbed more rapidly on an empty stomach. I was rather startled to find that H—'s preparations included two 1-cc. tuberculin syringes (for measurement), two 50-cc. flasks of distilled water, several black rubber stoppers, two bottles of thorazine solution for deep intramuscular (backside) injection (thorazine being a tranquilizer and supposedly an LSD antidote of sorts), two sterile 5-cc. syringes (for injection), a pad of notepaper, and at least three freshly sharpened pencils. As the bottles contained enough Thorazine to quiet an entire mental ward for days, I gathered that H— was rather transported at the prospect of my going insane, and envisioned saving me by administering the first deep intramuscular injection of his life. I was less than enthusiastic.

We had discussed the dosage, and had finally decided on 65 micrograms, which is not really considered a large dose. But I wished to be able to observe myself in a reasonably calm way, and I knew from seeing larger doses administered that they make rational observation impossible; they seem to put one into another world entirely. I wanted to remain enough in this world to say something useful perhaps, about what was happening.

But I must also admit to being somewhat afraid. I had seen subjects appear to enjoy the experience immensely. One of them, whom I knew personally, afterwards urged me to drop everything and try the drug immediately. Yet I had seen others scream and writhe in obvious agony or fright; several said later that nothing could ever induce them to repeat the experience, the most horrible, they insisted, of their lives. I had been warned that the slightest pressure, anxiety, or depression surrounding taking LSD can be enough to swing the balance from ecstasy to terror. I decided that by taking a smaller dose, I would accept the prospect of a milder Heaven, if it would guarantee a commensurably milder Hell.

As I began to crack open the ampoule, there was a knock at the door of H—'s room. We hid the equipment in a frenzy and opened the door. H—'s landlady stepped in and spoke for twenty minutes about her health until, with some adroitness, H— induced her, subtly, to leave. The incident unsettled me.

Again I began to saw off the top of the ampoule, laboriously, lest I smash it and lose all the LSD. H— took one of the small syringes and filled it to the proper mark, 65 micrograms, and then squirted the contents into one of the flasks of distilled water. (Ordinary tap water will inactivate LSD in seconds.)

I swirled the flask to mix the contents, an unnecessary gesture, paused for an inane toast, and drained the contents of the flask. H— recorded the time and asked me how I felt. I admitted to being a trifle nervous, and drank the other 50 ccs. of distilled water as a chaser. I then sat down in a large and comfortable armchair to wait for something to happen.

H— also sat down, in a chair opposite me. We had estimated forty-five minutes before an effect would be noticed. After the first ten or fifteen minutes, however, I noticed myself becoming more nervous, with sweating palms and a mild tremor of the fingertips. The room seemed unusually quiet. H— rose to pull down the shades, shutting out the daylight, and returned to his chair.

The pharmacopoeia says that LSD causes disturbances of the autonomic nervous system, including dilation of the pupils, nausea, sweating, increased heart rate and blood pressure; also, somatic disturbances such as muscular tremors and ataxia, which may end in violent shaking of the hands and loss of equilibrium. So it seems likely that even after these first ten minutes I was beginning to feel the initial effects of the drug. I especially remember that my presumably dilated pupils found the daylight very annoying.

Approximately twenty minutes later, I began to tense noticeably. A feeling of apprehension came over me, which I imagined to be a quality of the room rather than my own state of mind. H—, meanwhile, was obviously bored. He turned on his phonograph and took out a record of the Modern Jazz Quartet. With motions that seemed oddly deliberate, he placed the record on the turntable, set the volume at a low level, and returned to his chair. He seemed to be staring at me rather strangely; noted that forty minutes had passed.

I suppose at this point, with the feeling that H— was staring rather strangely at me, I was entering a somewhat paranoid stage, in which I felt that events around me were directed against me personally. I remembered one patient I had seen in an experiment; he had accused the doctors and nurses of deliberately provoking him, to test his reactions, The whole experiment, he decided, was a prearranged plot to annoy him. The odd thing in my own case was that at the same time I began to feel paranoid delusions, I began to think how paranoid it was of me to have them.

To see how far the paranoid theme would develop, I had asked H— earlier in the morning to refrain from acting in any but the most reassuring manner, and at the same time to point out any paranoid trends which he noticed in my thought. I had decided to give voice to such thoughts as they occurred to me. I asked H—, "Why are you staring at me like that?" "Like what?" "As though you thought I only pretended to take the drug." "Did you?" he asked. And he began to scribble on his note paper. Abruptly, I saw what was happening, and said: "Do you think that was a bit paranoid of me?" "Might be," he said, and went on scribbling. "Of course it was," I laughed, and added: "That's why you're writing it down, isn't it?" It struck me that the addendum was also in a rather paranoid vein, This amused me, and I began to laugh. H— looked up. "What's so funny?" he asked. It seemed too complicated to explain why I had laughed, so I said, "Don't worry, I'm not laughing at you." This provoked even greater hilarity.

In looking back, I tend to wonder about my laughter. Was it a case of finding things "funnier" under the drug, or was my laughter merely an involuntary reaction, independent of my thoughts? The truth is, it is hard for me to separate the two. My laughter seemed, more than anything else, the product of an altered emotional state. I did tend to see things as more "absurd" and hence funnier, but at the same time I was extracting humorous subtleties from a situation, my mood itself seemed to produce laughter which I could not control, and which pertained to more than simply this or that amusing thought. Even after I had forgotten the original joke, my hysteria continued with an apparent momentum of its own. I was, at any rate, extremely euphoric.

I felt that H— secretly doubted that the drug had caused my laughter, and that he believed I was only attempting to convince him, through a great show of merriment, that I had really taken it. We then discussed this delusion of mine as another paranoid idea, H— scribbling in a furious attempt to record my words verbatim, myself laughing as hard as I can remember ever laughing in my life.

Very soon after this I began to notice the first of the visual hallucinations. These originated as shifting patterns on the ceiling, and later became swirling fields of color whenever I closed my eyes.

In retrospect, I am not inclined to rhapsodize concerning these visions. They certainly did appear wonderfully splendid to me at the time. But I cannot forget that at the time I was in a state of wildly disturbed emotions. Insofar as one's aesthetic judgments are a function of his emotional condition, in part, I wonder to what extent my feelings about the beauty (or the horror) of my various hallucinations had to do with their actual appearance. Possibly this has been overlooked by many drug takers who, overcome with the intensity of the emotions which accompany their hallucinations, have been led to make statements about the extraordinary beauty of the hallucinatory visions themselves.

I rose from my chair and began to walk about the room. I felt a slight chill, and was moved to place my hands in my pockets. As we continued to talk, I burst into uncontrollable laughter at nearly everything said by H— or myself. This appeared to annoy H— who evidently felt himself excluded from a series of private jokes.

Another phenomenon was beginning to occur as the drug neared its full effect. In reply to H—'s inquiry as to how I felt, I replied, "I feel…" I hesitated for several seconds, and then concluded, "about the same as before." This brief hesitation is an example of what the observer often refers to, misleadingly, I think, as "thought blocking."

What I suspect happens is that one is able to go through several complete thoughts between the words of every sentence, at what must be a fantastic speed. It might go something like this: "I feel… (I wonder why he keeps asking me how I feel. Perhaps he wants to get as many notes as possible. But now supposing I told him that thought. He would write a note about it. Then I would have a new thought about that. And therefore, each time he wrote something, I would have another thought, and he would have to write it down, and it would go on forever. Ah, well. Imagine H— trying to interview me like a psychiatrist. I wonder what *he* would do if I were to ask him how *he* felt. Or if I took notes every time he asked a question. He would write down that I was writing something down, and I would write that he was writing something down. I wonder why I am laughing? Do I really feel "about the same as before," as I am about to tell H—? Or is the laughing a superficial effect of the drug, having nothing to do with the way I feel? Oh well, I am supposed to tell H— how I feel, so I might as well get it over with.) … about the same as before."

And this was only the beginning. Soon trains of thought started to appear between every word of every sentence. The speed of these thoughts seemed to promote euphoria, but it was a different matter when I tried putting my thoughts into words for H—'s benefit, and found intruding ideas between each pair of syllables; this can have a very demoralizing effect on a would-be speaker. I would begin a sentence, and by the time I had finished, so many thoughts had piled up that I was at a total loss where to begin the next sentence, And by the time the next sentence was begun, such a further backlog of ideas would have accumulated that finishing it would be out of the question. I had two alternatives: I could stop speaking, or I could resign myself to the fact that the words I spoke would have little to do with what I was thinking.

I cannot help wondering if a similar process is really part of our ordinary mental activity. It is possible that during a spoken sentence we are constantly editing, qualifying, and coloring our thoughts with associations that may range quite far afield. Only on the surface, perhaps, do we emerge with a verbal statement. Indeed, a covert thought which appears to us as being "true" or "logical" necessitates, in order to appear so, a great many assumptions and steps of reasoning which remain below the level of consciousness. Certainly, for a mechanism like the human brain, whose complexity dwarfs the comparatively childish digital computer, the mechanism of speech is a ridiculously slow readout device. Just as slow is the speed of what we call our "conscious" thought, by which we "read out" our thinking patterns to ourselves. It is quite plausible that our actual thought processes work at a much higher speed.

Another possibility, of course, is that under a hallucinogenic drug the process of thought is really sped up, so that one actually becomes a superfast thinker. It certainly feels that way, since all one is aware of under the drug is one's thoughts rushing at breakneck speed, and many drug-takers have put forth this latter view. But obviously, this is not a question to be decided by debate; at this point, all we can do is speculate.

As speech became increasingly difficult, I abandoned conversation altogether. Instead, I sat back down in the armchair and listened to the music. I tried closing my eyes. Instantly, the sound seemed to enclose me *physically,* and my sense of orientation with respect to the room vanished. The universe appeared to be occupied entirely by sound.

What followed was rather unlike any musical experience I have ever known. In the first place, my speeding brain seemed to assimilate the notes at a considerably greater rate than the musicians were able to play them. Thus, each note appeared to be separated from the next by a leisurely interval, so that I had ample time to consider the relationship of each note played to the entire composition, before the next note sounded. Secondly, my apparent ability to comprehend so many factors at once, enabled me to perceive the contribution of each musician to the entire musical production. The intentions of each musician became transparent: I knew "why" each one played the notes he did.

For my own peace of mind, I wish that I could arrive at some conclusion as to whether the above thoughts were delusional or not. But it's impossible for me now to even conceive of what it was like at the time. That hallucinogenic drugs give one the sense of an understanding quite beyond one's ordinary wisdom, is well known. Philosophically oriented persons, for instance, often report the ability to "understand" the total meaning and structure of the universe under the influence of hallucinogenic drugs. No one is as yet in a position to say exactly what this "understanding" entails.

However, one thing I can say is that whatever understanding I did have rapidly faded as the drug experience concluded, leaving only the ability to say that the understanding existed, and nothing more. At the time, I derived more meaning and more enjoyment from hearing the music than I had ever thought possible; yet upon listening to the same record since, I found that my level of musical appreciation was unchanged by the episode.

Apparently, one does not return from the hallucinogenic kingdom bearing any of its treasures.

When I reopened my eyes, H—— appeared to be sitting at a great distance from me, although his chair had not moved. As soon as I turned my full attention on him, he seemed to rush, in sitting position, towards me. Although my attention span was short, I was able to study him for perhaps half a minute, and as long as I did so, he remained immense and proximate, his face grotesquely distorted. When I lost interest in him, he immediately receded into the distance, and music again dominated my sensorium. This shifting back and forth of attention continued for perhaps an hour.

Although I felt fairly well-oriented at this time, I am perfectly sure I would have failed the simplest of psychological tests. I did not feel as though I had lost my ability to think (quite the contrary), but that I had lost most of my ability to *express* my thoughts. No sooner had H—— asked me a question than other thoughts would rapidly intrude, distracting my attention from the matter at hand, so that it was impossible to remain on one topic very long. Even when the answer to a question leapt instantly into consciousness, my mind was so preoccupied that it became simply too much trouble to go through the effort of mouthing the answer.

During this hour of intermittent conversation, H—— attempted to take advantage of my apparent spurts of subconscious wisdom to obtain my thoughts on some of his own personal problems, I answered all of his questions with an array of poorly executed puns, at which I laughed violently. Some of these struck me as funny because of inordinately complicated multiple meanings which I wove into them. As far as H—— was concerned, these highly hilarious super-puns were quite inscrutable, and in the matter of clarifying his own problems, the day was rather a total loss.

The rest of the time I devoted to listening to the music, out of contact with H—— or occasionally pacing around the room and joking with H—— in a disjointed way. As I paced, I happened to notice at one point the clock resting on the mantelpiece. It said, I clearly remember, 12:25. Then I lapsed into a train of thought whose various labyrinths seemed to lead me in thousands of directions for thousands of hours. And then I glanced at the clock again. This time it read 12:28, which led me to exclaim, "My God, so much has happened in the last three minutes."

H—— replied that as far as he had been able to see, I had walked around the room a few times, and that he failed to see what was meant by "so much has happened." I began to explain, but once again, my intended explanation swelled to such proportions that I was forced to let the matter drop in mid-sentence.

My sense of time was, of course, strikingly distorted. This may well have had something to do with the sudden unusual speed of my thoughts; the rate of mental processes must in some way provide a yardstick by which we measure the flow of time. If the yardstick were stretched, corresponding measurements would also be distorted. Seconds would literally become minutes, and minutes hours, which was exactly how things did seem to me. Once a subject told me that under a hallucinogen he had tried to take this distortion into account; he still ended up by estimating the time to be three hours later than it actually was. Thus each time I glanced at the clock in H—'s room, I was amazed at the brief interval in which "so much" had happened.

About three hours after taking the drug, I asked H— if he thought it might be safe for the two of us to venture out for a walk. He seemed unsure of himself, as he hesitated for a split second. I sensed the uncertainty and envisioned the conflict taking place in his thoughts.

Although this may have been somewhat delusional, I seemed to perceive a rapport between H—'s thoughts and my own. It appeared to be largely due to the fact that I was able to sense a number of nuances with regard to facial expression, eye movement, and voice inflection, details which I might ordinarily miss. I explained my feeling later to H——and he agreed that my interpretation of his thoughts was roughly correct.

H—'s hesitation was due to his fear of encountering either someone we knew, or a policeman, either of whom would immediately perceive my unusual behavior. On the other hand, he felt obligated to make my day as complete as possible, and did not wish to deprive me of a chance to walk in the park nearby, which I had expressed a desire to visit. He suggested at last that we wait for a half hour or so, to allow the drug's effect to level off, and possibly to wane a bit. I found myself rather relieved to have him take command of the situation, and gladly consented to wait.

Half an hour later, my nose emerged from the front doorway of the building. I suddenly bolted back into the hallway and seized H—'s coat. Feeling an absolute dearth of confidence, I imagined myself as a small child seeking its parents' protection in a crowd.

I could not remember ever feeling quite so unqualified to deal with the physical world. The presence of H— was reassuring to the point of being a necessity; I should have been utterly terrified if he had left me. Taking a potent hallucinogen by oneself, I imagine, would be likely to induce a state of panic, and to throw the entire tenor of the experience into the realm of horror. Did my dependence on H— cause me to feel like a small child, or did my feeling like a small child force me to rely on H—'s protection? When I ask myself this, I think immediately of the chicken and the egg.

A curious thing is that at the same time, I felt remarkably old and wise. But my wisdom seemed useless when applied to the problem of going outside. It seemed vaguely as though death awaited me there, in some innocuous disguise.

H— observed my uncertainty, and suggested I sit down on the step for a moment. When I had done so, I looked out at the scene before me and noticed the unusual distortions in my vision. The daylight was intense; the trees in the park were a gaudy shade of green; every object was outlined with strange clarity and precision, as though my normal vision were some sort of myopia. More striking yet was a confusion of my depth perception. As in a convex mirror, things appeared to recede more sharply into the distance. Things close to me were very large, while things at a greater distance were ridiculously small.

When I commented to this effect, H— handed me a pencil and paper and encouraged me to draw. Not wishing to offend him, I began a childlike sketch of a house, but between each painfully protracted line my attention drifted from the task, and I would begin to study the lines themselves. I finally abandoned the effort, and we rose to leave.

As we walked I kept my eyes directed downwards at my feet. Although I did not feel myself to be particularly unsteady, I had a great fear of tripping, and worse, of not being able to supply the correct responses to prevent a disastrous crash. The timing of our steps did not appear abnormal, yet when I looked up to survey our progress, I saw that we had hardly moved from our starting point.

I remember this part of the experience as "dream-like," yet it was not a dream. It was more like the state of semi-consciousness when awakening from sleep, an odd collage of events in which the real and the unreal merge. This is also the case with the drug psychosis.

Another difference was that in a dream, one believes his surroundings to exist; but I knew that, for example, the sensation I was having of floating over the sidewalk was hallucinatory, and did not believe in its reality, nor suppose myself to be in "another world."

But perhaps it is not that easy to distinguish the states. I remember reading of an experiment with subjects under hallucinogens, where the subjects were placed before stroboscopic flashes of light that coincided the alpha rhythm of the brain waves. It was a technique similar to that used in inducing another well-known dream-like state: hypnosis. Indeed, the subjects reported experiences of being transported to another world, a "dream-world" in whose reality they believed just as one believes that one's dreams are real. They remembered nothing that had gone on round them; it was as if they had been asleep.

I continued a steady stream of disorganized puns and wild hilarity until we passed by the door of a delicatessen, at which point H— mentioned that he was hungry and suggested getting something to eat. I told him I was not hungry, but would be glad to wait for him. He explained that he did not wish to leave me out in the street unguarded, and tried to impress upon me the importance of good behavior while we were inside the delicatessen.

When we got inside, I sat down at a booth while H— went to the counter to order a sandwich. He repeated his offer of a sandwich for me, which I declined. I watched him approach the proprietor.

As H— and the proprietor performed the ritual dance of ordering, preparing, and paying for a sandwich, I found myself absorbed in the scene. The counter seemed to rush away from me each time H— spoke, and then with each reply of the proprietor, to rush back again at breakneck speed. Behind the revolving meat slicer blade, I observed the broken pattern of moving hands with curious fascination. The proprietor himself, whom I had seen before, presented a striking caricature of his usual appearance, which in itself was a rather good caricature of a delicatessen proprietor. Now he seemed to satirize himself with gestures of low comedy.

I managed a resolute silence while we were in the establishment, but the moment we left, launched into an attempted description of the sandwich-buying, seeing that H— had evidently missed its comic aspect. This seemed to bore H—. For him, the sandwich was enough reminder of the encounter with the proprietor, and he munched on it as we walked towards the park.

Suddenly I began to stare intently at the sandwich. For no apparent reason, I began to doubt that the scene in the delicatessen had actually taken place, a doubt which disturbed me; I felt I was losing my faculties. But I found I was able to reassure myself by staring at H—'s sandwich, evidence that the scene I seemed to remember had actually occurred.

In the throes of hallucinogenic fantasy, I was now typically confused between reality and non-reality. It was, at times, greatly disturbing; I was frightened at "losing my grip on reality," and sought reassurance in material objects, specifically, the sandwich. I once saw a subject in experiment cling for hours to a small plastic drinking cup, talking endlessly of its being "real," and seeming to find immense assurance in fact. Later, however, he confessed to having been confused as to just what the word "real" meant.

A few moments after we had entered the park, and had begun to walk around a small lake, a boy of fifteen or so approached and asked us, laconically, for a match. H— reached into his pocket to produce one, but I had other ideas. I said: "What do you want a match for, kid?" The boy seemed startled, and H— glanced apprehensively, fearing that I intended to engage the boy in conversation. I intended exactly that, hugely amused by the idea.

"For this cigarette," the boy replied, with some irony. "You mean you want to light it?" I felt I ought to insist upon preciseness in our discourse. "Yeah. so what?"

"What will you do with it after you light it?" I inquired.

By now the boy seemed to regard me as odd. "What do you think I'm going to do with it, eat it?" he said. "Well, I suppose you could," I answered. "You could also put it out, or you could give it to my friend H— here to smoke, or you could give it to me, but I don't smoke, so I would put it out, or you could smoke the match and throw the cigarette in the lake." I followed this outburst with insane laughter. The boy seemed genuinely confused, and H— looked rather embarrassed.

It must appear as though I had lost all inhibitions. But this particular uninhibited state was unlike any other I had ever experienced, certainly nothing like drunkenness. I felt myself detached, to a large degree, from my physical "self," unrelated to the actions my body was performing.

"Schizophrenic" was, of course, the term that came first to mind. I felt no lurching sense of intoxication, no bravado; I should not have been inclined to perform rash feats. I merely felt as though the slightly giddy person expostulating about cigarettes was, quite simply, someone else.

H— finally struck a match for the boy's cigarette, and the latter breathed a cloud of smoke towards our faces with theatrical disdain. He turned to go, but I intercepted his escape, and began a wildly disorganized lecture on lung cancer and other inconveniences of smoking. This talk contained a large number of technical terms, deliberately misused. The boy seemed willing to listen, although apparently interested in my rather electric performance than in the content of my talk, and presently the two of us fell into step along the path, While H— trailed apprehensively behind.

As we talked, I was suddenly struck with the sinister appearance presented by the boy's face. I imagined I could detect in the deliberately "tough" expression he assumed, all the criminal fantasies which I supposed to be lurking within his malevolent mind. At the same time, two black lines appeared on his face, resembling Indian war paint. I stopped speaking and looked at him.

"Why don't you wash your face more often?" I said. I was aware of inviting misinterpretation, but enjoyed the secret of my private joke. The boy was clearly upset. He looked at me and said: "You know something, buddy? You're crazy." Then he walked away, rapidly. H— and I looked at each other, and though I felt the boy's parting remark to be objectively funny, felt no impulse to laugh. H— did not laugh either. I asked H— if I appeared crazy; he replied testily that I seemed slightly drunk. Then he decided we had better return to his room.

Back in H—'s room, about mid-afternoon, I lay on the bed gazing at the ceiling while H— sat in a chair by the window, reading. There was, as at the very beginning of the experience, a certain density in room, a feeling or quality of apprehension.

I now knew what was meant by the "feeling of apprehension" described by so many subjects under hallucinogens. It was as though each scene was viewed in the manner of a movie which focuses upon a silent and unpopulated scene, and thereby suggests an ominous significance.

Later, I began to speculate that perhaps this phenomenon indicates the connection between the effects of hallucinogens and the normal human response to a sudden stress. It was a theory I had often come across. I remember the familiar example of the automobile driver about to crash. Between the realization of the impending crash and the moment of impact, time seems to stand still. A vast number of thoughts occur: they may concern possible results of the crash, or indeed, one's life may "flash before one's eyes." Speech at such a time is impossible. Some psychiatrists have held that the effect of hallucinogens is a prolongation of a response to an artificially created stress.

On the ceiling, various areas of plaster seemed to become detached, to rotate one way or the other, and then to return to their proper places, as in a dance. The surface of the ceiling broke up into intersecting planes, which somehow seemed to suggest certain abstract thoughts on the nature of "reality" itself, though what these were I do not remember. Colored flashes of light appeared on the wall, which I identified as reflections from passing cars outside. I asked H—— if he thought the flashes were brightly colored, and he said they were not.

I noted the acuity of my sense of hearing. The sound of H—'s breathing, and his turning of pages, were strikingly loud. After a while I leaned over the edge of the bed and watched the patterns in the rug execute maneuvers similar to those of the ceiling. I was much impressed by the beauty and complexity of these arrangements, and imagined myself to possess an extraordinary aesthetic sense, unusually sensitive to visual beauty.

Although afterwards, of course, I was no keener an art critic than I had been previously, still I believe that the experience had a certain kind of effect. If nothing else, it taught me that seeing itself was an art, and that meanings not obvious on the surface might be derived by paying attention to color, line, formal structure, etc., things which every artist takes for granted, but of which the drug helped me to be more aware than I had. Also, on several occasions, I found that looking at, say, a painting, would suddenly bring to mind the association of what I had seen under LSD, and would be reminiscent of the experience.

As I lay on the bed, the effects of the drug began to dissipate. After an hour or two I arose and announced that I had "recovered." I had a general sense of well-being, except for a headache that probably was the result of prolonged and intense laughter.

H— and I discussed the events of the day, myself bubbling over at a fairly euphoric clip. He appeared glad to see me back on his own level of communication, but after a half-hour or so, he found even this a bit wearisome, and began to grow restive. Noticing this, I suggested seeing a movie, and he gladly assented.

H— drove me home in his car to change my clothes. When I entered the apartment, my roommate was lying on the couch, reading. He had not known where I had gone or what I had done, and after listening to my somewhat hypertensive conversation for a few minutes, asked me if I had been out drinking all day. "What makes you think I've been drinking?" I was a bit taken aback, for I drank infrequently, and my roommate knew this. "Well first of all," he said, "you seem to be acting rather oddly, and secondly your nose is bright red." I went over to him and breathed in his face. "Does it smell as if I've been drinking?" I demanded, loudly. He appeared indecisive. "I don't know," he said, "but your nose is awfully red." "That's ridiculous," I said, and went to the mirror to look. My nose was a gleaming shade of scarlet.

In retrospect, I find no great inclination to repeat the experiment. This may seem to contradict the apparently wondrous nature of the experience, as I, at least, seemed to find it. But I found the emotional state induced by the drug difficult to comprehend, once I had returned to ordinary consciousness. I could not conceive of what the experience had been like; it was not "vivid," as is the idea of eating food when one is hungry. The hallucinogenic experience lacked, for me, anticipatory pleasure. Instead, it seemed to provoke anxiety; I was vaguely afraid of what I had been through, and sensed a certain possible danger in the experience. It seemed though it might not always turn out to be so pleasant, and indeed, this was confirmed for me by others.

As for my original grandiose idea in taking the drug: I did not feel I learned very much, in an objective way, from the experience. But if the simple ingestion of a hallucinogenic drug does not provide answers, any more than our objective studies, how then, are we to explore it further?

I had to content myself with this answer: That the method used would probably depend on techniques of obtaining data that are presently unknown to us. Current studies were only tentatively referred to as "experiments," since the term implies that one is taking all the factors into account, and controlling all the variables. Actually, our experiments were, as most psychiatrists point out, gropings in the dark.

It seems, then, that until new methods of communication are devised, we must make do with what we have. At present, that consists of simple observations, comparisons with psychotic conditions such as schizophrenia (there are both similarities and differences), and the subjective experiences of those who are willing to experiment on their own. But the gap, alas, is not to be bridged simply by the magic act of drug taking, as I was so disappointed to discover.

CHAPTER 4

Personal Statement

by Paul W. Mosher, M.D.
04-09-2018

My involvement with computer technology goes back to the 1950s when as a college freshman I for a time changed my college major from "Premed" to "Applied Mathematics," the name used at Harvard in those days for what is now called "Computer Science." Torn between these two sets of interests I eventually changed back to medicine as a future vocation but I never lost what was at that early time a fascination with the possibilities of electronic computers. I was one of those kids with his nose pressed against the glass windows surrounding the "Mark I" computer dreaming of the day when everyone would have a computer of his or her own.

Steeped in technology during my teenage years I had by the time I graduated from high school already passed the examinations for the highest levels of radio licenses issued by the U.S. government in the amateur and commercial series; as a consequence I was able to work my way through college as a summer replacement broadcast transmitter engineer in one of the country's most well known broadcasting stations and later as a summer replacement member of the studio engineering staff of a major television station.

I have provided this and the following background information to make clear that my 1990 proposal to digitize the full text of psychoanalytic journal literature, which ultimately became PEP, was an organic outgrowth of years of work within APsaA on the problem of access to the journal literature and of my immersion in the early days of the computer revolution rather than a sudden inspiration or impulse.

At the dawn of the personal computer, in the so-called "golden age" (1978-1982), by which time I was already a practicing psychoanalyst, I was therefore well positioned to participate in the "personal computer revolution." I began to teach myself programming languages, and was an author and staff writer for a national computer hobbyist magazine. Ultimately, I wrote two commercial programs for the Apple II computer, one of which I personally sold to one of the inventors of the Apple II (Steve Wozniak) and which he used to display Apple II graphics on giant screens at the 1982 "US Festival" in California.

In the early 1980s, as a member of the American Psychoanalytic Association (APsaA), I joined a long-standing project and committee intended to create a computer based index to the psychoanalytic journal literature. That project had stalled and seemed to have little hope of success. In the meantime, two senior analysts and computer hobbyists, Stanley Goodman and Vann Spruiell, working on their own and with some colleagues had created a bibliographical database using a simple free program. While this database had great potential there was no convenient way to search the bibliography, which was split among a set of "floppy disks," the only affordable storage medium at that time. With their encouragement, I wrote a user-friendly program, which could read and search the entire database in a single pass and eventually made this program available to any analyst with a personal computer.

However, the number of analysts who could access the data with a computer was quite limited, and so I then wrote a much more complex computer program for my own use, which converted the entire database into a printed book using a format called a "key word index." I printed the entire book in camera-ready form using techniques that I had developed to control a printer from a computer for the original purpose of printing graphical images at home. The book made it possible to look up any article in the covered journals by the name of the author or any word in the title. It was published in 1986 by APsaA, to whom I had donated it under the name, *Title Key Word and Author Index to the Psychoanalytic Literature.* Ultimately two editions (1986 and 1990) were printed and were purchased by thousands of analysts, who for the first time had a consolidated index of sorts to the included journals.

Shortly after APsaA published the second edition of the book, I was asked by the APsaA leadership to oversee the "computerization" of APsaA's Central Office. As part of that task I established the Association's first Internet connection, a pioneering web site and an email system, with my chosen domain name "apsa.org," which is still in use today. Eventually I was able to make the bibliographic database available free of charge via the APsaA web site to any user anywhere in the world using an on-line search program (or "search engine") that I wrote myself. For several years that facility was utilized by thousands of psychoanalysts in numerous countries.

Although these facilities, the published books and the on-line bibliographical search, served a useful purpose, they most definitely did not take the place of a complete index, the making of which seemed to be a costly and otherwise impossible task. It was at that point that the alternative idea of a fully searchable collection of full text journal articles distributed on CD-ROMs, which had just come onto the scene, occurred to me. Distribution via the Internet was impractical in those early days.

Consequently, at the December 1991 meeting of the APsaA Committee on Scientific Activities, I submitted a formal proposal (attached) for the Association to fund the digitization of the *full text, since their inception*, of five journals whose tables of contents were listed in the Goodman *Jourlit* database.

After some considerable turmoil and doubt, one false start, and difficulties locating reliable vendors, which were few and far between in those days, APsaA and the Institute for Psychoanalysis in London agreed to form a non-profit subsidiary corporation equally owned by both organizations, and to fund the initial digitization and publication of the fully digitized and searchable text on a CD-ROM. The new corporation, named "Psychoanalytic Electronic Publishing" (PEP) at my suggestion, was governed by a six-member board of directors with three directors elected by each of the two-owner/partner organizations. I have served continuously as an unpaid member of the PEP Board of Directors since that time, mostly concerning myself with the technical aspects of PEP.

One of my first contributions to the effort was recruiting Neil Shapiro, a Ph.D. computer scientist and neighbor, who at the time was a consultant to major airlines, which were starting to distribute their voluminous repair manuals on CD-ROMs. Neil has been with PEP ever since, moving from the role of consultant to developer and technical whiz, negotiating on behalf of PEP with the various vendors with whom we need to deal. Our first CD-ROM was published in 1996.

Subsequently, as PEP and the Internet grew together, it became practical to distribute our data via the Internet and the CD-ROM version of PEP was gradually replaced with the current PEP website, http://pep-web.org.

To me over these ensuing 20 years, watching PEP grow into the influential and beneficial psychoanalytic institution it is today, far beyond the scope I originally imagined, has been an enormous thrill. We members of the PEP Board have functioned as a team, with Nadine Levinson and David Tuckett handling the complex management and business aspects of PEP. I will be forever grateful to the visionary leaders of the two owners of PEP who had the confidence and trust in us to give PEP its start.

Should We Consider Making Psychoanalytic Literature Available on CD-ROM?

A Proposal to the APsaA Committee on Scientific Activities

POINTS IN FAVOR:

1) CD-ROM is a relatively new medium for making LARGE amounts of text based material easily available to individual users. A single CD-ROM disk, physically identical to a CD digital audio recording, can hold the equivalent of about 250, 000 pages of text (or at least 550, 000, 000 characters). ONE disk could therefore contain the entire FULL TEXT of the greater part of our literature .

For reference, Dr. S. Goodman and I recently estimated the number of pages of text, and the number of characters on those pages, for ALL the full text of ALL the articles in the JOURLIT database. This represents ALL the text of all the articles in eight psychoanalytic periodicals from their inception, the entire Standard Edition, and the complete Writings of Anna Freud. Our estimate is that this huge mass of literature contains about 147,000 pages with about 350,000,000 characters.

2) In terms of space and cost, CD-ROM might be the best way for the individual analyst (and institute libraries) to gain access to this vast body of literature in his or her own office.

3) The entire body of text on a CD-ROM (usually) is automatically "indexed" through a text inversion, which allows rapid access to each place in the entire collection of text where a particular word (or combination of words) appears. It is not yet known whether this sort of "index" is as useful as a traditional

index. Even if it is not, having the literature available in CD-ROM form would (probably) enormously facilitate the preparation of a traditional index.

4) Other specialty groups are gaining access to their literature through distribution on CD-ROM. Therefore, there is a considerable body of experience already available from professional colleagues regarding ways to proceed with such a project.

POINTS AGAINST:

1) Cost. Unfortunately, most of our literature is available only in printed form. This makes the cost of creating a CD-ROM much more expensive than it would be if the material were already available in machine readable form. Most material on CD-ROMs being produced today existed in machine readable form. In fact, the major roadblock to this project is the problem of transforming the literature into computer text files. While such a task would only have to be done once, it is a daunting task because of the enormous size of the literature. Two possible ways of capturing the text are scanning and keyboarding. The cost of the text conversion could be anywhere from $50, 000 to $200,000. Once the text is available, the actual cost of producing the disks is surprisingly small. The cost of setting up the production of the disks would be about $20,000. Each individual disk would cost about $2.50 to make. Thus, for a run of 200 disks, the cost per disk would be about $100 each. Obviously, the cost falls rapidly for larger numbers of disks. Annual updates might be prepared at about half the cost of the first edition.

2) A CD-ROM drive and a personal computer are required to access the disk. The cost of CD-ROM drives has been a major impediment to this technology until recently. However; the cost of such drives is now falling fairly rapidly, and it is now possible to get a drive which will work with a PC for about $400.

3) It is difficult actually to READ large amounts of text from a computer screen. For analysts, a CD-ROM of the literature may therefore never be used as more than a way of locating material to be read in the printed version. Producing one's own hard copy from the CD-ROM is possible but raises copyright issues.

WHY US?

The amount of text in all the issues of our individual journals is too small to justify the production of CD-ROMs by the journals themselves. It seems natural to consider pooling all the material to make a single disk. Such a project would require the coordination by a trusted central body which could work with the journals in regard to issues of royalties, copyrights, and distribution. Other professional groups, including medical specialty groups, are active in this area.

A JOB NOT WORTH DOING IS NOT WORTH DOING WELL.

I hope the committee will consider this project, either for additional action, for future reference, or to reach the conclusion that it would not be worth the effort. A tremendous amount of Work would be required by Association members who have the organizational skills required to bring all the interested parties together in a collaborative effort. If it does appear that further exploration of this project is justified, l suggest that a small working group of interested persons be appointed to gather more information.

Paul W. Mosher, M.D. 12-18-1991

THE MAN

Personal Statements from the Wide Circle of Those He Touched

CHAPTER 5

A Shared Love of Computers and Programs

by Neil Lipson

The Apple I computer came out in April 1976, followed a year later by Apple II, independently embraced by Paul and me. By that time I had started my own company, Progressive Software and placed an ad in a computer magazine for software sales. Paul, who had written his Graphic Printing System software, contacted me about selling his programs, which we then made available in stores, in magazines and in computer shows up and down the east coast. Things went so well that I was able to quit my engineering job and devoted myself to computer sales, software and hardware and even invented the Lipson light pen!

Over the years he continued to write other programs, often the first of their kind; they also sold well but as our friendship developed and we worked together Paul also described the APsaA lists and his other projects that were not meant for the commercial market, although I don't remember specifically talking about *Jourlit.*

Over the more than 40-year period, 1980 to 2020, we spoke almost daily, about how the computer field was changing, how the world was changing in general and about our families. A positive, unanticipated benefit for me was Paul's instrumental role in helping me lose 130 pounds over that long period of time and keeping it off!

During those more than four decades, until his death, I enjoyed a special, life-long, reciprocal, trusting friendship with him and his family. I went to numerous family affairs and during our frequent phone calls we discussed such diverse topics like the stock market, politics and his children.

Paul had a deep understanding of the world and this country and always provided deep insights into what was happening and what to expect in the future. He often told me funny stories, once confiding that he'd seen someone he had had a relationship with years before his marriage and said to me, "Neil, I am so glad I didn't marry her."

He was a SPECIAL friend, and I will miss him dearly.

CHAPTER 6

A Train Ride Leading to New Directions

by Neil Shapiro

I started my career in 1982 at GE's Research and Development Center working on new technology for networks and interactive electronic documentation. After 8 years, I left to become a technology consultant. But it was my journey in the following years with PEP and particularly Paul Mosher that significantly impacted me personally, technically, and professionally. This is our story.

It was on an Amtrak train in June 1994, traveling with a colleague on our way to PC Expo in New York City when we struck up a conversation with the person in the seat across the aisle, who was on his way to the same convention. Like us, he was very excited to go and see the new technology being presented — it was about 7 years before the public adoption of the Internet, and stand-alone PC technology advances were still exciting and new.

The person across the aisle was Dr. Paul Mosher. Paul was an early adapter of PCs, and an avid technology enthusiast as well. Of future significance, I mentioned that I was a software consultant, specializing in full-text software (search) technology. I was working with the Air Transport Association (ATA) on standards for putting aircraft and engine maintenance manuals on CD-ROM.

This was the key that brought our worlds together. Some months later, Paul called me to ask if I would be interested in consulting on a project to build an archive of the major Psychoanalytic journals and books on CD-ROM. I was busy at the time with the ATA work, but my associate who was working with me submitted a proposal on our behalf. Later, I was told that a proposal from another consulting group had been chosen.

A year or so later, Paul called me that they needed a restart of the project, and he had an idea how to do it. He had found full-text software called Folio Views. Folio Views was very advanced full-text search software with a word-processor like front-end that could do very flexible and advanced indexing for both common word and phrase search, and advanced proximity and contextual searches. Paul was excited at the prospect of building the literature archive into a full-fledged full-text database with such unlimited prospects for searching. And that the full PEP Archive could be distributed and ported around by users so conveniently on a single CD-ROM. It was a lot of research power in the palm of your hands.

Paul wanted the user interface to the database to be different than what we've come to see as a publication database. Rather than focusing on the journal or book (sources) by source name, he saw it as a database of articles. The left pane of the interface would simply be a list of articles. And when you did a search, that pane would be filtered (limited) to the matching articles. Selecting an article from that list would then display the full-text of that article. A true database of articles, with a simple and straightforward interface. But the filtering was pure power: searches by article metadata (author, title, etc.), and searches of content: full-text searches for words within the article, or for words that are within the same paragraph, sentence, or even within a specified distance from each other.

I worked with Paul to find a company with experience with building databases with Folio Views (which they call infobases). We found a company in Atlanta called Galaxy, and together Paul and I worked with their technical person to design the first PEP infobase. We worked together in my office to come up with a design for the first version of the PEP Archive. And we designed the XML Document Type Definition (DTD) needed for the data input contractor to identify (markup) the core metadata, and document elements.

Galaxy produced a prototype of the infobase, which was essentially a version of the infobase with a smaller amount of data. We went through design reviews with the PEP Board, including David Tuckett, Nadine Levinson, Peter Fonagy, Alice Bartlett, and Martin Miller. Paul's and the PEP Board's vision of a full-text searchable database of Psychoanalytic Journals was about to become a reality.

Galaxy's participation in the project was limited to beta discs of the first version, due to issues in delivering the final version (and particularly delays and cost overruns). I was asked to take over development of the infobases, developing the software needed to add further intelligent markup to the instances and convert the data to the format needed by Folio Views. And here is another aspect where Paul's involvement, foresight, and academic breadth impacted my career and, for that matter, my day to day life. Paul, who was interested in software languages among his many interests, suggested I try to do the development in a relatively new language called Python. Although young, Python already had a strong following, and there were many utility libraries which would simplify development. He was right: not only did I do the development in Python, but I've continued to love it, and use it, for more than 25 years as my primary development language. Ninety-five percent of the development I've done for PEP subsequently has been in Python. The DTD he helped design has been expanded to accommodate new features and adopted to XML, but we are still using it today.

The CD-ROM based versions of Folio Views were continued very successfully for eight years. Paul and the board continued to make suggestions for new search and presentation features, but mostly, the database continued to grow in size, as new sources, and more recent years of sources, were added. In fact, it outgrew the CD-ROM format...first requiring us to distribute two CD-ROM sets, and later, switching over to DVD-ROMs. But by the 5th version, PEP had added a web version of the database, built by Global Village Publishing, and available for institutions only. After Version 7, this was extended for all users. The interface was changed from the primary view being a list of articles, to a list of journals, which could then be browsed by year and volume. The search engine was changed from Folio Views to DTSearch. But neither change was limiting. It added breadth: the search tab still quickly showed a list of matching articles following a search. The interface was simple, and accessible through the web which by then was readily available to all, and users loved that.

As the World Wide Web became the standard for the world, it became the *de facto* standard for PEP, and the disc version was discontinued. Each year as we added more journals and books, we kept improving it: we added new features, like a harmonized glossary of Psychoanalytic terms harvested from published Psychoanalytic glossaries, which my processing software linked to all the other PEP content. But as always, technology moved on. Users were using the web on mobile phones with small screens. The interface for PEP-Web was not readily adaptable to these smaller screen sizes. It could be used, but with some difficulty. And Paul, always on the forefront, pushed another idea: he wanted us to develop a very basic search interface for the phone: a search entry field, and a list of articles below it. To solve the problem in a general way, we had GVPi put an Application Programming Interface (API) into the backend of PEP-Web, so new user-interfaces specific to devices or usage could be easily added. The first of these, was PEP-Easy, which I developed for PEP. As Paul wanted, it eliminated the journal browse interface in favor of search only. Paul was happy with PEP-Easy, but in reality he wanted it to be simplified even further. I'm sure with Paul's technical knowledge, if he had the time, he would have personally designed or developed a second interface that was even better.

But neither Paul nor I developed other interfaces using the API that GVPi developed, because in 2019, GVPi was acquired by another company, and PEP needed to start over and build a new system. The board decided to build a completely open source platform based on the same principles where we would have a standard API between the user interface and the backend (search engine). While testing new search engines, I built a prototype system for the backend search engine, and we contracted for the front end from a development company in Troy, NY. The new user interface was designed by David Tuckett, with my design modifications to help it fit within a modern Web implementation, and of course, feedback from the board. This is the new PEP-Web, which adapts to screen size, so it's both desktop computer friendly, and mobile friendly. One feature I added, thinking of Paul's request, was the concept of Smart Search. This is essentially a search box which is not dedicated to a specific search type. Instead, it uses a limited form of AI to parse the user's request and perform an appropriate search, much like Google does with their search field. This is a key feature of the new search interface, and PEP has plans to extend this far beyond the limited AI that I implemented, working with an AI specialist. While Paul hadn't suggested this specifically, I'm sure he had it in mind. He was always a step ahead.

Besides Paul's many contributions to PEP, and our long term working relationship, we were friends. We had another shared interest—photography. Indeed, Paul was ahead of me in this aspect as well...at his house, he showed me boxes of fine art photographs he had taken before the digital days. We went out on day expeditions shooting, and indoor studio type work where Paul and I took each other's headshots. I still use mine today, though at this point, admittedly it looks younger than I do in person!

We will miss you Paul. Our collaboration and friendship will always be a part of my life.

CHAPTER 7

Paul Mosher: Coauthor and Friend

by Jeffrey Berman

Coauthorship, not quite a marriage, is a relationship based on trust, respect, and mutuality. Coauthors, like a married couple, do not always agree on everything, but they learn how to work together and forge consensus when there is disagreement. They know that their collaborative efforts will culminate in a creation, often a book, that would not have occurred without their combined efforts. The book affirms the coauthors' dedication to their offspring and, if the book is worthy enough to succeed on its own, it will survive its creators.

It was a joy to work with Paul Mosher as a coauthor. Through mutual friends, I first met Paul and Paula in the mid-1970s, when I first came to Albany to teach at what was then called SUNY-Albany (now the University at Albany). I remember that both Paul and Paula were friendly and welcoming. Decades passed, and I was pleased when Paul gave me a copy of his edited volume *Title Key Word and Author Index to Psychoanalytic Journals, 1920–1986*. Published by the American Psychoanalytic Association in 1987, the volume proved essential to scholars throughout the world, including psychoanalytic literary critics like myself. The *Index* preceded an even more momentous bibliographic work, PEP-WEB, which allows scholars to obtain online articles published in the major psychoanalytic journals and in dozens of noteworthy psychoanalytic books. Paul was the driving force behind the creation of PEP-WEB, which is now an indispensable guide for anyone interested in the history of psychoanalysis. The digitalization of psychoanalytic research is bound to further psychoanalytic scholarship and promote interdisciplinary work. This alone makes Paul an influential figure in the history of psychoanalysis—a true pioneer.

BECOMING COAUTHORS

Around 2011 Paul invited me to review a book with him, Mary Bergstein's *Mirrors of Memory: Freud, Photography and the History of Art.* I was delighted to work with Paul, but I recall wondering at the time why he wanted a coauthor: most scholarly books are reviewed by single authors. We wrote the review, which was published in *The Psychoanalytic Quarterly* in 2012. In retrospect, I realized that Paul was testing whether we would be able to work together on future projects. Over the years we coauthored four more reviews, excellent preparation for the two books we wrote together: *Confidentiality and Its Discontents*, published by Fordham University Press in 2015, and *Off the Tracks: Cautionary Tales about the Derailing of Mental Health Care*, published by IP Books in 2019.

Confidentiality and Its Discontents

The idea behind *Confidentiality and Its Discontents* was Paul's, as was the selection of the authors and the topics about which we wrote. While researching the book, I discovered that Paul was one of the country's leading experts on confidentiality—indeed, he had written many articles and book chapters on privacy in psychotherapy. In the 1990s he was chair of the Committee on Confidentiality of the American Psychoanalytic Association, and he also served as a member of the Confidentiality Committee of the American Psychiatric Association. Additionally, he coordinated the preparation of an amici curiae brief on behalf of four psychoanalytic organizations at the time of the U.S. Supreme Court's deliberations on the *Jaffee v. Redmond* case. He also maintained the *Jaffee v. Redmond* website.

Paul and I did extensive research for *Confidentiality and Its Discontents*. We interviewed several people who were involved in landmark privacy cases. Joseph Lifschutz, a San Francisco psychoanalyst who was arrested and briefly jailed in 1969 for refusing to testify about a former patient, gave us details that cast light on one of the earliest privacy stories. Frank Werner spoke to us about his mother's shock and horror upon learning that her psychoanalyst had betrayed confidentiality by publishing in 1973, without permission, a thousand-page case study, *In Search of a Response*. The resulting lawsuit was one of the oddest and most outrageous invasions of privacy in the history of psychotherapy. We interviewed two of the people who were centrally involved in the landmark 1996 Supreme Court decision *Jaffee v. Redmond*, which created for the first time a federal psychotherapist-patient privilege: Karen Beyer, the social worker whose heroic refusal to turn over her psychotherapy notes, as ordered by a Chicago judge, initiated the case; and her lawyer, Sandra Nye. Alayne Katz shared with us her recollections of Robert Birnbaum's brutal murder of her sister, Gail, in 1985, along with her perspective as a lawyer of the complex legal and psychiatric issues arising over whether a therapist's testimony could be used in the trial. We also interviewed former New York Chief Judge Sol Wachtler, who offered us his impressions about the stigma of mental illness that contributed to his bizarre behavior in 1992, arrest, and imprisonment.

We promised all of the people whom we interviewed that we would show them how we used the information they provided us—and they could withdraw permission at any time prior to publication if they felt we were not representing them fairly. This is an unusual step in interviewing people for a book, but we wanted to be as careful as possible, particularly since we were writing about privacy stories.

One of the unintended but serendipitous consequences of showing the interviewees how we used their words was that several of them found the experience "cathartic and positive," to quote one of them. Paul and I speculated that the interviewees felt this way because we encouraged them to tell their own stories, in their own words, without interrupting, contradicting, or "analyzing" them. I believe we created a model of interviewing research subjects that other scholars might wish to use in their own work. Interestingly, much of the research we relied on was made available through PEP. Thus one can see how Paul's past research made possible our own research. One of the strengths of *Confidentiality and Its Discontents*—and this was Paul's idea—was to end each chapter with a "take home lesson." To quote the take home lesson at the end of the Jaffee chapter:

> Confidential information deriving from a treatment conversation between a licensed psychotherapist and a patient is now protected from compelled disclosure in all federal courts of the United States by a very strong "absolute" privilege rule similar to the well-known and highly regarded attorney-client privilege. Many psychotherapists have failed to grasp the importance of this powerful protection for their patients. (p. 234)

Paul and I never had any serious disagreements during our years as coauthors, but we had different attitudes toward privacy in our chapter on the "Anne Sexton Controversy." The vexing question we confronted was whether it was permissible for a psychotherapist to release confidential tape recordings of a patient' psychotherapy sessions after the patient's death, and without the patient's consent? The question involved Anne Sexton, a Pulitzer-Prize winning "confessional" poet who was in therapy for many years with Martin Orne, who with her permission taped their sessions. After her death, her daughter and literary executor, Linda Grey Sexton, made the tapes available to Anne Sexton's biographer, Diane Middlebrook. There were many daunting issues surrounding the Anne Sexton controversy, including the risks and benefits posed to the psychotherapeutic and literary communities by the use of the tapes. The controversy was fierce, with mental health professionals and literary scholars taking opposite positions.

Paul was an absolutist when it came to preserving patient-therapist confidentiality, and he strongly disapproved of Orne's cooperation with Middlebrook. I, on the other hand, believed that Middlebrook's use of the tapes was crucial for understanding Anne Sexton's life. Paul and I tried to present *both* points of view. "In general, mental health professionals excoriated Dr. Orne, accusing him of acting unethically, while many humanities scholars believed the contribution the tapes make to understanding the sources of Sexton's poetry outweighs concerns about the breach of confidentiality" (p. 145). Throughout the chapter we explored the complexity of the story without resolving its many ambiguities. The two take home lessons of the story are worth repeating:

1. Disclosure of confidential tape recordings of a patient's psycho-therapy sessions, with the permission of the patient's executor, is probably not illegal and is probably not considered unethical by the psychiatric profession. Nonetheless, such an understanding is bound to be controversial.

2. An important principle of privacy protection is that information held about individuals should be used only for the purpose for which it was gathered in the first place. (p. 174)

In coauthoring *Confidentiality and Its Discontents*, which received the American Psychoanalytic Association's Courage to Dream Book Prize in

2017, I learned so much about the intersections of psychoanalysis and the law. Paul was exemplary in every way, an admirable coauthor and friend. A paragraph in the Acknowledgments page of *Confidentiality and Its Discontents* conveys our working relationship while writing the book:

> It was Paul's idea to create a book of this sort, and he did much of the psychiatric and legal research during his long personal career. He enlisted Jeff's help as a coauthor to convey the human interest in privacy stories. Paul believes he never could have written a book like this on his own. Jeff has long been an armchair analyst, and it has been a pleasure for him to work with a real psychoanalyst. Jeff has never been in psychoanalysis, preferring instead to muddle through life, but if he could begin his life over again, he would want to be in analysis with Paul. Paul appreciates the compliment but isn't accepting new patients. (p. xi-xii)

Off the Tracks

Working with Paul on *Off the Tracks* was an eye-opening experience. As with *Confidentiality and Its Discontents*, Paul selected the topics for *Off the Tracks*. We had no idea when we began the project that it would result in a massive two-volume tome, 1142 pages long. There are so many abuses in the history of the mental health profession that we could have spent the rest of our lives writing about these cautionary tales. Volume 1 discusses sexual and nonsexual boundary violations, while volume 2 calls attention to scientology, alien abduction, false memories, "black psychiatry," and the siren call of psychopharmacology. Many psychiatric abuses were horrifying, such as the "focal septic" approach to psychosis that led to the victimization of patients and widespread suffering at Trenton State Hospital, and the top-secret MKULTRA experiments that were conducted on patients at the Allan Memorial Institute in Montreal under D. Ewen Cameron. I wasn't aware of any of these psychiatric misadventures, and it was a sobering learning experience conducting research on these topics. As always, Paul guided me in my research.

Paul was, by both nature and training, cautious and skeptical, and I remember his incredulity when we were researching the chapter in volume 1 on Jules Masserman, who was called the "most prominent psychiatrist in the world." Several of Masserman's female patients, beginning with Barbara Noël, alleged that he had drugged and then raped them during therapy. The case made the national headlines. We interviewed two of the people involved with the story: Kathryn Watterson, an investigative journalist who coauthored a book, *You Must Be Dreaming* (1992), with Noël, and Brenda Solomon, who was the co-chair of the Illinois Psychiatric Society Ethics Committee that investigated the charges. When Solomon learned, as a result of our research, that Masserman's early scientific work involved stimulating cats by inserting sodium amytal in their vaginas, she was so troubled that the night before our interview, she dreamed of Masserman—a dream, she added, that was profoundly disturbing. Writing the chapter together, Paul and tried to convey the reader's dilemma in learning about the story:

Shock and horror were our first responses to the Noël story. Masserman must have been sick to have committed the deeds of which Barbara Noël accuses him. Next we felt doubt: maybe the patient actually had been dreaming or inventing these experiences. Then we felt doubt about our doubt: Masserman's actions were too incredible to have been fabricated. By the end of the story, we were convinced of the truth of her charges. (vol. 1, p. 261)

Paul's major concern when we were writing *Off the Tracks* was that readers might assume from our discussion of derailed psychotherapy that we were anti-psychiatry. (Paul was not amused by Nabokov's mordant remark in *Lolita* that the difference between "therapist" and "the rapist" is a matter of spacing.) The opposite was true. Paul was deeply knowledgeable about psychiatry's successes as well as failures, and he insisted that mental health practitioners must confront its often dark history to avoid making the same mistakes again. We end volume 2 of *Off the Tracks* with a statement by the great British novelist and poet Thomas Hardy: "If a way to the Better there be, it exacts a full look at the Worst." (p. 1006)

CREWS-DISCUSSION GROUP

Paul was a polymath, deeply knowledgeable about a wide range of subjects and academic disciplines. He was open minded and intellectually curious, always revising and expanding his understanding of psychoanalysis. After we completed *Off the Tracks*, Paul created a google group focusing on Frederick Crews's 2017 biography *Freud: The Making of an Illusion*. The group consisted of Paul and Paula Mosher, Gregory Lavigne, Warren Procci, Ralph Fishkin, and me. Paul assigned the readings, encouraged the members to submit brief responses to the readings, and offered his own point of view. "We have come to an agreement," he wrote in October 2019, "that reading Crews's book, while at times infuriating, is also turning out to be a worthwhile experience because it is taking us step by step through important parts of Freud's career in a way which is more stimulating than would be a review done through the reading of more idealizing Freud biographies which at this point would seem a bit boring by comparison." Paul resisted being a Freud basher, which is Crews's position, or a Crews's basher, which is largely my own position. "It seems to me that after all the years that each of us have spent immersed in Freud's achievements," Paul wrote, "we ARE in a position to be able to form our own balanced views of Freud rather than sorting to the Freud-bashing-bashing that seems to be so prevalent among psychoanalysts when they encounter people like Crews."

Reading Crews's biography enabled us to see a darker side of Freud that was ignored in the "standard origin myth of psychoanalysis as taught in the 1960s," as Paul noted:

> The one area in which I DID raise questions as a candidate, "libido theory," was so sacrosanct that my raising the issue could have resulted in my ejection from the institute had I not backed down and shut up. The whole idea of "psychic energy" struck me as so absurd, and so reeking of pseudoscience, that it took a big effort on my part to button my lip. The issue is addressed also in the third part of chapter 22 in which Crews describes Freud's use of the abstract but ultimately meaningless idea of "quantity" as if there actually was a "quantity" of "something" floating around in the brain. Where would Freud ever have gotten such a silly idea? I wrote a paper about that question as a candidate and was able to locate one root of the idea in the "theorizing" of Meynert and Brücke.
>
> However, an even more important source of the libido debacle is the fact that ENERGY, as a concept in itself, was NEW in the 1800s, and it was actually the hot (pun intended) new topic in science at very time when Freud was a student. Most Freud scholars seem to have overlooked this fact, but it wasn't hard to imagine that the idea of "energy" as a "new, new thing" fired the imaginations of many students of that era, including of course Freud. Today, we still hear people speak of "psychic energy" and even have healers whose work is devoted to "adjusting" the "energy fields" of the body!

Despite Paul's silence over libido theory when he was a psychoanalytic candidate, he did not remain intimidated for long. In his 1998 article "Frequency of Word Use as Indicator of Evolution of Psychoanalytic Thought," Paul determined that the word "libido" starts out at about the same frequency as "self" in the 1920s but then declines steadily every decade. In volume 1 of *Off the Tracks* we quote Joseph Schachter's wry observation about the history of psychoanalysis: "discarded theories—like old generals—didn't die, they just faded away" (p. 417).

Paul's Retirement

After working with Paul for several years on two writing projects, I felt bereft when our coauthorship came to an end. I wanted to continue our writing, but Paul had many other interests, talents, and passions that he wanted to pursue, including writing an autobiography. I don't think Paul would have minded if I share with you an email he sent me in April, 2020, describing his feelings about retirement and writing an autobiography:

Although I had definitely mixed feelings about retiring it wasn't difficult at all. Medical practice is a very demanding activity and for those of us who take the responsibility seriously (not all do!) it can create a background hum of low level stress in one's life, even with a roster of relatively stable patients. However, I can also see that my reaction to stopping practice is all tangled up with the strange change in all our lives caused by the current plague. (We counted it as the 11th at our tele-seder with my daughter's family.) At least on the surface, I am enjoying being home, getting more sleep and doing much more of what I really enjoy (i.e., programming!) On the other hand, as to issues such as loss of identity, my office stands largely untouched so far, nothing moved at all, the way a person leaves a closet of clothing of a deceased loved one untouched, so we will have to see how long that goes on. I can already sense that it is going to be difficult to part with my office building, a not so tiny Civil War era brick carriage house which I had remodeled as an ideal analyst's office in the early 80s.

I've been trying to write a bit about my traumatic separation from my parents when I was 10 and how I think in some odd way it led to my "career" in technology, eventuating in my having made the proposal which led to PEP. I think it will be published in TAP [*The American Psychoanalyst*] to mark the occasion of my stepping down from the BOD [Board of Directors] of PEP after about 35 years. If I ever get enough of it done I would like to show it to you for suggestions. So far, it has had to compete with my programming and seems to lose out much of the time.

Paul led a fascinating life, fulfilled in love and work, Freud's definition of mental health. Devoted to his wife, children, and grandchildren, he had many hobbies that competed with his dedication to psychoanalysis, including programming and photography. A few months before his death, he gave me a prize-winning photograph he had taken in 2005 of my university, a campus that, in its rigid symmetry, seems almost unphotographable. The last time I saw Paul, in early June, 2021, he and Paula were on their way to visit Pine Hollow Arboretum, a 22-acre public arboretum and natural preserve situated five miles from downtown Albany. The next day he emailed me four stunning photographs.

Working with Paul was one of the highlights of my life. In rereading *Confidentiality and Its Discontents* and *Off the Tracks*, I cannot tell which contributions were Paul's and which were my own. Our "Note about Double

Authorship," on which we close volume 1 of *Off the Tracks*, continues to strike me as true:

> Unlike most double authored books, in which one author writes some chapters and the other author writes the remaining chapters, both of us have contributed equally to every chapter in the two volumes. Consequently, *Off the Tracks* is truly collaborative. To emphasize this, Jeffrey Berman is the lead author of volume 1, and Paul Mosher is the lead author of volume 2—though the lead authors could have easily been reversed. There are stylistic differences between the two of us—one of us is an English professor, the other a psychoanalyst—but it's impossible for us to separate one's ideas from the other's. "Blessed are the forgetful," quipped Nietzsche, "for they get the better even of their blunders."

REFERENCES

Berman, J. & Mosher, P.W. (2012). Review of Mary Bergstein, *Mirrors of Memory: Freud, Photography, and the History of Art. The Psychoanalytic Quarterly* 81: 500-503.

——— & ——— (2015). *Confidentiality and Its Discontents: Dilemmas of Privacy in Psychotherapy*. New York: Fordham University Press.

——— & ——— (2019). *Off the Tracks: Cautionary Tales about the Derailing of Mental Health* Care. 2 vols. New York: IP Books.

Mosher, Paul W. (1998). Frequency of Word Use as an Indicator of Evolution of Psychoanalytic Thought. *Journal of the American Psychoanalytic Association* 46: 577-581.

Noël, Barbara and Kathryn Watterson. (1992). *You Must Be Dreaming*. New York: Poseidon Press.

CHAPTER 8

Paul Mosher: As I Knew Him

by Robert Galatzer-Levy

Paul was a different kind of analyst. His interests, commitments, and enormous efforts in psychoanalysis took a different form and derived from different sources than that of most of his colleagues. He sought to contribute to psychoanalysis through rational thought and technical expertise. Throughout his professional life, he used his fine intellect and well-honed sense of justice in the service of our field.

Over many years, I was able to work with Paul, and occasionally against him, in varied contexts. In this chapter I describe some of our interactions in the hope of preserving a few of the qualities that made Paul a good friend and, at times, the best of enemies.

It all started with computers. Paul and I first met in APsaA's Committee on Scientific Activities. George Klumpner, the Chair of the Committee, believed that psychoanalysis could move forward if its rich literature was made more accessible, and this could be achieved through the enormously time-consuming task of indexing it all. He had actually produced an index of the first quarter century of *JAPA*. Paul, had a substantial background in the then-novel use of computers, and George knew that some of the most tedious aspects of indexing could be done on computers and recruited Paul to the indexing project. But then, in a manner that was typical of him, Paul quickly recognized that putting the literature of psychoanalysis in a computer-stored format that could be searched directly was far more efficient and thorough than any on paper index could be.[6] Paul came up with the idea that the psychoanalytic literature could be put on the, at that time, novel technology of a CD-ROM and distributed to psychoanalysts to use on their home computers. Analysts could have a searchable library of the analytic literature at their fingertips. He was excited about the details of the project, and seemed to meet every objection and difficulty, which were quite numerous, in the spirit of an engineer, that is, focused on finding technical solutions to problems rather than struggling with their moral or emotional dimensions. While others of us, including myself, argued about the conceptual desirability of this or that aspect of the project, Paul focused on finding concrete solutions, moving ahead with no particular attention to the sentimental attachment some of us felt to reading on paper or browsing through ancient bound volumes.

Paul's capacity for very hard, very able, and very detailed work always approached with great confidence paid off in this project that ultimately developed into that amazing tool of psychoanalysis, PEP. Paul's extraordinary capacity to disagree clearly and effectively with colleagues seemingly without personal rancor was evident as he worked on this project and was a continuing theme throughout his efforts. He was really smart and enormously invested in being smart but remarkably uninterested in competition or winning for its own sake.

---

6   The psychological dimensions of the whole story are worth noting. For example, Klumpner had a long classical, and seemingly not very successful, analysis with Kohut. He succeeded Kohut in leading the Committee on Scientific Activities. The men's vision of science and psychoanalysis remained radically different. Kohut's approach rested on broad empathic engagement with patients (which ultimately led him to self-psychology). Klumpner believed that psychoanalytic research should focus on the detailed study of psychoanalytic processes. When it came to the literature of psychoanalysis Kohut's attitude was that analysts should carefully read and integrate as much as possible, making that literature part of the analyst worldview. Klumpner thought being able to reference specific statements and findings was far more useful — hence the idea of an index.

The Birth of the Listserv

Paul and I both believed, but perhaps for slightly different reasons, that open conversation about a range of psychoanalytic topics was necessary for the field. Well into the 1990s, public discourse about controversies in analysis was severely limited. Whether in journals, open meetings, classrooms, or personal analyses the very real and intense disagreements within the analytic community were treated as deviations or errors that required correction. This constricted sort of discourse had a long history in psychoanalysis beginning with Freud and gathering particular, but hardly exclusive support, from the Board on Professional Standards (BOPS) of APsaA, whose approval was needed for various steps in career advancement in the psychoanalytic community.

I discovered a refreshing exception to this situation of stifled discourse in an arrangement set up by Vann Spruiell when he was editor for North America of the *International Journal of Psychoanalysis*. Rather than simply having peer reviews of submitted papers used by the editor to decide on publication, Spruiell distributed all peer reviews to members of the editorial board and invited discussions of them within the editorial board either by mail or by email. These conversations in writing beat anything I had seen in the analytic world up until then. Curating these documents must have involved a great deal of work for Spruiell, but I thought if something like that could be extended to a larger community, analysis might have some hope of a renewed vigor.

This was in the early '90s when, thanks to the interests of my eldest son Daniel, I became aware of online bulletin boards where individuals could post messages to be read by other members of the bulletin board system. In 1993, I set up the Psychoanalytic Virtual Bulletin Board. It was officially sponsored by the Chicago Institute for Psychoanalysis, though it was actually a one man show. I discussed the project with Paul who was enthusiastic about it, and we agreed that he would pursue it with APsaA's central office, which was becoming increasingly computerized and had gradually turned to Paul as one of few analysts who understood computers.

A major feature of Paul's character was that whatever topic he approached he required himself to develop, at least, a near professional degree of expertise. Paul's rather extensive preexisting background in computers begun in his days at Columbia, while certainly important, was much less significant than the group of attitudes that seem to have long preceded that involvement but which are particularly useful in fields like software engineering — a deep commitment to details, proficiency and overall technical competence. Paul would use technical expertise in the service of multiple goals and derived considerable power and authority from it in multiple contexts. And, he had remarkably little narcissistic or super-egoish investment in it. He did things very, very well, regularly earning but almost never demanding the respect of others and never, in my experience, demeaning people who were less able than he.

This quality of technical expertise extended to an extraordinary skill in political and organizational affairs and a pragmatic capacity to deal with the realities of APsaA. This led to our first serious disagreement. Paul quickly realized that APsaA would never support a listserv that was open to a general public, that the leadership and likely the members of APsaA would not support a free-for-all bulletin board such as I was attempting to run. Paul took the position that the listserv should only be open to APsaA members and was able to win the support of the administration.[7] Paul understood, as I did not, that to win the support of APsaA leadership, it would be necessary

---

7 Paul's anticipation that the listserv would be experienced as divisive, and even heretical, by significant groups and that active measures would be necessary to keep it alive turned out to be more than correct. The struggle continues to this day. Paul was repeatedly called on to help intervene and repeatedly responded supporting technical solutions, such as separate listservs for elections, that calmed the waters sufficiently that imperfectly, but reasonably open discourse could continue.

to be respectful of their concerns about a membership organization and its wish for exclusivity and order. Although I realized, at the time, that this was a pragmatic solution arising out of Paul's more accurate understanding of organizational dynamics, I also was angry and frustrated with him because the decision ran counter to my main goal of opening a channel of active communication among those interested in psychoanalysis. I kept the Bulletin Board going for a few years until it petered out in the face of the much more active and effective APsaA listserv. History had proven Paul right. Creating and sustaining a listserv that has been able to survive and bring into open discussion the cardinal issues of organized psychoanalysis has done more to move forward the desperately needed changes in APsaA than any other factor in the past quarter century.

Paul and I continued to work together on the Committee on Scientific Activities, although with quite different interests. His consistently friendly demeanor, along with his enormous competence in those areas that interested him, always made him a pleasure to work with. Paul's focus, however, tended to be on technical problems like the development of what was to become PEP, and he showed relatively little interest in specifically psychoanalytic topics.

BOPS TROUBLES

At some point, it became evident that our interests converged in another arena. We both found BOPS' activities and structures, especially its certification processes and the training analyst system, repulsive. Paul and I shared the personal experience of authoritarian colleagues in positions of power, whose rigid thinking and fundamentally anti-intellectual attitudes made attempting to be part of the analytic community disappointing and painful. Paul's experiences centered around the New York psychoanalytic community where he was made to feel unwelcome, mine around my interview with representatives of the Certification Committee who conducted an interview that combined a remarkably blatant condescension, simple stupidity, and bias, based in the assumption that since I was from Chicago I must be one of those evil self psychologists.

Paul and I shared a common sense that if APsaA was to have any reasonable future the attitudes and institutions associated with BOPS had to be eliminated or at least drastically transformed. But our ideas about how to do this were strikingly different. Mine was to show that BOPS' clearly biased and extremely conservative certification committee was not evaluating applicants in a valid or legitimate way and to call on BOPS, if it was to continue to exercise its authority, to evaluate its methodology and, if possible, (a possibility I doubted and continue to doubt) to develop a legitimate method of evaluation. While this approach eventually succeeded in creating studies of how the certification process could be made more valid and attempts to reform it in that direction, the results were at best disappointing. They absorbed huge amounts of energy of researchers, whose time would have been better spent on other projects and, although they resulted in some improvement in the process, never resulted in anything close to a truly satisfactory evaluation process. The effort had a particularly unfortunate side effect of making the Committee on Scientific Activities an enemy of BOPS, which ultimately resulted in the committee's floundering and failing.

Paul, on the other hand, conceptualized the situation in political terms. He saw clearly that the only way to bring BOPS under control was to drastically limit its organizational powers and began a long and ultimately effective effort in that direction. In his usual fashion of developing first-rate technical expertise about issues that mattered to him, Paul recognized that APsaA is a professional membership organization and used this concept, and the resulting clarification of the principles that ordinarily govern such an organization, to radically transform this structure of power and authority within APsaA. Again, Paul developed and used technical competence to calmly and without rancor, at least on his part, bring about meaningful change. The stormy but slow transformation of APsaA over recent decades owes more to Paul than to any other individual.

SHOULD PAUL HAVE BEEN A LAWYER?

Paul's work on confidentiality and, in particular, his efforts in creating the *amicus* brief in *Jaffe v. Redmond* discussed elsewhere in this volume partook of this same highly effective intellectual-technical approach to a problem. I had the pleasure of working with the attorney, Sandra Nye, who represented the social worker – litigant in this case. Sandra thought it was a pity that Paul had become a psychoanalyst since "he would have made a very, very fine lawyer."

THE REORGANIZATION COMMITTEE

My final extended experience working with Paul was in some ways less happy but continued the major themes of his (and my) personality. A committee to reorganize the governance of APsaA had been appointed with me as chair by then president Jon Meyer. The major problem confronting the committee, despite its broad mandate, continued to be the role of BOPS, but another group of issues around the nature of members' representation in governance was also of great importance. Several of the oddities in the way in which the committee was set up should have warned both Paul and me that it was meant to fail. One of these oddities was that none of the committee's deliberation were to be made public except for its final report which was to be submitted to the Council. (The following account is truncated in accordance with this agreement.)

Paul and I had strongly opposed views about the committee's tasks, Paul taking the stance that the committee's job was to narrowly address the specific issues that were represented in our charge, whereas I thought the committee's job was more broadly intended. As might be expected, the committee's meetings became heated and complicated in ways that 20 years later are probably not of great interest but which, in any case, all members of the committee had been sworn not to divulge to the larger world. As Secretary of APsaA, I had learned that Paul was a superb guide to matters of procedure, and he had introduced me to that infinitely useful volume, Robert's Rules of Order. Thus, it was one day that, in the midst of debate which was heated on the part of several of the committee's members, including myself, and during which Paul maintained his ever present and I, think authentic, calm, Paul and I simultaneously reached into our respective briefcases and pulled out copies of Robert's Rules to support our opinions. Both of us started laughing hard as Paul referred to this as our having "drawn the real gun."

The committee efforts, which involved an enormous amount of work, came to nothing but in a way that left us both laughing. Ultimately, the committee's report went in directions with which Paul strongly disagreed. When it came time for the report to be discussed in Council, the same president who had commissioned the report set a strict deadline on the discussion. Paul, who was the first to speak, had a great deal to say and as the minutes ticked away, it became clear to me that no real discussion and therefore no real action would be taken on the report unless Paul was interrupted by the president, something the president refused to do despite my repeated urgings. By the time Paul was finished, there was no room for further discussion, much less action. It was only in retrospect that Paul and I recognized how brilliantly we had both been outfoxed. The president who liked neither the report nor the directions in which Paul sought to revise it, and brilliantly used a parliamentary trick to deep-six the whole thing and to later generate a proposal of his own making which was more to his liking, but which suffered a similar fate. I was furious, but Paul showed no hint of anger, though he was disappointed in himself for not having recognized the trick. He seemed to feel calmly that this was just something he would have to keep working on and an experience from which he could learn.

Paul had an extraordinary capacity to get difficult things done. He was not terribly interested in emotionally charged rhetoric nor in the interpersonal complexities of an organization like APsaA. In fact, I never saw him to be terribly interested in what we usually think of as psychological questions at all. Rather, he was dedicated to the power of the intellect and the value of deep technical knowledge to achieve ends that he thought important. He obviously achieved both great pleasure and maintained an authentic calm as well as achieving so much using this approach, a deep-seated attitude which, in my experience, is nearly unique among psychoanalysts.[8]

Paul was a friend and a very good enemy. He transformed APsaA. He will be sorely missed.

---

8   There are very few psychoanalytic administrators, almost all of them products of or descended from the post-war Menninger Foundation who seem to have had similar attitudes.

CHAPTER 9

Love Letter to Paul Mosher

by Luba Kessler

We were in the cavernous halls of the IPA Congress in Chicago in 2009, probably amidst the book displays. I was waxing enthusiastic about a novel presentation I had attended, while Paul was clearly nonplussed by the premises I was expounding on. The difference between my excitement and his skepticism was a challenge: a formidable force in questioning the established authorities within APsaA, he held for me the unquestionable authority of someone with the impeccable pedigree of integrity.

So this was interesting. As a Councilor sitting on APsaA's Executive Council for the past few years I had been absorbing the unfamiliar arcana of organizational law and procedure under Paul's tutelage. Who would have known that arriving to serve on the Council in 2003 portended that kind of additional, unexpected, education? Yet there was Paul Mosher, an unprepossessing looking man in his ubiquitous navy jacket holding us all in thrall by talking about the governance of the Not-For-Profits! In the halls of the IPA Meetings in July of 2009, however, he was not wearing a jacket, and our brief exchange was about a matter of psychoanalytic theory, not governance. I could make my own claims on such grounds.

I had known Paul's method of presenting his arguments in the Council as always based on a solid examination of relevant data and informed by a meticulous application of cogent guiding principles. But this time we were on equal footing, just two participant colleagues at a psychoanalytic conference. A rather seriously impressed disciple of Paul's governance discussions as I had been in the Council, I was quite confident in my own studies of the various theoretical and clinical idioms of psychoanalytic versatility. I, in particular, remember being stimulated by my first encounter in that Congress with the ideas of Donald Meltzer. Maybe that was what I was so enthused about in talking to Paul. He, however, seemed to be less adventurously inclined — hence a bit of non-committal bemusement on his part in response.

Paul's comment in this moment was memorable: perhaps our non-convergence, he said, was due to his being more a left brain creature, lacking in the right brain attributes of greater creative flexibility. I did not know that I was necessarily ready to concede my own left-brain prowess of reason and be consigned to the emotionality of the right brain in contrast to him, but the contest was disarmed by his own light-hearted—if not totally surrendering—self-reflection. I did not know then that he had studied mathematics before deciding to attend medical school, and later to become a psychoanalyst. It figures.

There were other times through the years when Paul's quips in the get-togethers of the Alliance 21 subscribers during APsaA meetings brought moments of low-keyed hilarity, toning down the heated emotions of our rhetoric. This was especially welcome in the face of the insufferable intransigence of the conservatives within APsaA resisting our efforts to democratize our membership organization. There was something corny and a bit dated about how he contained the frustrations shared by the rest of the Alliance subscribers, and at the same time disarmingly refreshing. His was not the stridency, the sharpness, the impatience, the cheapness, and the witticism of ready sarcasm. He was Paul, and his method was one of being learned, of having the staying power of diligence, and of a well earned clarity of vision. He gave shape to our irritable dissatisfactions with the existing system, and provided firm grounding for our reformative aspirations. The muted wisecracks were the cherry on top. They may not have delivered satisfying punches, but they did deliver helpings of quieting delight. I may not have know it then, but I think I was partial to them. It makes me smile to revisit those moments even now.

Paul was not a mentor to me, nor a friend, nor a personal collaborator as I jealously know him to have been to others. I can think only of one other time when I had a personal encounter with Paul. It was when, greeted after his hip replacement operation, he declared that, relieved of his limp, he could now again dance with his sweetheart! Of course the image of his Paula immediately floated up in my mind's eye. But perhaps freedom from the commitment of a personal relationship was the particular gift of the unbound generosity of what his presence gave me. I could enjoy and learn from him just from being in his presence.

Long before encountering Paul in the Council of APsaA I had come upon *Title Key Word and Author Index to Psychoanalytic Journals 1920-1990* which he had compiled and edited. An early precursor to the Psychoanalytic Electronic Publishing, it had served as an introduction to my greedy perusal in psychoanalytic articles. I was finishing my psychoanalytic training in the late 90s and beginning to explore the literature on my own when I spotted the compendium among the books at the Waldorf. The red covered book took up a place of importance in my beginning library. It holds it still. The name of the editor of that volume, however, seemed of little consequence to me. I could only appreciate its provenance from the retrospection of many years later. It was an unsuspected first building block of my treasury of Paul's giftedness. I also did not know that my arrival on the Council as a Councilor representing the small Long Island Psychoanalytic Society at APsaA was owed to that self-same editor, Paul Mosher, M.D. The intervening years after graduating from psychoanalytic training were a time of individuating professional emancipation from institutional edicts, leading to my election as Councilor from Long Island. If I was developing my own professional outlook, it was because it coincided with the advent of the electronic listserv at APsaA. And Paul was the digital architect of the listserv. Paul's mathematical literacy were bringing us into the 21st century.

Of course, both the psychoanalytic index and the listserv were immeasurable gifts to all APsaA members. I have repeated many times—and have had no reason to edit the comment—that the listserv felt like the much needed oxygen for my professional bronchi, constricted by the rigidly held hierarchy of the existing institutional surround. Perhaps it was that pervading hierarchical obeisance, largely organized and upheld by the Training Analyst system enforced by APsaA' Board on Professional Standards, that precluded giving due credit to Paul Mosher's profoundly reformative contributions. I could only truly begin to appreciate them once his seemingly unprepossessing presence took on its true dimensions in the observed deliberations on the Council, APsaA's BOD.

Boy, I had had no idea what a ride it was going to be! Coming in as a newly minted Councilor was like learning to swim by being thrown into a deep-water pool. Only slowly, the outlines of APsaA's organizational structure came into clearer focus. I learned that APsaA had bicameral governance shared by Council, its BOD representing the general membership, and the Board on Professional Standards (BOPS), comprised exclusively of Training Analysts representing APsaA-approved institutes. It was this bicameral governance structure that faced Paul Mosher's scrutiny.

There had been a prolonged simmering discontent and skepticism over the influence of BOPS on APsaA's policies due to its proprietary control over the educational system through the certification and assignation of Training Analysts. Those policies, administered by the BOPS and echoed by the Education Committees of the approved institutes, ruled over the professional life of APsaA's membership. They marked professional careers right from the beginning of training, assigning Training Analysts for required training analysis and supervision. The authority of Training Analyst was a given, the TA assignation being the badge of recognizable and honored distinction for superiority over other analysts. Most, if not all, of the newly graduated fledgling members of APsaA came to the Waldorf's meeting halls imbued with reverence for the Training Analysts who had been the analysts, supervisors and teachers at their training institutes. This deference extended to the governance structure of our membership organization.

Enter Paul Mosher. Some Eureka moment had led him to question APsaA's organizational arrangement, leading him to an immersive study of Not-For-Profits functioning, the organizational predicate of APsaA. The rest of us in the Council were the open-mouthed recipients of his discoveries of the relevant outlines and specifics. At any rate, an organizational novice, entirely ignorant of even such basics as the parliamentary Robert's Rules, I was. Born and raised in Soviet lands devoid of opportunities of participatory democracy, I was nearly giddy with the promise of exercising my new awareness and say. I remember a particularly liminal moment of that newfound confidence when, in response to an assertion of special authority presumably due to her position as BOPS Secretary, I retorted my opposing views, adding pointedly that I was *only* a little Councilor from a little local society. The Soviet-imbibed ideals of egalitarianism overtook the assumptions of privileged positions in the ranks of APsaA. And it was the membership listserv that served as the training ground for examining the assumptions ruling the lives of the membership of the American.

The listserv became the loudspeaker of an unfolding passionate debate, and it was thrilling to be articulating and communicating ethically held principles. The drama of it all was unbelievable. The intersection of the governance discussions on the listserv and in the Council, supplemented further by contributions from the Alliance Listserv subscribers, became the bloodline of APsaA's reformative movement. And Paul was the beating heart of its circulation. His brilliant expositions of structural organizational principles as the necessary scaffolding for optimal functioning became the so-called *Civic Lessons*, a democratizing *tour de force* offering to all the fellow readers of the APsaA Members' Listserv. It gave the rest of us a solid foundation for the arguments in favor of needed organizational reform, a confident launch pad for our individual flights into the impassioned debates that ensued. I know that it was how it worked for me.

Eventually, following the dramatic events of the Council's resolve to challenge the BOPS institutional power prerogatives and the BOPS lawsuit against APsaA, it became inevitable that only a member bylaw amendment petition could determine the will of the membership with regard to APsaA's governance. Armed with well practiced articulation and communication on the Listserv, ennobled by ethically held principles taught by Paul, I championed the initiative for the petition and the sustained campaign on its behalf. Against the odds of the enduring legacy of the accustomed governance status quo, and in the face of resigned disbelief by many in the possibility of progress, the bylaw amendment proposal was voted in by the membership of APsaA.

Paul, too, had been skeptical about the prospects of the amendment passing. The teacher of all of the principles involved, the architect draftsman of its premises and the master builder of the envisioned organizational edifice, after years of unceasing yet futile efforts to alter the APsaA's organizational course, he may have had little reason for optimism that the membership could be stirred out of the accustomed modus operandi. Yet, he was the essential machinery that made it happen, the engine that could, and that did.

A lot in all of this has caused me to come to love Paul Mosher. I can readily call up the picture of him sitting in the Council on the customary Thursdays in the course of the APsaA meetings, always to be found upon entering the room in the center of the left wing of councilors. I see him standing at the microphone calmly delivering the golden nuggets of his learning, crisp arguments for the espoused principles in opposition to unearned presumptions of the system that be; or looking up expectantly from his seat at any of us when we followed with our own declamations at the same microphone, always guided by his look of satisfied approbation when we hit judicious notes of our own. His was always a steadying presence, a tuning fork delivering the A note for the rest of us. Did he know that? There was never any indication that he did. He was simply being Paul.

On preceding Wednesdays Paul could predictably be found in the gallery of the BOPS meetings, where the membership class of Training Analysts was shaping issues pertaining to APsaA's organizational policies. Since the insights gleaned from those discussions anticipated the agenda of the Council the following day, attending the BOPS meetings became part of the "homework" in preparation for it. It was a remarkable exercise of suffering the tedium of the various reports pertaining to institute business, but important so as to discern organizational implications. It helped to have the company of other stalwarts such as Elise Snyder, with her long gorgeous cascade of greying hair and Judy Schachter, our own knitting Madame Defarge. Those insights could be digested in the customary Wednesday evening meetings of the Alliance Listserv subscribers, where again Paul's deep organizational understanding contextualized their significance and informed our outlook.

It was the unswerving staying power of this diligence, this patient perseverance, this dogged inquiry, this principled stand, this steadfastness, this learning, this putting of the pieces together into a vision thus giving it direction, this clarion moral integrity, this teaching, this leading by being who he was, and chuckling here and there along the way, and cursing mutedly at stumbles—it was all this, and more, that was Paul to me, an unbidden treasure.

What's not to love?

In memoriam: Paul Mosher, MD (1936-2021)

CHAPTER 10

Dialogue with Paul Mosher

by Leon Hoffman

As we remember Paul Mosher, others will describe his intelligence, his incredible knowledge of the world, both the psychoanalytic world, the world of psychotherapy privacy, and the general political world. Paul and I were friendly rivals who respected one another. We both served on the Executive Council for many years during the 1990's. Despite our differences during those day-long meetings we chatted about a variety of issues, not just the politics of the American Psychoanalytic Association. We both shared a knowledge and communicated the importance of *Jaffee v. Redmond*, 518 U.S. 1 (1996), a United States Supreme Court case in which the Court created a psychotherapist-patient privilege in the Federal Rules of Evidence (https://en.wikipedia.org/wiki/Jaffee_v._Redmond).

In looking at my old files, the first document I found was from exactly a quarter of a century ago. In this statement, I argued for the importance of the unique union of the American Psychoanalytic Association. Paul was very active in promoting a unitary Board of Directors.

Historically, Paul's position eventually became the by-laws of the organization of what came to be called APsaA. I last saw Paul at the 2019 meeting where we chatted over a coke. I will always remember him.

AN ARGUMENT FOR THE IMPORTANCE OF THE UNIQUE UNION OF THE AMERICAN PSYCHOANALYTIC ASSOCIATION
December 1996

The American Psychoanalytic Association is a unique union in that it combines under one umbrella the essence of three kinds of organizations. First, it is a membership organization fulfilling a variety of functions for its members. Second, it is a certifying and national parent organization of educational institutions, and third, it is a certifying organization for individuals. This particular blend of functions contributes greatly to our strength and shows that we are not simply a professional guild. Despite the seeming "de facto oligarchy in the governance of the organization" (Mosher 12/8/96) the structure of the American has led to the development of strong educational curricula. As long as such a union continues, tensions resulting from competing and at times conflicting interests will be inevitable. It is important to stress that these tensions are both a source of strength as well a source of problems. The needs of a general membership organization are different from those of a parent organization of educational institutions and both are different from the needs of an organization that certifies individuals. Those needs are not always, if ever, congruent. In addition, tensions between local interests and national interests are also inevitable.

Thus, one has to evaluate the significance of Paul Mosher's comment on 12/8/1996 when he says, that "If the Council currently offers the most democratic expression of the membership's views, and is the governing body of the American, why is it that the issue in question [External Credentialling] isn't simply subject to being managed through the expressed will of the Council?"

The major question for our organization is whether we can continue to develop strategies that foster the continued development of psychoanalysis: its impact in mental health treatment, medicine, and other areas of intellectual life; the development of psychoanalytic practice for our future members; and the development of psychoanalytic education and training that continues with the will to support and enhance the development of psychoanalysis.

We are at a crucial juncture in the development of The American Psychoanalytic Association. There has been greater democratization within the organization as well as greater interaction with other psychoanalytic and psychotherapy groups: in terms of intellectual intercourse as well as unified action in political and other public arenas. The current debate about External Credentialing has included a great deal of rancorous debate. Those who favor external credentialling with the other members of the Consortium report that the other members of the Consortium "have shown increasing distress in recent meetings about their perception that the American is stalling on external credentialling" (Rosenblatt, 12/5/96). This criticism is apparently leveled at the American, despite the By-Laws of the Consortium, which state that any action by the Consortium requires unanimous agreement by all members of the Consortium. Thus, it seems that unless the American agrees with the other members of the Consortium, it is violating a principle, which is considered to be virtuous by the other members of the Consortium.

CHAPTER 11

A Photography Memory

by Carolyn Gatto

In my role as Scientific Program and Meetings Director for the American Psychoanalytic Association I had many interactions with Paul over the years. During one of APsaA's Annual meetings held in Chicago, Paul took his camera to Crown Fountain in Millennium Park. The fountain consists of two 50-foot glass block towers at each end of a shallow reflecting pool. The towers project video images of faces from a broad social spectrum of Chicago citizens. On a hot June day, the reflecting pool is full of people – kids running through the fountains, parents on the sidelines watching, tourists taking selfies. Paul took a picture of two children, one black and one white, sitting in the middle of the pool, engrossed in conversation with each other. It was so striking because of its simplicity. Two children, untouched by racism, politics, or strife at that very moment. It was beautiful.

Paul displayed that photo at APsaA's National Meeting Photo Exhibit. Paul and Paula were always fixtures at the exhibit—happy to talk to participants about the pictures that Paul took. I commented about that picture—telling Paul that I thought it was beautiful. He thanked me for my comment, and I continued with my day.

A week after that meeting, I received a copy of that photo in the mail from Paul.

CHAPTER 12

A Mentor and a Teacher

by Tina Faison

My fondest memories of Paul are those centering around the APsaA elections. Paul was incredibly knowledgeable at understanding and explaining the vast number of election procedures and methods, especially the Preferential Voting Method. I recall consulting with him on many occasions regarding the APsaA elections. He took great joy in helping me maneuver my way around the process. I consider myself somewhat of an expert now after following his tutelage. I am forever grateful.

Paul was also very instrumental in bringing the National Office "on-line", working with the Staff to computerize operations.

I also remember Paul's enthusiasm as he served as APsaA's Director of Technology for the CD-ROM project (which is now known as PEP—*Psychoanalytic Electronic Publishing*). This was a major breakthrough in psychoanalytic publishing comprising editorial copy of six of the most significant psychoanalytic journals of its time. His knowledge of technology was immeasurable! The project was a great success, and continues today!

CHAPTER 13

A Generative Friend

by Thomas Bartlett

I was very sad to learn of Paul's passing. I always hoped he might be properly honored by APsaA during his lifetime. Countless Distinguished Service plaques, but never the large and public recognition that he deserved. Two candidates for President assured me that once elected they would see that he was invited to give a plenary, but they never followed through. Like Judy Schachter and Ralph Fishkin, I wrote a letter, in 2009, proposing Paul for the Sigourney Award, and people on the Sigourney Committee who should've been sympathetic were either themselves too conservative or just too cautious to risk offending conservatives. One took the 'out' of saying that this award was for a "different kind" of contribution than the countless listed in the Sigourney nomination letters.

Paul was just too controversial, despite all he had given APsaA, and for a reason. Does anyone doubt, but for Paul, that BOPS would still dominating the Executive Committee, still in de facto control, with the Executive Council meeting only to rubber stamp their decisions?

Paul once told me, "Some people have photographic memories. I may have something analogous. I noticed when I was young that I never forget a rule once I learn it." It was that intuitive grasp of rules, their ramifications, how they all fit into a coherent whole, that let him 'see' that the way APsaA was being operated could not be right, according to its bylaws, or legally, according to New York Not for Profit law. And whatever Paul needed, to follow such a hunch, he simply taught himself from scratch, until, for example, he understood the relevant law better than APsaA's then attorney; or grasped Robert's Rules to the standard of a parliamentarian. (He even introduced me to an online forum of parliamentarians, where he confirmed his hunches.)

Similarly, when he found it necessary, Paul taught himself the rules and logic of programming. He prided himself that once he sat next to Steve Wozniak on an airplane and impressed him with original programming he had done in creating the Freud Archive, or maybe it was the early PEP discs, I'm not sure. Anyway, the programming was so impressive that Wozniak asked if he could use it! During Covid, Paul created an interactive map which let you watch the spread of the disease in the US and zero in on the statistics county by county. http://mosher.com/covid/hotspots/hotspot_map.html

I first met Paul when I was coming to a meeting in which the Affiliate (i.e., Candidate) Council President had invited a major BOPS representative to talk with the Candidate representatives to garner their support for BOPS Certification. I wrote Paul to ask if he would represent the other side, but the Affiliate President would not let him participate. At that Winter Meeting, he invited me to the Wednesday group and I continued in its back and forth email exchanges between meetings. When I pointed out that people were constantly being accidentally dropped from the conversations replying to one another in this way, Paul 'volunteered' me to organize the Wednesday Group's "Delinkage" elist, and he taught me how to set up and manage it on Yahoo Groups. I later set up elists for the Affiliates, for IPSO (IPA Candidate organizations) in five languages, and for several APsaA Societies. Paul explained that whenever he started a list, as he had the Members List and Open Line, he would nurture it whenever discussion died off, by feeding it with interesting comments on various topics until the list took hold.

I say BOPS would still be running the show today but for Paul. It was not just the "Civics Lessons" or the creation of the Members List and Open Line, though these were greatly important. You also had to garner the votes. I got to work closely with Paul behind the scenes on many of the bylaw amendments, and none would have passed or in the beginning, nearly passed, but for his masterful use of the internet. I might help do the nuts and bolts of gathering information from this or that list, but Paul put it all to work. At meetings he always found time to meet with me at least once at this really cheap Korean restaurant on Second Avenue.

When Jon Meyer proposed the Reorganization Task Force, we were skeptical, especially upon learning that you had to agree to join before knowing who else had been invited. But Meyer's move to reorganize seemed like it would be a juggernaut at the time. If we refused to participate, the plan would be even worse and our objections would be less credible. The fifteen-member TFoR ended up being stacked in favor of TA's with only Paul and me from the Wednesday Group, despite our recent amendment having garnered 53% of the votes. Paul did more work than most anyone on that Task Force. It hurt to watch the eyes of the task force members glaze over every time Paul tried to impress on them that they were ignoring the wishes of a large portion of the members. "Forget politics, we are just fifteen individuals here" able to dream up something new." Once it became clear after a critical vote that he would simply be helping create something he would then work to oppose, he resigned. I stayed on to track what was to follow.

I could have stopped here and simply said that I feel very lucky to have had his friendship and to have learned from him but I wanted to add one more interesting accomplishment of Paul's. In the late 50's, Paul was a medical student doing research in the Harvard labs when LSD became of interest. He was testing something out on frogs and when his application was accepted, he was sent a huge quantity of really pure, still legal, LSD-25. Eventually, he tried it himself, only once, and wrote the first published piece about the LSD experience, for a 1961 book being compiled by David Eben called The Drug Experience. Paul loved being able to say he was published in a collection with William Burroughs, Aldous Huxley, Allen Ginsberg, Billie Holiday and others. His article is remarkably lucid, keeping his scientific curiosity alive amidst the experience. He did not "turn on, tune in, and drop out".

He used whatever opportunities came his way to learn and expand his knowledge and experience. For that reason, at my suggestion, the LSD chapter appears in this book and I've had the opportunity to reciprocate and enlarge Paul's reputation with those reading this book.

THE WORK

CHAPTER 14

Anticipating a *JAPA* Book Review;
The Review

by Helen Gediman

Just a few years ago, when APsaA meetings were live and not remote, I was sitting in an audience waiting for the start of a panel. Rosemary Balsam, a member of that panel, stepped down from the dais, and with her hand sort of covering her mouth, as though she were revealing a secret, told me with a big smile that I was sure to have a strong reaction when I would receive a copy of *JAPA*'s review of my book, ***Stalker, Hacker, Voyeur, Spy*** (Karnac, 2017). Rosemary, then book review editor of *JAPA*, was trying both to give me a heads up and to maintain the confidentiality of her reviewer's identity.

A few weeks later, I received a copy of the book review, totally surprised to see it was written by Paul Mosher and his coauthor, Jeffrey Berman. Paul Mosher, so well known for his magnificent work in developing the PEP, and for his accomplishments in advancing APsaA's governance, reviewing a book on "Stalking?" I had intended the book to appeal not simply to psychoanalysts, but to an audience of academics and other elitists interested in my topic. I had illustrated my examples with only a few clinical examples but mostly from films which I had suggested the reader might view along with the chapters each movie was intended to illustrate.

As it turned out, Paul and his wife, Paula had together read the book as I had hoped my general readership would. In the section on **Sexual Stalking,** they viewed the films *Play Misty for Me* (Clint Eastwood, 1971) and *Fatal Attractions* (Adrian Lyne, 1987). I knew Paul reasonably well from our work together in the Alliance, and from simultaneously being on the Executive Council, now the BOD, of APsaA. What a nice surprise to think his interests extended beyond what I might have guessed from our heretofore limited contextual milieus. When it came to the section on **Surveillance Stalking**, the couple viewed *Peeping Tom* (Michael Powell, 1960); *Rear Window* (Alfred Hitchcock, 1954); *The Conversation* (Francis Ford Coppola, 1974); *Caché*, (Michael Haneke, 2005); and *Red Road* (Andrea Arnold, 2007). Although I am not certain of this, I believe Paul's workman interests must have taken him into the world of photography and photographers, as portrayed by Jimmy Stewart in *Rear Window*. In that classic, Hitchcock makes us, the audience, complicit in the voyeurism of the photographer, so Paul, by virtue of being a member of that compact audience, knew that photographers were often cast in the roles of sexual and surveillance stalkers. I am ever grateful for the opportunity to have talked with him and Paula about their reactions at one of Joe and Judy's annual parties for Alliance members and their friends over Judy's omnipresent and delicious beef, barley and mushroom soup.

I would guess it was not until he reached the section on **Stalking and Hacking in Cyberspace** that I could recognize Paul Mosher at the movies as distinctly the same Paul Mosher who was deeply into computers and governance. I can easily imagine him watching the films *Enemy of the State* (Tony Scott, 1998) and *Citizenfour* (Laura Poitras, 2014) when he would have been stimulated not only in reviewing my book, but in formulating new ideas that could apply to his growing concerns with problems faced by the APsaA Board. He did not disappoint. These two films, which deal with the conflicts between privacy and security in present-day cyber attacks, might well have been examples of what Rosemary Balsam had on her mind when she said I was sure to have a strong reaction to the review.

I quote now what is most unusual to find in a book review, but the creativity and importance of which were obviously understood by *JAPA*'s book review section:

> "One cannot be blamed for worrying that the constant drumbeat of revelations of new intrusions into virtually everyone's privacy via the Internet has dulled even psychoanalysts' sensibilities about spying and being spied upon. After APsaA installed a new email list system, one of us, Paul Mosher, in examining the hidden code in the messages the system delivers to the members, discovered that every message the system distributes contains a concealed 'email web beacon' that silently sends back a message to the Association indicting the email address of the person who opened the message, exactly what message it is, and the exact time and date the message was opened by that individual. After having been informed of this spying six months ago as of the time of this writing, APsaA officers apparently accepted the vendor's claim that the breach cannot be removed. Although the issue was mentioned in committee minutes, ***APsaA officers had not explicitly notified the membership of this practice until shown a draft of this review.***" [Emphasis mine].

That is, the review itself had revealed that the Board had read the review of my book before I did, a revelation that had not been shared with me until I read a copy of the Mosher-Berman review. Was this why Rosemary's approach to me before her own panel began appeared somewhat stealthy (personally but I do not believe professionally)? Even Mosher says "We can only speculate how Helen Gediman would respond to this issue, but it's likely she would be concerned."

Well, whatever concern I have had about any possible secrecy about my book being discussed publicly behind my back, such concern is superseded by my deepest respect for Paul Mosher's motives and entirely well-meaning intentions. As for Rosemary Balsam, she recently, in a personal commutation said:

"So H — here is what I have in my coffers still. I think the influence of Jeffrey Berman brought out the straightforward scholarly aspect of Paul that, as I say, was a joy to interact with. Jeff is a fine writer too, and very interesting thinker. My impression was that they were best or at least very good friends. They were always very responsive as a duo when we invited them to review — and of course, they turned in excellent essays and did their work exquisitely on time (the way to the heart of an editor)…Paul always submitted mss. that were very clear, meticulous and needing little editing - if I remember rightly!! He was a pleasure to work with — and your book was terrific, so I don't think this particular task was very hard for him, and I think brought him a lot of pleasure…"

What a heartwarming thing to say about Paul. I hope by now we can all understand and appreciate Paul and his being chosen, along with Jeffrey, to write a review about stalking and the movies. I will leave it up to all of us to think about his belief that even psychoanalysts have taken steps at one time or another, toward a dystopian "surveillance" state. I will fondly remember him for his final sentence: "The value of **Stalker, Hacker, Voyeur, Spy** is that it warns of bedeviling problems we cannot yet imagine."

Stalker, Hacker, Voyeur, Spy: A Psychoanalytic Study of Erotomania, Voyeurism, Surveillance, and Invasions of Privacy. By Helen K. Gediman. London: Karnac Books, 2017, xxxix + 204 pp., $36.55, Reviewed by Paul Mosher and Jeffrey Berman.

"The world's most famous filing cabinet," an artifact now housed in the Smithsonian Museum of American History, once belonged to the Los Angeles psychoanalyst Lewis Fielding. The cabinet shows obvious damage from having been pried open on September 3, 1971, by President Richard Nixon's "Plumbers" in their first foray into illegal spying on fellow citizens. The Plumbers sought information about Fielding's patient Daniel Ellsberg's possible knowledge of Nixon's secret plans for expanding the war. The Plumbers may have wanted to "neutralize Ellsberg." When this matter came to public attention during Ellsberg's trial over his release of the "Pentagon Papers," the media reported that the Plumbers had found nothing. On the contrary: they had discovered Ellsberg's file in the cabinet. They saw in that file a copy of a paper Ellsberg had written indicating he had indeed seen relevant classified information (Edwards, 2012).

Terrible as this break-in was, and despite the fact that it unleashed a chain of events leading to Watergate and ultimately to Nixon's resignation three years later, the incident now seems quaint to us because the means used to access Ellsberg's file was a mere crowbar, hardly the high-tech tool by which such intrusion is carried out today. By 1991, tales in which analysts or their patients were intruded upon could still be the stuff of comedy, such as the 1991 film *What About Bob?*, which depicts a highly dependent patient (Bill Murray) who stalks his new analyst (Richard Dreyfuss) on his New Hampshire vacation. In the transformed world we work in today, however, reality has taken a darker turn, not only in the lives of psychoanalysts and their patients, but in virtually everyone's life.

If the lilting title *Stalker, Hacker, Voyeur, Spy* reminds readers of a John Le Carré story (such as the 1974 novel *Tinker Tailor Soldier Spy*), the connection is deliberate, as Helen K. Gediman readily acknowledges in the Preface. She rejected her original title, *Stalker, Hacker, Bugger, Spy*, because of the salacious connotations of the third word. No matter: the present title evokes the sinister implications of life in an age of ubiquitous surveillance.

The title's literary allusion is apt for another reason. Gediman's discussion centers less on clinical material, of which there is little, than on the growing number of novels, memoirs, films, and documentaries that dramatize various forms of stalking, hacking, and spying. In chapter 1 she remarks on the few references to the words "stalking" or "stalker" in the definitive research reference source, Psychoanalytic Electronic Publishing (PEP), created by Paul Mosher and others. She offers in chapter 2 case study vignettes on erotomania and unrequited love. Gediman then turns in chapter 3 to film portrayals of sexual stalking. Two classic films form the basis of her discussion: *Play Misty for Me* (1971), directed by Clint Eastwood, and *Fatal Attraction* (1987), directed by Adrian Lyne. Gediman offers convincing psychoanalytic interpretations of both iconic films. Noting that *Play Misty for Me* is a psychological study of the madness that sometimes results from being "in love," she suggests that Eastwood's screen persona "deconstructed the stereotypical male patriarchal image of refractory, ferocious, and seemingly invulnerable macho masculinity that he had projected in previous roles" (p. 25). *Fatal Attraction* is the most famous film portrayal of a vindictive, crazed, erotomanic sexual stalker. Played by Glenn Close in the film, Alex Forrest "projects the *femme fatale* image of erotomania, a perversion of idealized but unrequited romantic love commonly found in sexual stalking" (p. 28).

Chapter 4, film portrayals of stalking that involve voyeurism, sadism, and the primal scene, explores Hitchcock's 1954 masterpiece of suspense, *Rear Window*. Much has been written on the film, though not by psychoanalytically oriented scholars. Suggesting that sexual voyeurism is a form of stalking, Gediman argues that Hitchcock makes us complicit in the voyeurism of the injured photographer, played by James Stewart. "The film focuses on the layers of parallel subjective psychological points of view of filmer, camera, characters, and audience alike" (p. 40). This complicity, Gediman adds, is a result of what film critics call the "doubling technique": "You look, you see what the protagonist sees, and then you see how he reacts" (p. 40). One of Gediman's most prescient insights is that photographers are often cast in the roles of sexual and/or surveillance stalkers. This is also true in the eminently forgettable 1960 psycho-thriller *Peeping Tom*, directed by Michael Powell, which depicts the voyeurism inherent in the processes of filmmaking and film viewing.

Chapter 5, gender and sexual stalking, reveals an intriguing disconnect between film and real life. "By and large, female protagonists in films about sexual stalking are erotomanic and vengeful, whereas male protagonists are voyeuristic and often cruel" (p. 56). And yet, curiously, the female sexual stalking in the films she analyzes does not correspond to real life: "most sexual stalkers are men, not murderous women, no matter how common it is for women off the silver screen to feel vengeful toward their supposed lovers who do not support their erotomania—a quasi-delusional belief that their love is romantically returned" (pp. 56–57). How do we explain this contradiction? The question leads Gediman into a discussion of second-wave feminism of the 1970s followed by the "backlash films" of later decades that portray women as seeking to dominate, castrate, or destroy helpless male protagonists.

Chapter 6, film portrayals of surveillance stalking, considers a number of films, including Francis Ford Coppola's 1974 *The Conversation*, the forerunner of films in the surveillance-stalking genre. In a witty reference to the "loneliness of the long distance stalker" (p. 70), Gediman asserts that as we gaze closely at the film, we invade the privacy of Henry Caul, played by Gene Hackman, in the same way that he and his associates invade the privacy of those on whom he eavesdrops. Gediman discusses other films in this genre, include *Caché*, directed by Michael Haneke and starring Daniel Auteuil and Juliette Binoche, and the little-known Scottish film *Red Road*.

Chapters 7 through 9 focus on stalking and hacking in cyberspace. These chapters are the most unsettling, for they describe a brave new world that affects all of us in the most alarming way. The week we began our review, for example, the credit reporting company Equifax announced begrudgingly, a month after the fact, a massive data breach affecting 143 million Americans whose credit card numbers, drivers' license numbers, and Social Security numbers were stolen. No one can predict the frightening implications of identity theft made possible by advanced technology. Privacy no longer exists in an age of surveillance, leading to Gediman's rueful conclusion of "justified paranoia" (p. 152).

Most of us are not famous enough to worry about celebrity stalking, but Gediman has much to say about the subject in chapter 7, which highlights Ron Galella and Jacqueline Kennedy Onassis: the paparazzo stalker and his stalkee. Chapter 8—stalking in cyberspace: hacking and spying—presents three case vignettes that came to Gediman's attention around the time of the media's disclosure of rampant invasions of privacy by two government agencies, the Central Intelligence Agency (CIA) and the National Security Agency (NSA). Chapter 9, the conflicts between privacy and security in present-day cyber attacks, offers a thoughtful discussion of the 1998 film *Enemy of the State*, directed by Tony Scott, prophetic in its vision of high-tech identity theft, and the 2013 documentary *Citizenfour*, directed by Laura Poitras, about the former NSA contractor Edward Snowden's whistleblowing. Gediman is rightly troubled by the American government's willingness to eavesdrop on any telephone call it wants "and does so much more often than the law suggests it should" (p. 144).

In the epilogue, Gediman explores the implications of learning that our privacy has been invaded by various forms of stalking, including cyberstalking. She gives an example of a subtle form of stalking that probably all of us have experienced—our purchasing preferences in advertisements that pop up on the right side of our computer screens when we sign on to our personal email accounts. Unnervingly, we may not initially realize we are being pursued with unexpected and unrequested information.

The shortage of clinical vignettes in Gediman's book reveals, as Karnac's series editor Fredric Perlman indicates in the Preface, that stalkers generally do not seek treatment. Gediman estimates that about ten percent of therapists have been stalked by patients. Few of these therapists, Perlman admits, "including myself (unhappily, one of the ten percent), ever speak or write about it publicly" (p. xiv). Gediman, Adjunct Clinical Professor of Psychology at the New York University Postdoctoral Program in Psychotherapy and Psychoanalysis, acknowledges that, because of confidentiality, she is reluctant to speak about being stalked by her patients. This explains her emphasis on film portrayals of stalking, hacking, and spying.

The possibility of a psychoanalyst's being stalked by a patient, however, cannot be ignored in today's world. Indeed, in the current television series *Mr. Robot*, the protagonist, Elliot Alderson, is a computer security consultant by day and a hacker by night. In a gripping three minute segment in episode seven of the first season, the seriously depressed and schizoid Elliot confronts his therapist, Krista Gordon, with the confession, "I've been lying to you." He then reveals, apart from the fact that he takes none of his prescribed medication, everything he has learned about her personal and professional life by breaking into her online accounts — her loneliness, her sexual proclivities, her romantic relationships, and even her thoughts about other patients. Subsequently, in a subplot, he discovers that Krista's current male friend is cheating on her and takes it upon himself to set things right. Elliot tells Krista, "I don't just hack you, Krista. I hack everyone."

One cannot be blamed for worrying that the constant drumbeat of revelations of new intrusions into virtually everyone's privacy via the Internet has dulled even psychoanalysts' sensibilities about spying or being spied on. After APsaA installed a new email list system, one of us, Paul Mosher, in examining the hidden code in the messages the system delivers to the members, discovered that every message the system distributes contains a concealed "email web beacon" that silently sends back a message to the Association indicating the email address of the person who opened the message, exactly which message it is, and the exact time and date the message was opened by that individual. After having been informed of this "spying" six months ago as of the time off this writing, APsaA officers apparently accepted the vendor's claim that the beacon cannot be removed. Although the issue was mentioned in committee minutes, APsaA officers had not explicitly notified the membership of this practice until shown a draft of this review. APsaA officers seem to have been caught between the contrasting views that the hidden code in the new email list system is a benign non-issue, on the one hand, and that the membership would be irrationally alarmed by being informed of its existence, on the other. Following the notice, no member complained. Considering that such invisible beacons were described as "Orwellian" and "carbon monoxide for Internet privacy" when they first came to public attention a mere 15 years ago (Olsen), it is clear that even psychoanalysts — leadership and members alike — now take for granted one more step toward a dystopian "surveillance state."

We can only speculate how Helen Gediman would respond to this issue, but it's likely she would be concerned. The author of many articles on the subject, she shares her expertise with readers in a probing and well written book. To her credit, she points out the parallels between the sexual stalker's voyeurism and that of reporters, analysts, and scholars like herself. "Arguably, filmmakers, cinematographers, and editors and writers like me voyeuristically watch and take pleasure as their creative products take shape"

(p. 53). Sometimes Gediman expands the definition of stalking to include activities that may not strike everyone as illicit. "Today, many patients, perhaps most, Google their analysts simply to check out their credentials or to conjecture if they would be a good match" (p. xxxiv). She then states that several of her patients have confessed, or simply disclosed, without guilt, that they "web-stalked" her, aided by Google. Such internet investigations are now so common that it may be impossible to separate legitimate research from stalking. The value of *Stalker, Hacker, Voyeur, Spy* is that it warns of bedeviling problems we cannot yet imagine.

REFERENCES

Edwards, O. (October 2012). The Ellsberg files: A 1971 burglary unleashed a chain of events that altered American history. *Smithsonian Magazine* 70-71.

Olsen, S. (January 2, 2002). "Nearly undetectable tracking device raises concern." *C|net*.

https://www.cnet.com/news/nearly-undetectable-tracking-device-raises-concern/ (accessed 10-11-2017)

CHAPTER 15

Civics Lessons

Introduction by Paul Brinich

My interactions with Paul Mosher stretched over a quarter of a century. A quick review of a year's worth of our email correspondence back in 2010 shows that we discussed:

1. the central role of privacy in our field and how HIPAA was problematic;
2. the use and misuse of statistics in mental health (and especially medication trials);
3. the seduction of psychoanalytic psychiatrists by the pharmaceutical industry;
4. the problems created when training analysts play a role in candidate advancement;
5. the PEP database and its evolution;
6. the aging of APsaA's membership (with data);
7. the Jaffee v. Redmond (518 U.S. 1; 1996) landmark Supreme Court case which granted communications between psychotherapists and their patients privileged status in federal courts;
8. the benefits and problems associated with electronic medical records;

9. Marcia Angell's trenchant remarks regarding the corruption of medical research and resultant publications by pharmaceutical interests;

10. the vagaries of the "certification" process as implemented by BoPS;

11. the brave new world of on-line therapy; and

12. the explosion of diagnoses in DSM-III, IV, and 5.

My contact with Paul began when I took on the role of the North Carolina Psychoanalytic Society's representative to APsaA's board of directors (then called the Executive Council). It was then that Paul generously shared with me his "Civics Lessons." This series of 13 essays provided me and many other APsaA members with a remarkable and very useful introduction to the idiosyncrasies of APsaA's governance. Paul wrote clearly, with a sense of history, and (at times) a wry humor regarding the ways in which APsaA had created for itself a governing structure in which the Executive Council was responsible for everything, but had little real authority over one of APsaA's major components, the Board on Professional Standards (BoPS).

Paul was no radical; he believed in law and order — but he also believed in being truthful, and in speaking truth to power. From his position in Albany he carefully laid out how APsaA's governance had evolved, sometimes in line with then-current New York State laws regarding not-for-profit organizations, and sometimes in ignorance or disregard of those laws.

I was a neophyte in APsaA's organizational politics and, as such, it took me a while to recognize the importance of some of the distinctions Paul made in his civics lessons. However, when I was asked to chair the Compliance Task Force (set up in 2006 to review the ways in which APsaA's bylaws complied or failed to comply with NY State laws), I found myself returning again and again to Paul's essays.

Paul's careful work was appreciated by many of his fellow APsaA members. Some of these organized themselves into an "alliance" [the

146

Alliance Listserve], which sought to highlight ways in which APsaA might evolve from an organization run by a *de facto* oligarchy to one in which all members had a say in the future of the organization.

Changes in APsaA's bylaws came slowly, but they came. And while Paul would be the first to acknowledge that APsaA will need to continue its evolution, it is impossible to deny that Paul's civics lessons contributed to changes that have created a more flexible, member-responsive organization, one that is able to adapt to present and future needs.

Paul's death has deprived us of a loyal gadfly whose erudition and multiple talents contributed greatly to APsaA for half a century. We won't see another like him anytime soon.

CIVICS LESSONS
Paul W. Mosher

Date: Wed, 12 Dec 2001:
Civics Lesson — Part 1 —

A Civics Lesson to Myself
This Note was Written in Defense of the Non-Binding Referendum Proposal and Shows That Power to Make APsaA Policy Belongs to the Members

For those who are having trouble understanding what's going on in the discussion in advance of the APsaA Executive Council meeting, here's my brief "civics lesson" to myself on how APsaA is governed. I think that some of the information posted on this list during the discussion on the referendum proposal (including a remark of mine suggesting that APsaA is a representative democracy) might have been misleading. I put the following together for my own edification but I think it could be of general interest, as well.

The Nature of APsaA Democracy

Some list contributors have suggested that the idea of a non-binding referendum is undermining of the "representative democracy" of APsaA. The fact is, however, that APsaA is really more of a hybrid of "Representative Democracy" and "Direct Democracy." In that light, the idea of a non-binding referendum ballot seems perfectly appropriate:

Although the Executive Council functions as the Board of Directors of APsaA and therefore ordinarily is responsible for all policy decisions of the Association, APsaA is not a representative democracy in the strictest sense of the word. This is because the by-laws are written in a way that introduces something of a "direct democracy" element into the governance of APsaA: the general members have the option of a DIRECT veto of the Executive Council's actions, not just an indirect voice through the election of their Councilor representatives. This is true whether (c) or not (d) the Council invites a membership review of its actions:

SECTION 6. GENERAL POWERS OF EXECUTIVE COUNCIL. Except as otherwise limited herein, the Executive Council shall have all of the powers in the management of the property, affairs and business of the Association, of a Board of Directors under the New York Not-for-Profit Corporation Law, provided:

...

"(c) The Executive Council MAY determine with respect to any action taken by it that such action shall be subject to the approval of the members, and in any such case the action so taken by the Executive Council shall not become final unless and until it has been approved (a) by a majority vote of the members eligible to vote present at a Meeting of Members, or (b) by mail as hereinafter provided in Section 8 of this Article V.

"(d) Any action taken by the Executive Council pursuant to the powers vested in it by this Article V and not referred by it to, or for the approval of, the Active Members shall nevertheless be final and binding on the Association; PROVIDED, HOWEVER, THAT NOTHING HEREIN CONTAINED SHALL BE CONSTRUED TO LIMIT THE POWER OF A MAJORITY OF THE MEMBERS ELIGIBLE TO VOTE PRESENT AT A MEETING AT WHICH A QUORUM IS PRESENT TO DISAPPROVE ANY ACTION TAKEN BY THE EXECUTIVE COUNCIL TO THE EXTENT THAT SUCH ACTION HAS NOT THERETOFORE BEEN CONSUMMATED." … [emphasis added]

Note added May, 2003
Since I wrote this I have learned that the New York State Law does not permit the actions of the Board of Directors to be overridden by the membership. Prior to the incorporation, the bylaws read "to veto and disapprove" but the word "veto" was struck out at that time. Exactly what the remaining "disapprove" means is not clear.

Note added December, 2010
More recently, an attorney has informed APsaA that the entire "Approval by Mail" scheme in the APsaA bylaws does not comply with the New York State Not-for-Profit Corporation Law.

The members may also directly initiate a deliberation by the Executive Council on an issue:

SECTION 7. DIRECTIONS TO THE EXECUTIVE COUNCIL. By a majority vote of the legally constituted Meeting of Members present at a meeting at which a quorum is present, the Executive Council may be directed to investigate, report and recommend as to any course of action proposed to be taken by the members. (Article III, Sec. 7) … and the Council may then report back to take the members (but the Executive Council may NOT act on the matter itself):

(e) When the Executive Council shall have been directed as hereinbefore provided, to investigate, report and recommend as to any proposed course of action, it shall have no authority to take any further action with regard to such proposed course of action, except in accordance with the action of the members taken upon its report.

In other words, the members of APsaA, as expressed through their votes in the often disparaged (and frequently ceremonial) meeting of members have the FINAL WORD on any policy decision in APsaA. The by-laws envision a kind of partnership between the Executive Council acting as a representative body, on the one hand, and the general membership acting through a direct-democracy-like voting mechanism on the other. Unlike the Executive Council, where no one may vote without being present at the meeting, the by-laws specifically recognize a proxy mechanism for votes taken at the meeting of members so that the votes of members who are not present can be counted on any issue that is referred to in their proxy.

The Executive Committee

The Executive Committee is empowered to act in place of the Executive Council between Council meetings, but it is clearly subordinate to the Executive Council.

"Unless otherwise provided from time to time by the Executive Council, the Executive Committee shall have and may exercise any and all powers of the Executive Council between meetings of the Executive Council to the extent permitted by New York law … … the Executive Committee shall normally handle contacts between the Association and outside agencies; shall help Affiliate Societies with matters of organization and in their relationship to the Association; and shall advise and assist the Executive Council in the management of the property, affairs and business of the Association." (Article VI, Section 2)

An Executive Council meeting can be called at any time by a request of any six members of the Executive Council and at such a meeting almost any action of the Executive Committee may be "subject to rescission:"

"… Any action taken by the Executive Committee shall be subject to rescission or change by the Executive Council, provided, however, that no such rescission or change shall invalidate any acts of any officers or other persons taken pursuant to such action of the Executive Committee prior to such rescission or change by the Executive Council." (Article VI, Section 5)

Governance in APsaA

The President and Secretary of APsaA are ex-officio voting members of the Executive Council and serve, respectively as the Chair and Secretary of the Executive Council. The chair is required to act impartially and should only vote if his/her vote if necessary to decide an issue. The by-laws require that the meetings of the Executive Council be conducted in accordance with Robert's Rules of Order which the APsaA by-laws designate as APsaA's "parliamentary authority." (Article 15, Sec. 3)

As APsaA has grown much larger than it was at the time the by-laws were constructed, the "direct democracy" aspect of our governance has tended to be forgotten. The Executive Committee (hopefully by accident) and the officers who comprise it, have come to be seen as the policy making body of the Association and the Council has somewhat abdicated its role as the spark plug (subject to review by the entire membership) of APsaA policy.

But now that we have member-to-member communication via these lists, and also a new resolve to empower the Executive Council, there seems to be no reason that we can't do better in governing the organization in the spirit of the by-laws. I think it's in that spirit that the people who circulated the request for proxies for the forthcoming members meeting took their initiative.

To put this another way, there's no point in carping about the way "the leadership" is running APsaA, because, as long as the leadership is following the rules, the way APsaA is run is up to all of us. (In the words of the old Pogo cartoon, "We have met the enemy and he is us.")

A complete version of the most recently amended by-laws of APsaA (effective 12/01) is available in the "members only" section of the WWW site at: http://apsa.org/closed/

Date: Fri, 28 Dec 2001:

Civics Lesson — **Part 2** —

This Note was Written after Defeat of the Non-Binding Referendum Proposal and Shows That (a) Our Meetings Must be Conducted According To "Robert's Rules of Order" (b) Certain Important Formalities Related to Our Governance are Being Ignored

Although those of us supporting the non-binding referendum proposal [about Certification] in the Executive Council were disappointed that the proposal did not pass, I believe that the December meeting of the Association marks a watershed in our governance and that APsaA is entering a new era because of that. The discussions leading up to the meetings, and the meeting itself, led to some important clarifications of the principles which apply to the governing of our profession (I'll leave the referendum issue itself alone until after the holidays.)

In my December, 12 "civics lesson" note I wrote:

"… there's no point in carping about the way "the leadership" is running APsaA, because, as long as the leadership is following the rules, the way APsaA is run is up to all of us. (In the words of the old Pogo cartoon, "We have met the enemy and he is us.").

Robert's Rules

For the first time in my memory, the Executive Council debate and vote on a contentious subject roughly followed the format required in the Council by Robert's Rules of Order: that is, a motion was made and seconded; a debate took place in which each speaker identified him/herself as speaking for or against the motion; the for and against speakers alternated; and no one spoke twice until each Councilor who wished to speak had spoken at least once. Dick Fox deserves our thanks for chairing the meeting impartially and according to the rules.

I always thought the Robert's Rules was a boring book of confusing and overly technical rules about motions and I never took it seriously until recently. It turns out, however, that Robert's is much more than that. Robert's is a wonderful distillation of hundreds of years of experience about how democratic organizations should be run; Robert's contains, in addition to the mind-bending rules, a great deal of wisdom about how differences of opinion in democratic organizations can lead to effective action by the majority, while still respecting the rights of the minority.

The primary premise of Robert's is that all decisions (other than those which take away a member's rights) must be made by a simple majority vote in a face-to-face MEETING in which all participants can simultaneously hear all other participants. In general, to prevent instability, any action already decided by a majority can be undone only by a 2/3 majority rather than a simple majority. This is the basis of the rule that requires a 2/3 vote, rather than a simple majority vote, to change the bylaws of an organization. The APsaA Bylaws adopt Robert's as the rulebook for our Association (RONR 10th Ed., Note 1):

SECTION 3. RULES OF ORDER. Parliamentary usage, as set forth in Roberts'[sic] Rules of Order, as periodically revised, shall govern all meetings of the Association. (Article XV, Sec. 3)

Commentators on Robert's advise against being overly legalistic or technical in applying the rules. However, I believe that to ignore the rules and Bylaws altogether is to invite trouble, chaos, and instability in an organization, so I hope you will forgive my referring to Robert's and our Bylaws in what follows.

Not Following the Bylaws and the Consequences

Our APsaA Bylaws constitute a surprisingly democratic document and delegate all ultimate authority regarding APsaA policies to the will of the general membership. For reasons which are not entirely clear to me, it seems that over the past two decades (at least) we have drifted away from the democratic principles embodied in the Bylaws. In effect, the power, which actually belongs to the general membership and the Executive Council has been assumed (hopefully not arrogated) by the Executive Committee and the Board of Professional Standards. I'd like to give three examples, which show what has happened:

1. NOT FOLLOWING THE RULES FOR BUSINESS MEETINGS OF MEMBERS:

The Bylaws require the Executive Council to meet twice a year (the "Annual Meeting" and the "Fall Meeting.") The Bylaws also refer to an "Annual Meeting" and "Fall Meeting" of the members, but appear to require only an Annual meeting. At meetings of the members, any action of the Executive Council can be rescinded. However, in order for ANY action to take place at such a meeting a QUORUM is required to be present and in our Bylaws this is

"...the presence of one-tenth of the members entitled to vote..." (Article III, Section 3)

According to Robert's, any action taken at a meeting at which a quorum is NOT present is NULL AND VOID. (RONR 10th Ed. p. 336,l. 25–27) In addition, "The prohibition against transacting business in the absence of a quorum cannot be waived even by unanimous consent (p. 337, 14–15).

Since the first delinkage and up until this month's meeting, the number of members eligible to vote has been in the range of 2400 so that it is extremely unlikely that a quorum of 240 members has been present at most of the meetings which were held in the 1990's. All actions taken in those meetings (if any) may therefore be null and void. Now under the revised Bylaws, with about 3100 members eligible to vote, a quorum will constitute 310 members. It is the responsibility of the Chair of the meeting (The APsaA President) to determine that a quorum is present and, if it is not, he must adjourn the meeting.

According to Robert's, if a quorum is not present at a required meeting and the meeting is adjourned, the requirement that the meeting be held is nonetheless met. In other words, if the members don't show up for the meeting, it's their loss!

The Bylaws also require that one of the meetings of the Executive Council be a "Fall" meeting, which has now been changed to a "winter" meeting despite what the Bylaws say AND that:

"Whenever possible, however, the Annual Meeting shall be held in the spring of the year IN CONJUNCTION WITH THE ANNUAL MEETING OF THE AMERICAN PSYCHIATRIC ASSOCIATION." (Article III, Sec. 1) [emphasis added]

So not only do the Meetings of Members appear to lack any ability to do anything unless more of us start showing up, it also appears that the recent changes in our meeting schedule (changing the "fall" meeting to winter, and changing the Annual meeting so it is not in conjunction with the APA) have been made without regard to the Bylaws! If the changes in the meeting schedules further decrease the chances of a quorum at the meetings, then these changes, in addition to violating the Bylaws, could also be seen as constituting a decrease in the authority of the general membership.

2. NOT MAILING PROXIES FOR THE MEETINGS OF MEMBERS

The Bylaws of APsaA are absolutely unambiguous in stating that every voting member MUST be sent a proxy in advance of every meeting of members:

SECTION 6. PROXIES. At least 30 days but not more than 90 days before each Meeting of Members, the Secretary of the Association shall send to each member of the Association entitled to vote a proxy form and return envelope, marked "proxy." The proxy form, which must be signed by the member, shall contain instructions, including the final return date, and such matters as may be required pursuant to Article III, Section 2. The Secretary shall retain the proxies as a record of proxies cast at the Meeting, except that, at the Meeting any member attending who wishes to vote in person on matters contained in the proxy may have the proxy returned on request. (Article III, Sec. 6)

About six years ago, for reasons which are not at all clear to me, the Secretary ceased following the Bylaws in this regard. While this fact is of no practical consequence, since in all probability none of the meetings affected by this have had a quorum present anyway, I believe that the absence of the proxy mailings has had a psychological effect on the membership because receiving the proxy reminded each of us of the fact that WE have the ultimate authority in APsaA.

When Dick Fox wrote to us on December 11 …

"As Chair of the Executive Council, I have serious concern that a proxy drive occurring BEFORE the Council has even addressed the issue undermines the Council's role as Board of Directors of APsaA. The consequences of such a precedent would be very far reaching."

… he appeared to have been unaware of the fact that the Bylaw REQUIREMENT that proxies be sent to ALL members was not being followed.

3. FOSTERING MYTHS REGARDING REQUIREMENTS FOR AMENDING THE BYLAWS

Somehow, a myth has existed, and has not been corrected by the leadership, that the general membership has no power to change APsaA's educational or certification policies.

The Bylaws themselves are subject to amendment (change) by the membership. All authority delegated by the members to the Executive Council, the Executive Committee, AND THE BOARD OF PROFESSIONAL STANDARDS, is subject to change through such a Bylaws change.

In a recent e-mail to me, the Parliamentarian wrote the following:

"Any change in the current certification procedures proposed in the referendum would require an amendment to the Bylaws. Since certification is an educational issue it falls under the aegis of the Board on Professional Standards, WHICH WOULD HAVE TO ORIGINATE OR APPROVE ANY BYLAW CHANGE undertaken in response to the result of the referendum." [emphasis added]

The highlighted part of the above statement is absolutely false. While it is true that UNDER THE CURRENT BYLAWS educational issues generally fall under the aegis (syn. sponsorship, protection) of BOPS, there is absolutely NO REQUIREMENT that bylaw changes affecting our educational policies must originate in BOPS or must be approved by BOPS. Any 50 members (or any officer, or the Executive Council) can originate such a proposal. The proposal is subject to review by BOPS at its discretion but this can result only in an ADVISORY opinion. The Bylaws proposal MUST still be submitted to the entire membership for a formal vote.

The Members Have Ultimate Authority Through the Bylaws

The minutes of the last meeting of the BOPS Coordinating Committee contains the following unattributed statement:

> "The discussion on certification will have to follow our by-laws. The Executive Council is consultative to the Board. A decision about the continuation or discontinuation or altering of certification WILL BE a decision made in the Board On Professional Standards." [emphasis added]

This statement, once again, seems to indicate an unawareness that the Board of Professional Standards operates under authority delegated by the entire APsaA membership via the Bylaws and that this authority, including the authority to have a certification process of any kind, can be withdrawn by the members if and when 2/3 of the members choose to amend the Bylaws in a vote triggered by the signatures of ANY 50 members. In other words, while BOPS CURRENTLY has the authority described above, this authority is not carved in stone. BOPS, thus, has a constituency which encompasses the entire profession and it cannot ignore the WILL OF THE MEMBERSHIP AS A WHOLE. In this regard, the fact that only about 30 to 40% of the members currently apply for certification should most definitely not be ignored.

Note 1: There are many books around which purport to be Robert's but the official version to which the by-laws of organizations actually refer is "Robert's Rules of Order Newly Revised," currently in its 10th edition (2000.) The ISBN of the paperback edition is #0738203076.

Date: Wed, 9 Jan 2002:

Civics Lesson — Part 3 —

Some History

This Note was Describes the 1951 Dispute over the Role of the Board on Professional Standards and Includes a Citation from the APsaA Legal Counsel to the Effect that The Executive Council has FINAL AUTHORITY over APsaA Policy

To me, the last paragraph (5) of the legal opinion at the end of this note says it all in a very insightful way. However, to understand what is often referred to (inaccurately, I think) by APsaA "insiders players" as Board/Council conflicts, I believe it would be helpful to read the following introductory material here first.

FIFTY YEARS AGO, at the meeting of members of APsaA on December 9, 1951 the following resolution was introduced by Dr. John A. P. Millet and was APPROVED by a large majority of the members:

"[WHEREAS] It is no longer possible for the Association to blind itself to widespread dissatisfaction with the present functions of and the relationship between the executive bodies of the American Psychoanalytic Association. [and]

"[WHEREAS] The Board on Professional Standards was originally conceived as a deliberative body for the exchange of ideas between the constituent institutes. [and]

"[WHEREAS] At the present time it exercises authority and makes decisions as to membership and training procedures which are not submitted directly to the membership for their approval before becoming effective,

"BE IT THEREFORE RESOLVED that the Executive Council re-examine the functions and procedures of the Board on Professional Standards and the authority independently exercised by it." [bracketed words added for clarity]

This dramatic event took place only 5 years after the adoption of the "new" 1946 Bylaws, which give APsaA its current form (and problems.) In only 5 years the issue of certification (it was then referred to as "membership") had turned into a major controversy because, prior to 1946, there was no centralized control over who could become a member of APsaA; simply belonging to a component society automatically made an analyst a member of APsaA. But in 1946 the Association adopted our "new" Bylaws which changed the organization from a federation of Society/Institutes to a membership organization.

In the "new" 1946 Bylaws, the Board of Professional Standards was created to replace what had been the "The Council on Professional Training" in the 1932-1946 Association. In the earlier Constitution, that Council was given a strictly advisory role. That is to say that before 1946, no education policy could be adopted as official APsaA policy unless it was unanimously approved by all Society/Institutes. After 1946, some people thought everything had changed — others didn't.

Between 1947 and 1951 the "membership committee" (equivalent to today's Certification Committee) had reached the following point, triggering Dr. Millet's resolution:

"...applications for membership since 1947 revealed that of 219 applications for membership 153 were certified to the membership for action with a minimum of delay. Forty-three applicants were deferred, largely in terms of technical and administrative difficulties and were subsequently certified to the membership. Twenty-two applicants are at present in the status of deferral, one applicant was rejected, and two withdrew their applications."

Some of the additional complaints about the functioning of the Membership Committee included these:

(1) The Committee refused to reveal the names of the applicants who were deferred, even to the Board of Professional Standards, so the Board could not review the Committee's decisions.

(2) The Board itself was promulgating training standards and making them binding on Institutes through the mechanism of withholding approval of those graduates not trained in accordance with the Board's standards.

(3) Some applicants had been waiting for over a year from the time of submission of their applications to hear from the Committee.

(4) "The penalizing of institute graduates for the "sins" of their institutes, and the upping of requirements mid-way in their training and then applying these standards retroactively." (R. Knight, Bulletin, 9:328)

At the time of Dr. Millet's 1951 resolution, the President of APsaA was Robert Knight and the Chairman of The Board of Professional Standards was Ives Hendrick, both very strong proponents of centralized control over training standards. The Millet resolution immediately started a huge dispute over the following question, which is still unresolved in APsaA:

Under the current Bylaws, does The Board of Professional Standards have ABSOLUTE authority to create and implement educational and membership (certification) standards?

OR, on the other hand,

Are the policies adopted by The Board of Professional Standards subject to review and possible change by the Executive Council and/or the membership of APsaA?

One side argued that since the Executive Council in the old Bylaws was specifically denied any authority in education and training ("shall have no authority with reference to matters of training, teaching and psychoanalytic institutes"); and the "new" Bylaws assigned the function of developing educational standards to The Board of Professional Standards; and since it is called a "board" and not a "committee" it is intended not to be subordinate to the Executive Council and/or the membership — in other words the intent is for the Board to exercise "absolute" authority over educational matters, absent an actual change in the Bylaws.

The other side argued that since the predecessor of The Board of Professional Standards had only an "advisory" function, and since the Executive Council was designated (by a 1951 amendment to the 1946 Bylaws) as the "Board of Directors of APsaA" all acts of The Board of Professional Standards were subject to oversight by the Executive Council which is legally responsible for all actions of APsaA.

Since the new Bylaws ACTUALLY SAID NOTHING about the relationship between the Executive Council and The Board of Professional Standards, it was more or less agreed by all that the Bylaws were (and are) AMBIGUOUS in this respect. THIS AMBIGUITY HAS NEVER BEEN RESOLVED.

Instead, a seemingly unending sequence of political fights has plagued the Association. Some have promoted an unconvincing (to me) view that APsaA is governed by something like a two-body legislature with two co-equal bodies. Others have believed that The Board of Professional Standards is more like a large committee, subordinate to the membership and/or the Executive Council. This doesn't seem quite right, either. (In fact, the distinction between the terms "board" and "committee" has to do with procedures during meetings, not to the authority of the entity. Robert's refers to "committees" and "subsidiary boards" as being similar in the way they make reports.)

In an attempt to resolve the question of whether Dr. Millet's resolution (remember, this was ADOPTED by a large majority of the membership — the supposed final authority in APsaA) actually was required to be implemented, the leadership, which appears to have viewed the resolution as a nuisance-like revolt by a small group of dissidents, requested and obtained an opinion from the APsaA legal counsel. They probably didn't like what they heard.

"Each Society Decides for Itself the Meaning of its Bylaws"-RONR

First, some necessary background:

Robert's Rules of Order, which is the Bylaws-designated authority for APsaA, has a section to deal with this exact situation of AMBIGUOUS BYLAWS called "Some Principles of Interpretation" (RONR 10th Ed. pp. 570-573)

According to Robert's, the guiding principle is that EACH SOCIETY DECIDES FOR ITSELF THE MEANING OF ITS BYLAWS. In other words, the opinion of a legal counsel, or a committee, is of interest but determines nothing because, according to Robert's, the following principles have to be employed (my paraphrase):

(1) No "interpretation" of Bylaws can take place unless an ambiguity actually exists — when the meaning is clear even a unanimous vote cannot change their meaning except through the formal process of amending the Bylaws.

(2) Consistency with other parts of the Bylaws is an important component of interpretation.

(3) In reaching an interpretation, the interpretation should be in accordance with the original intent at the time the Bylaw was adopted to the extent to which this can be determined.

(4) Where an ambiguity actually does exist, and there is a dispute as to what was the original intent, THE MATTER IS SETTLED BY A MAJORITY VOTE OF THE MEMBERS.

(5) Once an ambiguity is thus resolved, the Bylaws of the organization should be amended as soon as possible to resolve the ambiguity.

The legal counsel to APsaA was evidently well aware of what Robert's says about a situation like ours. Here's the substance of the APsaA legal counsel's opinion as explicated by Robert Knight who, following this report went on to appoint an investigating committee of the Executive Council [emphases added by me]:

"The Association's legal counsel makes the following points:

"1. As to the Original Intent of the By-Laws: While the By-Law provisions indicate the areas within which the Board on Professional Standards is to function, they are silent as to whether the intention was that the Board have final authority in these areas or whether the Board's conclusions were subject to final action by the Executive Council or by the membership. IT IS SO UNUSUAL TO CONFER FINAL AUTHORITY ON FUNDAMENTAL QUESTIONS ON A BOARD OR COMMITTEE OF THIS KIND THAT ONE WOULD EXPECT TO FIND CLEAR LANGUAGE TO THIS EFFECT IF THAT WERE ACTUALLY THE INTENT.

"2. As to the New York Law, Applicable since Incorporation: The Executive Council has the powers of a "Board of Directors." This would normally give it supervisory control over other committees and boards, EXCEPT TO THE EXTENT THAT A CONTRARY RESULT WAS ESTABLISHED BY CLEAR AND VALID BY-LAW PROVISIONS. With respect to the establishment of training standards — a matter which is specifically set forth in the Certificate of Incorporation as one of the basic purposes of the organization — this would be normally considered so fundamental that IT WOULD PROBABLY NOT BE PROPER UNDER NEW YORK LAW TO GIVE FINAL AUTHORITY IN THIS AREA TO ANY ADMINISTRATIVE BODY OTHER THAN THE EXECUTIVE COUNCIL. CONSEQUENTLY, ANY DETERMINATIONS MADE BY THE BOARD ON PROFESSIONAL STANDARDS IN THIS AREA SHOULD BE MADE SUBJECT TO ACTION EITHER BY THE EXECUTIVE COUNCIL OR BY THE MEMBERSHIP. It would be possible to make valid provision in the By-Laws that the Board on Professional Standards have final authority with respect to less fundamental matters such as the determination of whether individuals or institutes applying for membership or recognition conform to established standards.

"3. As to Procedure of Sub-Committees: There seems to be no basis in the present By-Laws for the practice which has grown up under which a sub-committee of the Board on Professional Standards, such as the Membership Committee, can withhold from the full committee facts requested by a majority of the Board on Professional Standards.

"4. Necessity for Clarifying Amendments: The By-Laws should be amended to clarify the various questions WHICH ARE NOW AMBIGUOUS as to the possession of authority of the Board on Professional Standards, etc.

"5. Broader Considerations: The specific questions which are now in issue are tied into BROADER FUNDAMENTAL QUESTIONS RELATING TO THE CONCEPTION OF THE MEMBERSHIP AS TO THE PROPER FUNCTION OF THE AMERICAN IN THE ENTIRE FIELD OF PSYCHOANALYSIS. Is the American to be considered primarily as the guardian of "orthodoxy" or is it to be inclusive of various shades of theory and practice? Should it exercise actual central control in matters of training or should it merely make recommendations and permit local autonomy to the institutes? If it is to exercise central control over standards of training in the institutes, should it also pass upon the adequacy of training of particular individuals who have complied fully with the training requirements of a particular institute? IF AGREEMENT IS REACHED ON SUCH BASIC QUESTIONS, the more specific by-law questions as to how the American should administratively exercise its powers can be resolved more readily." (Bulletin, 9:316-317) [emphases added]

Of course, agreement has never been reached on these basic questions, and the Bylaws changes, which presumably could follow from such an agreement, have never happened. Stay tuned for the next installment to see what happened instead.

References:

Committee on the Function of the Board of Professional Standards, & Committee Report (1993) Report Bul. Amer. Psychoanal. Assn. 9:319-330.

Hale, N.G. (1995) The Rise and Crisis of Psychoanalysis in the United States: Volume II, Freud and the Americans 1917-1985, Oxford: New York.

Robert's Rules of Order Newly Revised (2000), Perseus: Cambridge.

Date: Wed, 16 Jan 2002:
Civics Lesson — Part 4 —

More History

This Note Shows That The Bylaws are "Ambiguous" in Describing the Relationship between the EC and BOPS

I concluded the 3rd installment in this series by quoting in its entirety APsaA President Robert Knight's account of the 1951 opinion of the APsaA legal counsel to the effect that the Bylaws of APsaA are ambiguous as regards the question of whether the Board on Professional Standards is extended ABSOLUTE authority to determine educational and professional standards, OR whether standards set up by that Board are subject to review by the Executive Council and/or the entire voting membership of APsaA.

As you will also recall from the previous installment, Robert's Rules of Order specify how such a situation of ambiguity should be dealt with, that is, when an ambiguity exists, and the original intent is not clear, the ambiguity must be resolved (STEP 1) by a majority vote of the MEMBERS. (STEP 2) Robert's advises that following such a determination, the Bylaws should be amended "as soon as practicable." (See Note 1) Of course, the second step of this sequence has never taken place.

As a result of the large vote in favor of Dr. Millet's motion at the December, 1951 meeting, and possibly following the opinion from the APsaA legal counsel, which I quoted last time, Dr. Robert Knight, the President of APsaA, appointed a Committee of the Executive Council to investigate the functioning of the Board on Professional Standards.

The fact that such a Committee was appointed by Dr. Knight, in itself, served as an acknowledgment that the two bodies, the Executive Council and the Board on Professional Standards, are not co-equal. A further argument in support of this understanding was found in the Bylaws themselves in the provisions for amending the Bylaws. (Note 2) Even Ives Hendrick, who was Chairman of the Board on Professional Standards at the time, and a man who never seemed to accept that there had been a valid basis for the appointment of such a Council Committee, wrote this review of the 1951-1952 episode in his 1955 Presidential address:

> "... There were a few sardonic mumbles as to the paradox that an Executive Council, which had no constitutional rights under our By-Laws to examine the Board, should examine the Board for exceeding its constitutional rights. BUT THE EXECUTIVE COUNCIL DID HAVE POWER TO AMEND THE BY-LAWS, WHICH GAVE THE BOARD ITS POWERS, AND UNDER THIS PROVISION. President Knight had then appointed a Task Committee on Function of the Board..." (J. Amer. Psychoanal. Assn., 3:578)

The "Task Committee on the Function of the Board on Professional Standards" was placed under the chairmanship of Dr. M. Ralph Kaufman. Dr. Kaufman (1947-8) had preceded Drs. Knight (1949-50) and Hendrick (1951-2) as Board Chairman, and had been, in fact, the first Chairman of the Board on Professional Standards. (See Note 3) (Can you see where this is going?)

The full report of the Committee was published in the APsaA Bulletin. (Note 4) The committee report was in two parts corresponding, in reverse order, to the two parts of the Millet resolution, (1) authority and (2) functions and procedures:

"BE IT THEREFORE RESOLVED that the Executive Council re-examine the functions and procedures of the Board on Professional Standards and the authority independently exercised by it."

In the first part, presumably, but not actually, addressing the issue of the Board's having ABSOLUTE authority, the Committee examined the history of the 1932 and 1946 Bylaws. It reached the conclusion that the way the Board was functioning was in the best interest of the training programs:

"It seemed to this Committee that the purpose of this change [in the Bylaws as a result of the reorganization in 1946] was to give authority to the Board on Professional Standards as the standard-setting and accrediting body of the American Psychoanalytic Association and to divorce this body as far as possible from any sort of political pressure. In other words, one had within the American Psychoanalytic Association a group made up of representatives of teaching faculties of all accredited institutes and training centers, whose duty it was to deal with professional standards. This in theory made for as independent a body as possible. ...

"The consensus of your Committee was that the present constitutional set-up of the Board on Professional Standards guarantees the maximum degree of academic freedom, the maximum opportunity for functioning as a body, representing psychoanalysis as a whole and a judicial atmosphere free from external pressures. The Committee unanimously recommends that no change in the relation of the Board on Professional Standards either to the Executive Council or to the membership be made. The Board on Professional Standards as constituted, with direct free representation of the individual teaching faculties, provides for maximum flexibility and the maintenance of the highest standards, while at the same time providing for the freest expression of all points of view. Therefore, it is further recommended that if any legal changes become necessary, they should be in the direction of the maintenance of the present status of the Board on Professional Standards through any necessary amendments to the By-Laws, and your Committee stands ready to confer with legal counsel if so indicated."

However, the report was completely silent as to the issue of whether the Board had ABSOLUTE authority in such matters. The Committee report did not make any mention at all of the APsaA's Counsel's opinion.

In other words, the Committee responded to its charge simply by affirming that the Board on Professional Standards was granted by the Bylaws the authority it exercised to review applicants for membership. It further affirmed the completely murky "present constitutional set-up" or "present status" but in its recommendations at the end of the report [it] seemed to suggest that this "present status" might not actually be supported by the current Bylaws. It recommended:

" 1. No change in the relation of the Board on Professional Standards either to the Executive Council or to the membership be made. However, if legal changes become necessary, they should be in the direction of the maintenance of the present status of the Board on Professional Standards, through amendments of the By-Laws."

In the second part of it's report, the Committee examined the details of the functioning of the Board's Membership Committee. As a result, it came up with several specific recommendations for changes in the certification procedures of the Committee.

The most significant of these was a recommendation, which appears to me to have been intended to address the concerns that the Membership Committee was being unfair to some applicants, possibly ones from particular institutes, and thereby offered a compromise to Dr. Millet (who was included on the Committee) and the others who raised the issue to start with. This recommendation appeared intended to extend "due process rights" to applicants who were not approved. However, the Committee evidently was at odds over whether this relief should take the form of a MANDATORY REVIEW WHICH COULD OVERRIDE THE COMMITTEE's decision or an OPTIONAL APPEALS PROCESS, because the report seems to say both things:

In the report body we find:

"In those instances where the Committee cannot certify their approval of the candidate, on request of the Chairman of the Membership Committee, an ad hoc Committee MAY BE APPOINTED, one of whose members shall always be from the applicant's training institution, to re-examine all aspects of the applicant's record, including the recommendations of the Membership Committee. The ad hoc Committee SHOULD then make final recommendations to the Board on Professional Standards. The provision for such an ad hoc Committee will help to resolve the knotty problem of maintaining adequate protection of confidential information regarding the candidates." [in body of report, p.328] [emphasis added]

But in its FINAL RECOMMENDATIONS section, the Task Committee report reads:

7 (ii). In those instances where [the] Membership Committee cannot certify approval of candidate, an ad hoc Committee SHALL BE APPOINTED to re-examine applicant's record and to make final recommendations to the Board on Professional Standards. [p. 330] [emphasis added]

No matter though, because when the report was presented to the entire Executive Council, this recommendation was the ONLY ONE that was modified in the Council as follows:

"The Seventh Recommendation is approved, subject to changing the phrase, in subsection (ii), "an Ad Hoc Committee shall be appointed," to read "an Ad Hoc Committee may be appointed." [Executive Council Minutes, December, 1952]

Finally, the Task Committee did, in its report, make the following statement:

"Your Committee wishes to re-emphasize its belief that the basic principle involved in the accrediting of a candidate, in regard to his academic training, should be that it is the responsibility of the training institution rather than the individual onus of the trainee. There is the hope that when this principle is fully implemented THE NEED FOR ELABORATE INVESTIGATION OF THE TRAINING

OF THE INDIVIDUAL WILL BE MATERIALLY REDUCED." [p. 328] [emphasis added]

However, the Board on Professional Standards has evidently had only limited luck in getting institutes to adhere to its standards, so the graduates end up paying the price. Anton O. Kris has elaborated on this point in his illuminating 1976 article (Note 5). He wrote:

"... Candidates are encouraged to believe that they are entering an approved training program, which meets the minimal standards of the Association, only to find upon graduation that the Association wants proof from the graduate that he has indeed met these minimal standards. The fundamental operating basis of the Committee is, therefore, in conflict with the spirit of the by-laws and the purposes of the Association.

"Historically, this situation has evolved as a result of the political weakness of the Board relative to the institutes. Only the newly graduated analyst seeking membership and the new training center seeking approval as an institute are weaker than the Board. Functionally, this situation compromises the integrity of the Association. It is inimical to psychoanalysis and, in its ramifications, tends to violate the central aspirations of the Association and its members.

"Naturally, the Board and the Committee have been aware all along of difficulties and imperfections in their procedures. As we have noted, at the heart of these procedures lie two dominant factors: distrust of the institutes, and lack of power. Yet, the Board is composed exclusively of the elected representatives of the institutes (except for four ex officio administrative officers of the Association). To a much greater extent than it likes to acknowledge, therefore, the Board speaks for the institutes rather than for the Association."

And so, the Membership/Certification process went forward (with some modifications) until now. The incredibly rapid growth of psychoanalysis in the 50's and 60's papered over the fact that many of our graduates were not applying for membership in APsaA, because APsaA continued to grow anyway, but as interest in analysis began to show signs of a coming plateau in the 1970's, the makings of a crisis appeared. By 1976, of the 2,200 graduates of APsaA institutes, only 1,400 belonged to APsaA, and many of the other 800 had ill-will (or worse) toward APsaA, even though many actually belonged to our societies and were practicing psychoanalysts.

In a subsequent installment, for those who can stand more of these "lessons", I'll go back to the 1932-1946 period to try to show why the ambiguity came to exist in the Bylaws in the first place, and why it led to the myth of a Board with ABSOLUTE authority within APsaA. However, it might be enlightening to quote at this point a paragraph in a letter written by Bertram Lewin to Robert Knight dated May 8,1945, the year our "new" 1946 Bylaws were finalized to replace those of 1932:

"... It has not escaped your attention surely that for some reason so far as the affairs of our societies are concerned, analysts consider themselves incomparable business men, financiers, constitutional lawyers, etc., though in practice they do not always produce the goods, and indeed often make a hell of a mess." (Note 6)

Note 1: It could be argued that following the adoption of Dr. Millet's resolution "by a large majority" at the December 1951 meeting of members of APsaA, Step 1 had already taken place because in the preamble to Dr. Millet's resolution [was] the straightforward statement:

"... The Board on Professional Standards was originally conceived as a deliberative body for the exchange of ideas between the constituent institutes..." which seems clearly to indicate the majority of the members' conception of the intent of the Bylaws.

————————

Note 2: A little-known provision added to the Bylaws in 1951 actually allows the EXECUTIVE COUNCIL to ADOPT a Bylaws change, rather than relying on the membership to do so. Such a change, however, is subject to "approval" by a 2/3 vote of the members at the next meeting or by a mail ballot.

————————

Note 3: In the interest of full disclosure, I just want to point out that my Aunt, Dr. H. R. Klein, was a member of the Task Committee. Of course, I never discussed this subject with her since, at the time, I was a high school student in Albany, New York and had not even heard of APsaA.

————————

Note 4: Minutes of 1952 Midwinter Meeting, *Bul Amer. Psychoan. Assn.* 9:317-330 (1953)

————————

Note 5: Kris, A.O. (1976), The Problem of Membership in the American Psychoanalytic Association, J. Philadelphia Assn. for Psychoanalysis 3(1 & 2):22-36.

————————

Note 6: Quoted in Hale, N.G. (1995) The Rise and Crisis of Psychoanalysis in the United States: Volume II, Freud and the Americans 1917-1985, Oxford: New York., p. 218.

Date: Wed, 23 Jan 2002:
Civics Lesson — Part 5 —

Ambivalence Creates Ambiguity

This Note Shows That The 1946 Transition of APsaA to a Membership Society is Where the Ambiguity Originated

When, in the meeting of members of APsaA in December 1951, Dr. Millet introduced his resolution instructing the Executive Council to investigate the functioning of the Board on Professional Standards, a resolution which was approved by a "large majority," of the members voting, he included within the resolution the statements:

"The Board on Professional Standards was originally conceived as a deliberative body for the exchange of ideas between the constituent institutes.

"At the present time it exercises authority and makes decisions as to membership and training procedures which are not submitted directly to the membership for their approval before becoming effective." (Note 1, p. 311)

The question then arose as to whether the Board on Professional Standards is subject to an investigation by anyone or whether it exercises ABSOLUTE or "FINAL" authority in the areas of education, training, and professional standards for the entire profession (Note 2).

In seeking clarification on this point, APsaA sought an opinion from the APsaA legal counsel who made it clear that:

"While the By-Law provisions indicate the areas within which the Board on Professional Standards is to function, they are silent as to whether the intention was that the Board have final authority in these areas, or whether the Board's conclusions were subject to final action by the Executive Council or by the membership. It is so unusual to confer final authority on fundamental questions on a board or committee of this kind that one would expect to find clear language to this effect if that were actually the intent…. It would probably not be proper under New York law to give final authority in this area to any administrative body other than the Executive Council. Consequently, any determinations made by the Board on Professional Standards in this area should be made subject to action either by the Executive Council or by the membership." (Note 1, p. 316)

To better understand the reason our current Bylaws are ambiguous as to the question of whether the Board on Professional Standards has ABSOLUTE authority regarding the professional and educational standards of APsaA, let's look back at the period from 1932 to 1945, the period in APsaA history before our current Bylaws were adopted in 1946.

In 1932, a rather simple membership organization which had been in existence since 1911, now known as the "Old American," was abandoned and a new organization was formed. This new American Psychoanalytic Association was organized as a FEDERATION (or in some ways a "confederation") of constituent societies. The new organization had both a "Constitution" which contained more general material and a set of "Bylaws" with some additional details (these taken together correspond to our current Bylaws).

A major reason for the formation of the new organization was to establish TRAINING STANDARDS to counteract the influx of those styled as "quacks", non-MD's, and other interlopers into the burgeoning field of "psychoanalysis" — and to limit membership in APsaA Societies to individuals who had been trained as psychoanalysts.

There were only four societies in the original 1932 APsaA, and three of these societies "owned" a training institute (the 4th was in the process of forming one.) There was no concept of a Society without, or separate from, an Institute and no concept of an Institute not attached to a Society.

The "new" 1932 APsaA, which was formed under the 1932 Bylaws had two classes of voting "members." One class of members consisted of the SOCIETIES themselves. Each of the four societies was a "CONSTITUENT SOCIETY MEMBER." In addition, each individual member of each Society was made an "INDIVIDUAL MEMBER" of APsaA automatically, simply by virtue of being a member of the constituent society. When matters came to a vote in the 1932 APsaA, voting was done by the "Constituent Societies" in some circumstances, and by the "Individual Members" in others.

However, in the 1932 APsaA we can see the ancestors of today's APsaA institutions: There was an Executive Council, and there was a Council on Professional Training — the predecessor of today's Board on Professional

Standards. Significantly, neither of these entities was given the power to IMPOSE any educational or training standards.

The Executive Council was charged with " the control and management of the business, property, affairs and funds of this Association" but:

"The Executive Council shall be an administrative body only AND SHALL HAVE NO AUTHORITY WITH REFERENCE TO MATTERS OF TRAINING, TEACHING and psychoanalytic institutes." (Article 6, Sec. 3, 1932 Constitution) [emphasis added]

Just as stated in Dr. Millet's resolution, and affirmed by the 1951 vote of the membership, the Council on Professional Training was conceived as a forum in which representatives of SOCIETIES would discuss education and training:

"To ADVISE together and MAKE RECOMMENDATIONS for the purpose of coordinating the work of the several constituent society members in matters of training, teaching and psychoanalytic institutes in relation to each other, to this Association and to the International Psychoanalytic Association..." (Article 7, Sec. 4(b), 1932 Constitution) [emphases added]

These recommendations would then be submitted to the Societies. Only if ALL THE SOCIETIES approved the proposed standards could they become the official policy of APsaA.

The 1932 Constitution is perfectly clear on this point:

"To prepare RECOMMENDATIONS which shall be submitted to the several constituent society members for approval as the official recommendations on professional training of this Association…" … "The authority of the Council on Professional Training SHALL BE LIMITED TO MAKING RECOMMENDATIONS AS ABOVE PROVIDED. Recommendations of the Council on Professional Training as to matters of training, teaching, and psychoanalytic institutes, WHICH HAVE RECEIVED THE APPROVAL OF ALL CONSTITUENT SOCIETY MEMBERS as hereinabove provided, shall be promulgated as the official recommendations on professional training of this Association." (Article 7, Sec. 4(c), 1932 Constitution) [emphases added]

Clearly that the structure (and spirit) of the 1932 APsaA supported the concept that any standards which were created were based on the collective views of the entire profession, not just the views of a select group, or the views of a committee or board elected by a select, or self-selected, group.

In the first place, the Council on Professional Training itself consisted of representatives of the SOCIETIES, presumably elected by the entire Society memberships. Secondly, no policy suggested by that Council could become official APsaA policy unless that policy was UNANIMOUSLY approved by the "constituent society members." It's impossible to imagine that an arrangement so strongly geared toward the preservation of local autonomy could later be changed in the direction of greater central control without considerable ambivalence.

In addition, a striking feature of the 1932 Bylaws was a set of incredibly detailed (and iron clad) rules preventing the existence of two APsaA Societies in the same geographical area. (Note 3, p. 31)

The 1932 structure came to grief in the 1st half of the 1940's when it became clear that APsaA was growing rapidly through the addition of more societies. Those who were intent on strengthening standards of training were frustrated that getting unanimous agreement from all the constituent societies for each suggestion of the Council on Professional Training was either impossible or took a very long time.

But even more problematic was the secession of Sandor Rado and a group of his followers from the New York Society. These prominent members intended to form a new training facility in New York (the Columbia Institute), and a new Society (The Association for Psychoanalytic Medicine) which did not "own" the new institute, but this was in violation of the 1932 Constitution and Bylaws. Somewhat analogous problems arose in California.

In large part, it was for both these reasons that APsaA was completely reorganized in 1946 creating the structure we have today. In the 1946 APsaA (essentially today's APsaA), the following changes were made (many details are omitted here for clarity):

(1) The new organization had only individual members. Societies were no longer "members" but were rather "affiliated societies."

(2) Institutes and Societies were no longer considered to be a single entity. Societies could exist without institutes and institutes could exist without societies. The rules prohibiting more than one institute or society in a geographical area were dropped.

(3) The Executive Council was strengthened, in that the following 1932 provision was omitted after 1946 (note 4):

"The Executive Council shall be an administrative body only and shall have no authority with reference to matters of training, teaching and psychoanalytic institutes."

(4) The Council on Professional Training was replaced by the Board on Professional Standards. The following crucial changes were made:

(a) The representatives on the new Board (now referred to as "Fellows") were selected by the INSTITUTES, not the Societies. In other words, the new Board no longer represented the entire profession.

(b) Only a member who was a "Senior Member of the Faculty of an Institute" was eligible to be a Fellow. (The term "Senior Member" was undefined.)

(c) The duties of the new Board were described in importantly different language: Instead of using expressions such as "RECOMMEND standards…" the new bylaws said that the duty of the Board was to "SET UP minimal standards…"

There was no provision in the 1946 (or current) bylaws for any mandatory ratification of the actions of the Board on Professional Standards by either the Executive Council or by the membership, as had been present in the 1932-1945 Constitution. On the other hand, there was no statement that the Board had any kind of ABSOLUTE authority in the area of its responsibilities. The Legal Counsel to APsaA, in his 1951 opinion, saw clearly that this vagueness was the result of an inability of the profession to come to an agreement on the intended role of APsaA in becoming either the bastion of 1950's style "psychoanalytic orthodoxy" on the one hand or the nurturer of so-called "innovation" on the other.

However, those advocating stronger national standards for training (generally, but not all, promoters of "orthodoxy") found it convenient to pretend to themselves, and to act, as if the Board did have ABSOLUTE authority. In making their case, they tended to engage in a kind of revisionism or false memory about the 1932-1945 period. For example, Ives Hendrick, in a footnote to the published version of his 1955 Presidential address wrote:

"It has repetitively been stated in important discussions that the Council on Professional Training (1932-46) was only a body for consultation and discussion, without policy powers. Such statements are erroneous, both as to constitutional intent and as to history of the former Council…" (Note 5)

Even Robert Knight seemed to "forget" what the 1932 Constitution said because in his 1952 Presidential Address he wrote:

"During the federation period each local society voted as a unit in matters submitted by the national organization, a two-thirds affirmative vote of the member societies being required for adoption of a principle which then became binding on all…" (Note 6)

when, in fact, all policy decisions regarding training and standards had to be approved UNANIMOUSLY by the Societies before 1946.

The "assumption," (or as I prefer to call it, the "the myth") that the Board on Professional Standards had ABSOLUTE authority in the areas of its functioning leads to some absurd results, but the absurdity of those results was barely visible in the 1950's. In effect, an autonomous Board with ABSOLUTE or FINAL authority would be a body which is elected by only a select few members of the profession, a selection process in which those members of the profession who were not associated with Institutes would be COMPLETELY DISENFRANCHISED. In addition, membership on the Board would be limited to even a smaller segment of the profession ("Senior Members of Institute Faculties" and in a later version "Training Analysts").

In the 1950's there were about twice as many CANDIDATES in training as there were members in APsaA, so a much large proportion of the profession was concerned with matters of training. However, in today's world only about 25% of the active members of APsaA are Training Analysts, and are thus eligible to serve as Fellows of the Board on Professional Standards. The absurd result of assuming that the Board could have any kind of ABSOLUTE authority then would suggest that 25% of the entire profession would have the authority to dictate standards to the entire profession (to the extent that "training standards" are related to "professional standards.") In particular, it would lead to a situation best described as an "oligarchy" in which a subset of the profession was in the position to establish rules absolutely controlling the rights of other members of the profession to enter that subset.

Religions are organized in such a way. In all professions, the standards of the profession are agreed to, and evolve, by a process in which all members of the profession have some degree of authority in shaping the profession. Certainly, deference in a field such as ours deserves to be paid to senior members, scholars, academics, researchers, and so forth, but this cannot lead to a situation in which other members of the profession are completely excluded from the process, or only included when a self-chosen elite decides to allow their participation.

Otherwise we end up with a situation as described by Douglas Kirsner:

"Anointment and genealogy fill a vacuum created by uncertainty in the field. Instead of developing through an accumulation of evidence, psychoanalytic knowledge is often assumed to develop via a pipeline of certain people with supposed knowledge. Those purported to have the truth pass on the torch to selected members the next generation. For a qualification to be conferred, a level of skill and knowledge is assumed, an assumption that is not really warranted. Therefore, the gap between real knowledge and presumed 'pretend' knowledge is filled through particular 'anointed' people. The story of the NYPsaI [New York Psychoanalytic Society and Institute] is an exemplary tale of anointment, of what fills the gap when there is a contradiction between the nature of the psychoanalytic field-experiential, subjective, and yet (if ever) to be established scientifically-and the assumption that qualification as an analyst reflects a high level of knowledge."

However, control by a small ruling clique has not been limited to the NYPsaI. Authoritarianism in psychoanalysis is not the property of the particular personalities who are in control. (Note 7)

Because APsaA has been mired in a situation in which no formal authority is (or isn't) granted to the Executive Council or the General Membership to review, and, if desired, to reverse the actions of the Board on Professional Standards, the only recourse left to the membership as whole is to take the route of expressing itself through a vote to change the Bylaws of APsaA, an authority which the membership unquestionably possesses.

In the final "installment" of these notes, I will review the various mechanisms through which Bylaws changes in APsaA can be brought about.

————————

Note 1: Bulletin of APsaA, 9:311-317 (1953)

Note 2: I am using the term "profession" narrowly here to indicate the entire universe of psychoanalysts who are eligible for membership in APsaA. Clearly, in the year 2002 when there are so many non-APsaA psychoanalysts, this is much less accurate than it would have been in 1951.

"There are currently about 20,000 analytic practitioners in the US most of whom have trained through and remain members of psychoanalytic institutes [sic]. The major national umbrella organizations are the American Psychoanalytic Association (3,200 members), the American Academy of Psychoanalysis, the American Psychological Association's Division 39 on psychoanalysis (the number of psychologists indicating their specialty area as psychoanalysis is 4,109 in 1998), and the National Association for the Advancement of Psychoanalysis (1,700 members including 17 accredited institutes)." [Kirsner, Introduction, see Note 6]

Note 3: "Basic Instruments," Bulletin of APsaA, 1:20-43 (1938)

Note 4: In 1951, because of the incorporation of APsaA under the laws of New York State, the Executive Council was strengthened even further by being designated in the Bylaws as having "all the powers, in the management of the property, affairs, and business of the Association, of a Board of Directors under the General Corporation Law or the Membership Corporations Law of New York..." (1946 Bylaws as amended through 1951)

Note 5: Hendrick, I (1955) Presidential Address, J. Amer. Psychoanal. Assn., 3:561-599

Note 6: Knight, R. (1953) The Present Status of Organized Psychoanalysis in the United States. J. Amer. Psychoanal. Assn., 1:197-221

Note 7: Kirsner, D., (2000) Unfree associations: inside psychoanalytic institutes, Process Press. (Chapter 1) ISBN #1899209123.

Date: Wed, 30 Jan 2002:
Civics Lesson — Part 6 —

Amending the Bylaws

This Note Shows That The APsaA Bylaws Can be Amended, but Not by a Mail Ballot Unless the Amendment is ADOPTED by the Executive Council

In this "civics lesson" I will try to explain the mechanism by which the Bylaws of APsaA may be amended. Obviously, I'm not a lawyer and I would urge that this understanding should be confirmed by a New York Attorney.

To clarify the issues related to our governance, one must take account of the following four documents:

(1) The New York State Not-For-Profit Corporations Law (N-PCL) under which APsaA is now incorporated (see Note 1).
(2) The APsaA Certificate of Incorporation. (Not needed for this particular issue.)
(3) Robert's Rules of Order. (RONR, 10th Ed.)
(4) The Bylaws of APsaA.

Because APsaA is a Corporation in the State of New York, the Bylaws represent a contract between each member of the Corporation and the Corporation, and so it is important for each of us to understand what obligations we have to APsaA as a result of our being members of the APsaA Corporation.

In addition, because the Bylaws of APsaA currently REQUIRE the Board on Professional Standards to certify some members who choose to apply [ARTICLE XII, Section 2(d)], — and the Bylaws also REQUIRE a member to be so certified in order to be an Officer or Fellow of the Board (BOPS), a member of the Committees of the Board, or a Training and Supervising Analyst (Article XII, Section 5], none of these requirements can be eliminated without Bylaws amendments. (The Board on Professional Standards is, of course, free on its own to change the way its certification process is carried out.) From a practical standpoint these Bylaws requirements in Article XII, Section 5 are the only ways in which being certified matters today, and probably, if those actually were eliminated by a Bylaws amendment, few would even apply for certification (unless being certified took on some new significance.)

The relevant provision, Article XIV, Section 2, on amending the Bylaws in the current version of the Bylaws (Note 2.3), is so convoluted that to figure out what it actually means is, as "Reb" Tevye says in *Fiddler on the Roof,* like "posing problems that would cross a Rabbi's eyes." To figure it out, which took me the last couple weeks, I had to go back and read the old New York Membership Corporation Law and earlier versions of that same APsaA Bylaws Article. I started with the original 1946 version which described the process in a pretty clear way (See Note 2.1 for actual 1946 text.) Here, schematically, is how it went:

————————

Step 1: The proposed amendment is originated by
    (a) Any Officer OR
    (b) The Executive Council OR
    (c) Any 10 Members

Step 2: The Amendment is REVIEWED by The LEGAL COUNSEL as to "form"

Step 3: If approved AS TO FORM by the Legal Counsel, the amendment is then PROPOSED by whoever submitted it.

Step 4: The Executive Council APPROVES or DISAPPROVES of the proposed amendment. (This is ONLY an expression of opinion and is decided by majority vote; the opinion must be sent along with the amendment for Step 5.)

Step 5: (2 Options).
  (a) The proposed amendment is SUBMITTED to the members at the next meeting and is ADOPTED if it is approved by 2/3 of the members "present." (Provided a quorum is "present")

  OR

  (b) The proposed amendment is submitted to the members in a mail ballot and is ADOPTED if approved by 2/3 of the members voting.

—————————

Before going on to see how things got so convoluted after this (relative) simplicity, you need to know more about the use of the triple-A words AMEND, APPROVE and ADOPT:

AMEND: This means ANY change in the Bylaws whether it actually ADDS something to the Bylaws, changes something in the Bylaws, or entirely replaces the entire Bylaws. [RONR, 10th Ed. p. 564 l. 6-14]

APPROVE (or DISAPPROVE): This could mean that the members or body give an advisory OPINION about a proposal, but an APPROVAL could occur either before or after something happens. In the 1946 bylaws above, the (advisory) approval (or disapproval) of a proposed amendment by the

Council takes place BEFORE the Bylaw is ADOPTED by the members. If something done earlier depends on a subsequent APPROVAL then that APPROVAL has more than an advisory significance, and in that case "TO APPROVE" is equivalent to "TO RATIFY." (In our current Bylaws, the term is used in both senses within the same paragraph (Note 2.3) so pay attention here.) Usually, an approval requires a majority vote, but a special rule could require a different majority, such as 2/3, in a particular instance.

ADOPT (a bylaw amendment): A proposed Bylaw amendment becomes part of the Bylaws or modifies the Bylaws as soon it is ADOPTED. However, a Bylaw can be ADOPTED with a "proviso" which means that the ADOPTED Bylaw doesn't go INTO EFFECT until some other thing happens, even though it is now in the Bylaws. If the other thing doesn't happen, then the Bylaw amendment is nullified, but according to Robert's it would remain in the Bylaws with a footnote until removed by another amendment. [RONR 10th Ed. p. 578 l. 21 et. seq.] However, ADOPTING the Bylaw amendment is the critical step.

You will notice that in both of the options in Step 5 above, the amendment is ADOPTED by a vote of the members — in one instance at a MEETING, and in the other instance, by a MAIL BALLOT.

In 1951, APsaA was INCORPORATED in New York State under what was then the "Membership corporation Law" (The MCL.) To permit this incorporation, the Bylaws had to be changed, and one of the most important changes was a change in the way the Bylaws are amended. This is because, under the MCL (and its 1969 successor, the current N-PCL) it is illegal to ADOPT Bylaw amendments BY A MAIL VOTE (unless every single eligible voter agrees in writing). So in practical terms, Bylaw amendments can ONLY BE ADOPTED at a meeting. (see Note 1) This means that the (b) option in Step 5 above had to be changed.

The "clever" change which was made to the APsaA Bylaws in 1951 took advantage of a provision in the MCL which allows the Board of Directors of a Corporation (in our case, the Executive Council) to ADOPT Bylaws on its own. But clearly, the membership was not willing to grant this unfettered power to the Executive Council. So in the Bylaws as revised in 1951 (see Note 2.2) (and in the current Bylaws, see Note 2.3) the following change was made in Step 4, above, effectively replacing Step 5:

New Step 4: Either of these courses of action is followed:
   (a) The Executive Council APPROVES or DISAPPROVES (advisory) the amendment and it is then sent to the next meeting of members where it can be ADOPTED by a 2/3 vote of the members "present." This combined the old Step 4 and Step 5(a) above.

OR, TO DO IT BY MAIL,

   (b) The Executive Council can ADOPT the amendment at a MEETING of the Council with the PROVISION that the amendment must subsequently be APPROVED (i.e., ratified) in a mail ballot of the members, and with the additional requirement that such an APPROVAL requires a 2/3 vote of the members voting. (The "approval" in this alternative is NOT simply "advisory" because it is required to trigger the "proviso" which allows the adopted bylaw amendment to take effect.)

Does this change make any difference? It certainly does! In the first place, if the Executive Council does not ADOPT a proposed Bylaw amendment, then that amendment MUST be sent to a MEETING of members for a vote on adoption — it CANNOT be sent out in a mail ballot. And in order to ADOPT a Bylaw amendment, the Executive Council must vote in favor of adoption by a 2/3 majority (see note 3). To repeat: the only legal way that a Bylaw amendment can become effective by a mail ballot is if the Executive

Council first ADOPTS it. Otherwise, if the vote in the Council in favor is anything less than 2/3 in favor (i.e., simply approves or disapproves), the proposed amendment MUST be sent to the next MEETING of the members for a vote on ADOPTION.

The fact that the above set of requirements has been in effect since 1951 has apparently gotten lost to our leaders and possibly to the Legal Counsel to APsaA. Here's what has happened recently:

(1) In December 2000, Dr. Bhaskar Sripada presented to the Executive Council a proposed Bylaws amendment, endorsed by 10 members and approved by the Legal Counsel, to add a definition of psychoanalysis to our Bylaws. A motion that the Executive Council DISAPPROVES of the proposal was passed with one vote against and two abstentions. In other words, the Executive Council did not ADOPT the amendment. NEVERTHELESS, the proposed amendment was MAILED to the members. Doing this served no useful purpose. Instead, the proposed Bylaw should have been sent to a MEETING of the members because even if the members had voted in favor of the proposal by mail (they didn't) it could NOT HAVE BEEN ADOPTED BY MAIL.

(2) In the most recent 2001 amendments to the Bylaws, in an attempt to implement part of the proposals of the Joint Ad Hoc Task Force on Education and Membership, a new provision was added to Article XIV, SECTION 2 of the Bylaws which gives The Board on Professional Standards the option to offer "an advisory opinion … commenting on a proposed amendment" along with the approval or disapproval of the Executive Council. Reasonable as this new provision may be, it has been added in words which only serves to make even more obscure the meaning of the entire paragraph on

amendments. If you don't believe this, I challenge you to read the paragraph yourself! (It's in note 2.3).

Next time: Since the subject of Committee appointments has come up in our discussions, I decided that there will be another one of these lessons soon. The next one deals with some laws and rules I stumbled across about appointments to Committees and contains some really surprising (even startling) information.

Note 1:

You can read the New York Not-For-Profit Corporation Law at

——————

Note 2.1: ——— 1946 Version, BEFORE INCORPORATION: FROM 1946 Bylaws as amended through June 1948:

ARTICLE XI Section 2. Amendments - How Proposed. Any officer of the Association or the Executive Council or any 10 Active Members may offer a proposed amendment to the By-Laws, in writing, provided the form of the amendment has been submitted to counsel to the Association for his prior APPROVAL as to form and bears a proper notation as to such APPROVAL. Any such amendment not offered by the Executive Council shall be submitted to the Executive Council for its APPROVAL or DISAPPROVAL. Thereafter the full text of each amendment shall be submitted to each Active Member of the Association with a notation thereon indicating whether the Executive Council has APPROVED or DISAPPROVED the proposed amendment. Each such amendment shall be submitted to the members at the next Meeting and shall be deemed ADOPTED if

APPROVED by at least two-thirds of the Active Members present at such meeting, a quorum being present; provided, however, that the Executive Council may submit such amendment to the Membership for APPROVAL, by a mail ballot in the manner hereinbefore provided in Section 8 of ARTICLE V, and such amendment shall be ADOPTED if it is APPROVED by two-thirds of the Active Members voting. [emphases added]

Note 2.2: ———- 1952 Version, AFTER INCORPORATION From 1946 Bylaws effective 1951 amended through 1952:

ARTICLE XI SECTION 2. Amendments - How Proposed. Any officer of the Association or the Executive Council or any 10 Active Members may offer a proposed amendment to the By-laws, in writing, provided the form of amendment has been submitted to counsel to the Association for his prior APPROVAL as to form and bears a proper notation as to such APPROVAL. Any such amendment not offered by the Executive Council shall be submitted to the Executive Council for its APPROVAL or DISAPPROVAL Thereafter the full text of each amendment shall he submitted to each Active Member of the Association with a notation thereon indicating whether the Executive Council has APPROVED or DISAPPROVED the proposed amendment. Each such amendment shall he submitted to the members at the next Meeting and shall be deemed ADOPTED if APPROVED by at least two-thirds of the Active Members present at such meeting, a quorum being present; PROVIDED, however, that the Executive Council may, in its discretion, ADOPT such amendment, subject to the APPROVAL of the members as hereinbefore provided in Section 8 of ARTICLE V; and PROVIDED, further, that an amendment referred to the members for APPROVAL by mail shall not be deemed to be APPROVED by the members of the Association unless it receives the APPROVAL of two-thirds of those indicating their APPROVAL or DISAPPROVAL. [emphases added]

Note 2.3: ———- CURRENT VERSION AS AMENDED THROUGH DECEMBER 2001:

ARTICLE XIV SECTION 2. AMENDMENTS - HOW PROPOSED. Any officer of the Association, the Executive Council, or any fifty* (50) members** eligible to vote may offer a proposed amendment to the Bylaws, in writing, provided the form of amendment has been submitted to counsel to the Association for his/her prior APPROVAL as to Form and bears a proper notation as to such APPROVAL. Any such amendment not offered by the Executive Council shall be submitted to the Executive Council for its APPROVAL or DISAPPROVAL. Thereafter, the full text of each amendment shall be submitted to each member eligible to vote of the Association with (a) a notation thereon indicating the source of the proposed amendment and whether the Executive Council has APPROVED or DISAPPROVED the proposed amendment, and (b) if requested by the Board on Professional Standards, an advisory opinion of the Board on Professional Standards commenting on the proposed amendment. Each such amendment shall be submitted to the members at the next meeting and shall be deemed ADOPTED if APPROVED by at least two-thirds of the members eligible to vote present at such a meeting, a quorum being present, PROVIDED, however, that the Executive Council may, in its discretion, ADOPT such amendment, subject to the APPROVAL of the members eligible to vote as hereinbefore provided in Section 8 of Article V; and

PROVIDED, further, that an amendment referred to the members eligible to vote for APPROVAL by mail shall not be deemed to be APPROVED by the members of the Association unless it receives the APPROVAL of at least two-thirds of those members eligible to vote indicating their APPROVAL or DISAPPROVAL. [emphases added] * Changed from ten (10) in 2001. ** "active," before members was dropped in 2001.

————————

Note 3: Whoever wrote this change in the 1951 Bylaws failed to specify how large a majority is required in the Executive Council to ADOPT a Bylaws amendment. Robert's seems to me unclear on this particular situation. It doesn't matter, however, because The N-PCL, which controls the situation, specifies that the adoption of a Bylaws amendment by the Board of Directors requires a 2/3 vote unless the Bylaws specify an even larger super-majority. [Section 709(b)]

Date: Sun, 10 Feb 2002:
Civics Lesson — Part 7 —

Appointments to Committees
The President has only Limited Powers to make Appointments to Council Committees

Topics Covered here:
    A. Committee appointments
    B. Legal requirement for Councilors on Council Committees
    C. Legal limit on size of Executive Council

D. Question on selection of Fellows of the Board on Professional Standards

In this "civics lesson," I will tell you what I learned about committee appointments in APsaA and the selection of Fellows of the Board on Professional Standards. As a result of my looking up some of this material, it seems to me that the way many committee appointments are being made in APsaA could be contrary to the Bylaws and, in some respects, does not conform to a requirement of The New York State Not-For-Profit Corporations Law (N-PCL) under which APsaA is incorporated (Note 1).

Like the other issues I have addressed in these notes, I think the effect of these possible deviations from the Bylaws is to undermine the democratic principles on which APsaA was founded and the democratic principles underlying the N-PCL. This seems to have happened because the subset of members who have been accustomed to leading APsaA and making APsaA policy (those who are TA's, are associated with Institutes, and have served on BOPS) have over the years become a smaller and smaller fraction of the organization as (1) the organization has grown and (2) the training functions of APsaA have become RELATIVELY less important to the overall mission of APsaA.

In addition, for a number of years the current legal limit on the size of the Executive Council seems to have been exceeded by a large margin. While from the standpoint of the democratic process within APsaA this nitpicky point is of uncertain significance, I think it does serve to illustrate the way in which the rules under which we are organized seem to be overlooked or set aside in favor of improvisation — a phenomenon which, in itself, is a threat to democratic governance.

In the first part of this discussion I will show how there seems to have been an inadvertent transfer of power from the BOARD OF DIRECTORS (The Executive Council) to the President and President-Elect in the area of Committee appointments. (It should be noted that the elected officers of APsaA are almost EXCLUSIVELY TA's even though TA's represent a diminishing fraction of APsaA members — fewer than 20%, I believe, at present. To this point in time, only two individuals who are not TA's have ever been elected President of APsaA in the past 50 years! There has NEVER been a Secretary of APsaA who is not a TA!)

The power to appoint Committee members is the power to shape much of the deliberations which go on in the organization and to some extent the activities and policies of the organization itself. (Note 2)

A. HOW COMMITTEE APPOINTMENTS ARE MADE ACCORDING TO ROBERT'S RULES OF ORDER AND UNDER OUR BYLAWS

This discussion refers to "Committees of the Council" or "Council Committees" but with obvious modifications applies to appointments of Committees of the Board on Professional Standards as well. All told we have about 22 standing "Committees of the Executive Council" contributing their efforts to the work of APsaA. In APsaA, standing committees of the Executive Council can be established only by a vote of the Executive Council, but the members of such Council Committees are appointed exclusively by the President. As we will see, however, this presidential power to appoint MAY NOT BE AN UNLIMITED POWER even though it has incorrectly been exercised as such.

A Committee of the Board of Directors of an organization may act for the Board of Directors in a specific area but is always under the supervision of the Board itself, which is ultimately responsible for the Committee's actions. It is therefore logical, and in fact is usually the case, that a committee of a body is made up of MEMBERS of that body (e.g. members of Committees of the U.S. Senate are ALWAYS Senators, not other people.) You might then ask how is it that APsaA members who are not actually Executive Councilors are able to be appointed to Committees of the Executive Council? It turns

199

out that such appointments, while they are allowed, are not within the sole discretion of the President of APsaA, even though such appointments have been made as if such a power actually exists.

Robert's lists five distinct ways that appointments to committees may be made. (RONR 10th Ed. pp. 474 -482) Since four of these methods would refer to appointments made by the Executive Council itself, they can be ignored, because under the APsaA Bylaws such methods cannot be used. As recommended in Robert's for large groups, the only way members of standing Council Committees can be appointed in APsaA is by the President:

ARTICLE VIII AMENDMENT ON COMMITTEE APPOINTMENTS

SECTION 1. COUNCIL OR BOARD COMMITTEES:

The President of the Association shall make all appointments to committees of the Executive Council. The Chair of the Board on Professional Standards shall make all appointments to committees of the Board on Professional Standards. Appointments made by either the President or the Chair also convey the power to terminate such appointments... [APsaA Bylaws, current through Dec. 2001]

THIS DOES NOT MEAN HOWEVER, THAT THE PRESIDENT CAN APPOINT ANYONE HE OR SHE CHOOSES. According to Robert's:

"It is possible for persons who are not members of the assembly or the society to be appointed to committees — even to the position of committee chairman — but control over all such appointments is reserved to the assembly in the individual case, unless the bylaws provide otherwise... When ... the chair appoints either a standing or a special committee, however, the governing rule regarding the appointment of non-assembly members is as stated under "NAMING MEMBERS TO A SPECIAL COMMITTEE," on page 167." [RONR 10th Ed. p. 475] [emphasis in original]

"Whenever it is stated in the bylaws (with or without the proper exceptions just noted) that the president "shall appoint all committees," this means that the president shall select the persons to serve on such committees as the bylaws prescribe to be established or the assembly may direct to be appointed; it does not mean that the president can himself decide to appoint and assign a task to a group and thereby give it the status of a committee of the society. When the chair appoints a committee, no vote is taken on the appointees, EXCEPT ANY WHO ARE NOT MEMBERS OF THE ASSEMBLY IN CASES WHERE THERE IS NO PRIOR AUTHORIZATION FOR THE CHAIR TO APPOINT NON-ASSEMBLY MEMBERS TO THE COMMITTEE – either in the bylaws or in a motion directing the appointment of the particular committee (see also p. 167)." [RONR 10th Ed. p. 478] [emphasis added]

On page 167 Robert's says:

"A standing or special committee may include, or even have as its chairman, one or more persons who are not members of the assembly or the society; but if the chair appoints the committee, the names of all such nonmembers being appointed must be submitted to the assembly for approval, unless the bylaws or the motion to appoint the committee SPECIFICALLY AUTHORIZES THE PRESIDING OFFICER TO APPOINT NONMEMBERS (see also pp. 475, 478-79)." [emphasis added]

Since no specific authorization to appoint non-members of the Council to Council Committees exists in the APsaA Bylaws, this means that the President can, with no vote by the Council, appoint ONLY MEMBERS OF THE COUNCIL to Council Committees. Other appointments are possible, (and in APsaA's case quite important) but these appointments must be APPROVED INDIVIDUALLY by a vote of the Executive Council.

B. ADDITIONAL LEGAL CONSTRAINT ON APPOINTMENT OF COMMITTEES OF THE BOARD OF DIRECTORS (The Executive Council)

Under the N-PCL, the law under which APsaA is incorporated, the Board of Directors (The Executive Council) has legal responsibility and authority for the organization and all of its policies. Under the N-PCL, the Board of Directors is permitted to create committees provided that each such committee has AT LEAST THREE DIRECTORS (i.e. Executive Councilors) as members:

N-PCL, Section 712:

(a) If the certificate of incorporation or the by-laws so provide, the board, by resolution adopted by a majority of the entire board, may designate from among its members an executive committee and other standing committees, EACH CONSISTING OF THREE OR MORE DIRECTORS, and each of which, to the extent provided in the resolution or in the certificate of incorporation or by-laws, shall have all the authority of the board… [emphasis added]

This legal requirement that no Committee of the Board of Directors may have fewer than three Directors as members cannot be overridden in the Bylaws of an Not-for-Profit Corporation.

[Note added 2010: Over the years since I wrote the above I have become aware that I seriously understated the legal restriction on the President's appointment powers. Under the N-PCL only the board itself may make appointments to its own committees. In addition, any non-Director appointed to such a committee, even by the board itself, cannot vote in such a board committee.]

C. LEGAL RESTRICTION ON THE SIZE OF THE EXECUTIVE COUNCIL

When the APsaA was incorporated on November 26, 1951, the law (the now obsolete "Membership Corporation Law") required that the Certificate of Incorporation must state the minimum and maximum number of Directors on the Board of Directors. Therefore, the APsaA Certificate of Incorporation had, and apparently still has, the following provision:

"5. The number of its directors shall be not less than eleven (11) nor more than thirty-five (35)."

The currently constituted Executive Council seems to have somewhere around 60 members (including Councilors-at-Large, Officers, and ex-officio members) so it is very far out of compliance with our Certificate — which needs to be amended — and the law!

[Note: The Certificate of Incorporation was changed in 2004 to indicate that the Board of Directors would determine the number of Directors, two years after Paul Mosher wrote this Civic Lesson. JSS.]

D. SELECTION OF FELLOWS FOR THE BOARD OF/ON PROFESSIONAL STANDARDS (note 3)

The Board on Professional Standards is empowered to act on behalf of the Association in certain matters within its area of responsibility. For example, the "approval" of a training facility by the Board makes that facility an "Approved" training facility without any needed confirmation by the Executive Council or the Members. (This is not intended to address the question of whether such a decision could be rescinded by the Executive Council or the members. In the opposite case "disapproval" - i.e., withdrawal of approval — of a training facility clearly DOES require ratification by BOTH the Executive Council AND the members)

Since the Board on Professional Standards is an official body of the Corporation, but not a Committee or Board (Note 4) of the Executive Council, it must be what the N-PCL calls a "committee of the corporation":

"(e) Committees, other than standing or special committees of the board [of directors], whether created by the board [of directors] or by the members, shall be committees of the corporation. Such committees may be elected or appointed in the same manner as officers of the corporation. Provisions of this chapter applicable to officers generally shall apply to members of such committees." [N-PCL, Sec. 712(e)]

Selection of members of such a committee or board must be done "in the same manner as officers of the corporation," which in APsaA means selection by the members through an election. Since each Approved Institute or Training Center chooses its own Fellows of the Board on Professional Standards, it seems logical that there would be an electoral or appointment process in each such facility, but this could be only a process in which involvement in the selection is limited to APsaA members. NO such process is spelled out in the bylaws.

For example, in the somewhat analogous case (Note 5), in which the Executive Councilors are selected by the Societies, the bylaws specify that:

"[each] Affiliate Society shall select, BY ACTION OF ITS MEMBERS WHO ARE VOTING MEMBERS OF THE ASSOCIATION, in such manner as such Affiliate Society may determine, one of its members to be a member of the Executive Council..." [Article V, Sec. 2(b)(ii)] [emphasis added]

Logically enough, in other words, any society member who is NOT a member of APsaA may NOT participate in the selection of the Councilor. Most importantly, observe that the Councilor is selected by the APsaA MEMBERS in that society, not by the Society itself. The highlighted phrase in the Bylaw excerpt cited above was added at the time of the 1951 incorporation when it was recognized that the 1946 change in APsaA from a FEDERATION OF SOCIETIES to a MEMBERSHIP ORGANIZATION had opened the door to membership in societies to psychoanalysts who were not also APsaA members. Under the N-PCL such non-member/members cannot vote in APsaA elections. (In the "federation years" prior to 1946 EVERY society member was automatically an APsaA member.)

Now, returning to the selection of Fellows of the Board on Professional Standards: The 1932 Bylaws, under the Federation, said that the "members" (now "Fellows") of the Council on Professional Training

"...shall be designated ... in such a manner as each constituent SOCIETY MEMBER may designate."

In other words, in the days when the Societies themselves were a class of MEMBER of APsaA, that class of MEMBER selected the "Fellows" any way they chose.

When the 1946 transformation to a membership organization took place, the wording was changed slightly to:

[each institute] "shall designate its 2 Fellows in such manner as IT shall determine..." [1946 Bylaws, Article IX, Sec. 1] [emphasis added]

This wording was NOT UPDATED at the time of the incorporation in 1951 and remains unchanged today. A reasonable question is: to whom does the IT in this Bylaw provision refer when it comes to this important matter of selecting individuals who act on behalf of the Corporation? It cannot refer to the entire Institute because we do not have a membership class called "Institute." It must instead refer to individuals who are "members" of the Institute FACULTY. But what about the voting rights of the affiliate members (candidates) who have recently been given "full voting rights" in APsaA? Are they part of the "Institute?" Must they be allowed to participate in the selection of Fellows of the Board on Professional Standards? What about Institute Faculty members who are NOT members of APsaA (if any)? Would they have a say?

Because of my unfamiliarity with the inner workings of Institutes, I cannot add much more to this. However, the fact that the Board on Professional Standards actually makes "policies" for the entire APsaA in its area of responsibility suggests to me that the rules for selecting the Fellows need some major clarification. And finally this uncertainty provides just one more sound reason (beyond those cited by the APsaA legal counsel in 1951) why THE FINAL AUTHORITY FOR POLICY DECISIONS OF APsaA MUST RESIDE WITH THE BOARD OF DIRECTORS (the Executive Council) and the Members themselves.

As some of the commentary on the N-PCL in "McKinney's Consolidated Laws of New York, Annotated" (Vol 37) notes:

"The internal affairs, questions of policy or management, and expediency of contracts of a corporation are subject to control of a board of directors, and in so far as those directors are honest, capable, and independent, their judgment is final."

"Ordinarily, the management of property and affairs of a corporation is vested in its board of directors, so that except in unusual or extraordinary case, an officer should not be permitted to determine corporate policy or action."

"No agreement or by-law which deprives directors of corporation of their power to act for and in best interest of corporation is valid."

————————

Note 1: You can read the New York Not-For-Profit Corporation Law at https://www.nysenate.gov/legislation/laws/NPC

Note 2: As a newcomer to APsaA some 25 years ago I heard it said that political manipulation of Committee appointments was one way that certain politically domineering leadership types controlled APsaA. I never though about that much until a few years ago when I personally was blackballed from a Committee appointment by a zealous President who disagreed with me about certain activities of a Committee for which I was otherwise reasonably well suited and whose chairman had requested my appointment.

Note 3: In the 1946 Bylaws as amended through 1948 the "BOPS" is called the "Board OF Professional Standards" but in subsequent versions, and with no indication that any Bylaw amendment changed the name, it is referred to as the Board ON Professional Standards which seems to be the more common usage today.

Note 4: The distinction between a "committee" and a "board," according to Robert's is mainly one relating to the relative formality of the meetings they hold, with boards being the more formal. In addition, Boards typically have more authority to act independently within the area of their assigned responsibility than do committees, but otherwise the terms are roughly equivalent (See RONR 10th Ed. pp. 472-473)

Note 5: I am referring here to the process of selection. The Executive Councilors are not "Officers" of the Corporation; they are "Directors" of the Corporation.

Wed, 27 Feb. 2002:

Civics Lesson — Part 8 —

Membership Power Has Been Eroded By Ignoring Rules Related to Meetings of Members

In reply to two requests, this and my other "civics lessons" notes are now available on the WWW at:

http://mosher.com/apsaastuff/APsaAcivics.htm

[URL updated 09-21-05 pwm]

As I have been doing my own personal review of the governance of APsaA the phenomenon that is most striking to me is the extent to which the governing power, which belongs to the general membership of APsaA, has been transferred to the Executive Council, The Executive Committee, and the Board on Professional Standards.

My own view of why this has happened is this: In the 1950's, when APsaA was a newly organized MEMBERSHIP organization (membership organization formed in 1946, incorporation as such in 11/20/51) the profession was undergoing tremendous growth, and training and standards issues were a major preoccupation. There were nearly twice as many candidates in training as there were graduate analysts in APsaA. A much larger percentage of APsaA members were therefore involved in training activities than is the case today, so that those involved in "training" came to see themselves AS BEING THE "MEMBERSHIP." A completely unbalanced view (and set of customs) developed as to the relative roles of the "profession" as a whole vs. the role of academics and educators in the governance of the organization and the establishment of standards.

As time went by, and the relative role of training activities diminished as the exceptionally rapid growth tapered off, the arrangements, which were set in the 1950's prevented the organization from adapting to the changing circumstances. The Board on Professional Standards had come to see itself (falsely) as a co-equal body with the Executive Council and tried to maintain a position of ABSOLUTE rather than RELATIVE autonomy with regard to regulation of the profession. As one historian has put it:

"All these issues crystallized in debates over the structure of psychoanalytic organizations, which had remained unresolved during the war. The decisions made between 1946 and 1957 by the American Psychoanalytic Association held momentous consequences for psychoanalysis, many of them unintended, some of them damaging in retrospect." (Note 1, p. 212)

Gradually, the Board on Professional Standards sought greater representation on the Executive Committee, even though the Executive Committee is a COMMITTEE OF THE EXECUTIVE COUNCIL,

"There shall be an Executive Committee of the Executive Council..." [Bylaws Article 6, Section 1(a)]

and, in the interest of promoting the myth of co-equal bodies, appears to have abetted the transfer of powers from the membership to the Executive Council, and then from the Executive Council to the Executive Committee.

It wouldn't surprise me to discover that some members of the Executive Committee today don't even realize that the Executive Committee is a Committee of the Executive Council, and instead imagine that the Executive Committee has the power to make policy decisions for APsaA, whereas in fact that Committee is simply empowered to act for the Executive Council between Council meetings.

Just to show how far from the correct organizational "spirit" we have strayed: in the 1950's, the legal counsel to APsaA frowned at the fact that the Chair of the Board on Professional Standards was a member of the Executive Committee BECAUSE AT THAT TIME S/HE WAS NOT A MEMBER OF THE EXECUTIVE COUNCIL. (This issue was subsequently resolved by making the Chairman of the Board on Professional Standards an ex officio member of the Council, but it is that membership which makes the non-Council members of the Board on Professional Standards eligible to sit on the Executive Committee.)

A. CHANGES IN THE BUSINESS MEETING OF MEMBERS IN VIOLATION OF THE LAW AND THE BYLAWS:

Nowhere has this process been more evident than in the gradual erosion of the decision-making role of the general membership.

What seems to have happened is that the Bylaws of the Association and the New York State Not-For-Profit Corporation Law (N-PCL), under which the Association is incorporated, have gradually been ignored. This is most striking in the changes in the BUSINESS MEETING OF MEMBERS which has devolved into a sort of dog and pony show rather than a serious meeting at which business is transacted.

Membership in a Not-For-Profit Corporation is analogous to the role of stockholder in a Business Corporation in which each member owns, and can vote, a single share. According to a book on the subject:

"The [New York] Not-for-Profit Corporation Law was consciously patterned on the Business Corporation Law so that attorneys experienced with corporate practice could readily adapt to and be familiar with the principles of the not-for-profit statute. Nowhere is this more evident than in the rules of nonprofit governance, which closely parallel corporate practices.

"MEMBERS OF NEW YORK NOT-FOR-PROFIT CORPORATIONS HAVE A BROAD ARRAY OF MEMBERSHIP RIGHTS, including the power to adopt, amend, or appeal the bylaws or to restrict the rights of the board of directors to amend the same, to elect and remove directors, and to change the size of the board; to vote upon or approve fundamental changes in the structure of the corporation such as mergers or consolidations, disposition of all or substantially all of the assets of the corporation ... and dissolution. ...

"Members also have several monitoring rights, including: the right to inspect the corporations book and records; ... the right to receive an annual report of the organization containing financial information and indicating the number of members and changes in membership; the right to obtain lists of members of record at a members' meeting ... ...

"Bylaws are the internal rules of governance of the corporation and represent a contract between the organization and its members..." (Note 3, pp. 298-299) [emphasis added]

The N-PCL REQUIRES that a meeting of members be held at least once a year. The meeting of members is of great importance because, under the law, most governance actions initiated by the members must be enacted at such a meeting. For example, NO NEW MEMBERS CAN BE ADDED TO APsaA WITHOUT A VALID VOTE AT A VALID MEETING OF MEMBERS. And, of course, any proposed changes in the Association Bylaws (which have not been adopted by the Executive Council) can only be adopted by the members at such a meeting — not by a mail ballot.

Meetings of members are subject to a number of rules some of which are mandated in the N-PCL and others in the Bylaws. Of these rules, the following have evidently been overlooked or ignored in recent years:

(1) A QUORUM MUST BE "PRESENT" AT THE MEETING FOR BUSINESS TO TAKE PLACE. The President is responsible for determining the presence of a quorum before convening the meeting. I have never seen this done. In addition, with last year's change in our bylaws now granting about 3300 members the right to vote at meetings, the 10% quorum definition in the APsaA Bylaws now requires the "presence" of about 330 members.

(2) Under the N-PCL, A RECORD MUST BE KEPT OF THE NAMES OF THE MEMBERS WHO ATTEND THE MEETING and are eligible to vote:

"Sec. 607. LIST OR RECORD OF MEMBERS AT MEETINGS. A list or record of members entitled to vote, certified by the corporate officer responsible for its preparation or by a transfer agent, shall be produced at any meeting of members upon the request therefor of any member who has given written notice to the corporation that such request will be made at least ten days prior to such meeting. If the right to vote at any meeting is challenged, the inspectors of election, or the person presiding thereat, shall require such list or record of members to be produced as evidence of the right of the persons challenged to vote at such meeting, and all persons who appear from such list or record to be members entitled to vote thereat may vote at such meeting. (N-PCL)

In the last 10 years, I have not seen anyone bother to record the names of the members present at our business meetings.

(3) Under the APsaA Bylaws, every member eligible to vote MUST be sent a proxy in advance of each meeting. NO PROXIES HAVE BEEN MAILED BY THE SECRETARY OF APsaA FOR THE PAST SEVERAL YEARS. I understand that this lapse will be remedied starting with the May meeting, but presumably only because it has been pointed out that not to do so is a violation of the bylaws.

An additional minor complication is the fact that in the 2001 amendments to our bylaws, which obviously intended to extend full voting privileges to our affiliate members, poor drafting appears to have extended that power to affiliate members to vote AT MEETINGS, but possibly not in mail ballots! This is because the Bylaws, following our recent change, now say, as they did before:

"(d) All Active Members have voting rights." [Article 2, Section 2(d)]

But, under the section spelling out the rights of Affiliate Members now say:

"(d) An Affiliate Member shall have the following rights, privileges, powers, duties and obligations, in addition to any other rights, privileges, powers, duties or obligations that may be set forth elsewhere in these Bylaws:

(i) To attend any Meeting of Members of the Association, AND TO PARTICIPATE IN ANY SUCH MEETING to the same extent as an Active Member, and to attend any meeting of the Executive

Council, the Board on Professional Standards or any committee of the Association."
[Article 2, Section 6(d)(i)]

As far as I can see, there is no other mention of wider voting rights for Affiliate Members! This potential ambiguity must be resolved while the intent of the 2001 change is still in everyone's mind. This is only one example that has led me to believe we should review APsaA's relationship with the legal counsel who does our routine work in such matters.

B. PROXY VOTING IN APsaA

When you recognize the importance of the Business Meeting of Members, and the increasing difficulty of assembling a quorum to convene such a meeting with our increased number of members eligible to vote, it becomes self-evident that the role of proxies in our organization is taking on new importance. The problem, however, is that our rules are murky to the point of inscrutability when it comes to the question of whether the kind of proxies our organization allows can be counted toward a quorum at meeting.

In general, a proxy is a document which give another person permission to vote in place of someone who is absent. (The word "proxy" can also refer to that designated person.)

The New York N-PCL has some rules which apply to all Not-for-Profit Corporations and cannot be overridden in the Bylaws of the Corporation. There are other rules which come into play if the situation they address is not handled in the Bylaws, but otherwise may be overridden in the Bylaws. However, rules for some issues are simply not addressed in the law, but may be spelled out in the Bylaws, which are permitted to set any rules the organization desires so long as those rules are not contrary to the N-PCL or another law.

Most parliamentary authorities, including Robert and Sturgis, advise against allowing any proxies because they are very messy, cause no end of controversies, and are contrary to the principles of parliamentary law, but most state laws permit such voting in membership organizations anyway.

The N-PCL PERMITS but does not REQUIRE the use of proxies in a membership corporation. In the 1946 Bylaws of APsaA, proxy voting was forbidden, but in the 1951 revision at the time of incorporation, the right to use proxy voting was explicitly extended to the members.

There are, however, two kinds of proxies: general proxies and limited proxies. A GENERAL proxy usually means that another person is empowered to vote at the meeting in place of the person issuing the proxy on any matter which comes up and the holder of the proxy can vote however s/he wishes. A LIMITED proxy spells out certain issues on which the proxy can be voted and may also specify which way the holder must vote on each issue. According to one authority, however:

"Limited proxies for annual meetings usually have a general statement to the effect that proxy holders may vote as they choose on any other matters to legitimately come before the meeting" (Note 4, p. 54).

However, the APsaA Bylaws are very restrictive with regard to the kind of proxies that are allowed. Not only are proxies required to be limited to specific issues, but also they are NOT allowed to be voted on any issue not mentioned in the proxy:

"… no proxy may be voted on any matter other than the matters referred to in the notice of such meeting (unless such other matter is specified in the proxy)."
[Article III, Section 2]

All this matters because:

(1) The kind of proxies which are allowed may bear on the question of whether the proxies can be counted toward a quorum to convene a meeting and
(2) With the new right of affiliate members to vote at meetings, and the possibility that affiliates are less likely to be able personally to attend our semiannual meetings than active members, the rules for proxy voting have taken on new significance for APsaA.

C. CONFUSION ABOUT THE ROLE OF PROXIES AT MEETINGS COMPOUNDED BY POORLY WRITTEN BYLAWS AND UNCLEAR (in my opinion) LEGAL ADVICE:

In the APsaA Bylaws, a quorum is defined as "THE PRESENCE of one-tenth of the members entitled to vote." Whoever wrote the 1951 bylaws changes, which allowed proxy voting failed to change this requirement to say whether or not proxies should be counted in determining the presence of a quorum.

I spent considerable time in the last couple weeks trying to find the answer to this question. Here's what I found out:

(1) The N-PCL speaks of "members attending, in person or by proxy" in certain limited circumstances [e.g.. Sec. 604(b)] but is silent on the general issue of defining a quorum:

> "Members entitled to cast [some proportion] of the total number
> of votes entitled to be cast thereat shall constitute a quorum at a
> meeting of members for the transaction of any business."
> [Sec. 608(a)]

The New York N-PCL doesn't mention the words "present" or "proxy." By contrast, the comparable law in Texas is quite specific that proxies DO COUNT UNLESS the Bylaws say otherwise:

"Art. 1396–2.12. Quorum of Members A. Unless otherwise provided in the articles of incorporation or in the by-laws, members holding one-tenth of the votes entitled to be cast, represented in person OR BY PROXY, shall constitute a quorum."

Whereas, in California the law says that proxies MUST be counted no matter what the Bylaws say:

"(d) The votes represented, either in person or by proxy, at a meeting called or by written ballot ordered pursuant to subdivision (c) and entitled to be cast on the business to be transacted shall constitute a quorum, NOTWITHSTANDING ANY PROVISION OF THE ARTICLES OR BYLAWS or in this part to the contrary. [Sec. 7510] [emphasis added]

Furthermore, and without going into the details, authorities who write on this subject are divided on whether or not LIMITED proxies should count toward a quorum, even in situations where general proxies clearly count. The only reasonable way to deal with all this is to spell out the precise rule in each organization's Bylaws, according to the leading authority in the field:

"The presiding officer should determine whether a quorum is present at the beginning of the meeting. ... Proxies may or may not be counted, depending on statutory and bylaws provisions." Note 5, p. 47)

Due to poor drafting, the APsaA Bylaws don't offer any help in this matter. A 1994 letter from the association's legal counsel offers the view that proxies DO count toward a quorum on the matter to which they are addressed, but does not clearly state an opinion as to whether such limited proxies count for the purposes of convening the meeting.

It doesn't really matter what the legal counsel says, however, because the only way to resolve an ambiguity in the Bylaws of an organization is by a majority vote of the members. So there would have to be a quorum PHYSICALLY PRESENT at a meeting to decide this issue. Is this a good reason to show up for the meeting in Philadelphia?

If you look at the Bylaws of other organizations on the Internet (there are many of them) you can see how, by comparison, ours are poorly written.

Here's an example of a Bylaw in which only general proxies count toward a quorum:

"6. Proxy voting. At all membership meetings, written proxies shall be accepted and validated by the Secretary. Proxies presented by e-mail shall be accepted with the approval of the President and the Secretary. Copies of e-mail proxies must be presented at the meeting. General proxies are those that allow any Member to vote for the proxy at the discretion of the attending Member. GENERAL PROXIES shall count toward a quorum." [emphasis added]

Here's an example in which ALL proxies count toward a quorum:

"… All shares represented at the meeting, whether in person or by a GENERAL OR LIMITED PROXY, will be counted for the purpose of establishing a quorum." [emphasis added]

The bottom line in all this is that if APsaA is going to return to its intended form of governance, with the power to make decisions for the profession (or at least the part of the profession we represent) in the hands of the members, we better learn the rules, and where the rules aren't clear, straighten them out.

————————

Note 1: You can read the New York Not-For-Profit Corporation Law at https://www.nysenate.gov/legislation/laws/NPC

Note 2: Hale, N.G. (1995) The Rise and Crisis of Psychoanalysis in the United States: Volume II, Freud and the Americans 1917-1985, Oxford: New York.

Note 3: Bjorklund, V. B., et al. (1997) New York Nonprofit Law and Practice: With Tax Analysis. Michie: Charlottesville, VA.

Note 4: Stephens, J.L. (1993) A Guide to Voting: Procedures for Voluntary Organizations, Fredrick: Clearwater FL.

Note 5: Oleck, H.L. (1977) Parliamentary Law for Nonprofit Organizations, American Law Institute/ABA.

Date: Mon, 29 April, 2002:
Civics Lesson — Part 9 —

Voting, Meetings, Proxies (more)
Important Information about the INTENT of Some Unclear APsaA Bylaws

In this note I'd like to expand on and clarify some issue I raised in some earlier "civics lessons."

Since our governing rules, the Bylaws, were written half a century ago it's not surprising that we have trouble remembering the meaning of certain parts of them today. However, the age of the Bylaws is no excuse for ignoring the Bylaws, nor is it a reason to give up on trying to understand these rules that, after all, are a contract between the Association and each of us.

Covered here:
1. PRINCIPLES FOR UNDERSTANDING THE BYLAWS
2. AMENDING THE BYLAWS - REVISITED
3. VOTING (AT MEETINGS)
4. PROXIES
5. THE QUORUM

Here for orientation is a compressed timeline of APsaA:

1938 – APsaA is formed as a federation of Societies. A set of Bylaws and a Constitution are the governing documents.

1946 – The 1938 organization is dissolved and the new APsaA (today's) is formed with a new set of Bylaws. It is now a MEMBERSHIP ORGANIZATION.

1951 – The Association is incorporated under the New York State "Membership Corporation Law" (MCL). The Bylaws are revised in several ways but only to make the organization compliant with the law; the Executive Council is designated in the Bylaws as the Board of Directors of the Corporation. From this date forward, the organization MUST function as a corporation under New York law. The vote on these Bylaws changes was almost unanimous. (236 to 1.)

1969 – The New York Membership Corporation Law is repealed and replaced with the Not for Profit Corporation Law (the N-PCL) under which APsaA is regulated today. This law makes the regulation of all Corporations in New York State more uniform, including the "principle of a strong board of directors."

1994 – The Bylaws are amended to provide for the election of officers by a mail ballot and the central mailing of proxies, mainly intended for that purpose, is discontinued even though the Bylaws continue to mandate such mailings.

1. PRINCIPLES FOR UNDERSTANDING THE BYLAWS

Where a passage in the Bylaws (or in another document) of our organization is "unclear or uncertain," Robert's Rules lays out the protocol we should follow to determine its meaning (pp. 570 - 571).

So long as an interpretation doesn't conflict with other Bylaws (and the law) the meaning can be determined by understanding the INTENT of the Bylaw. If the intent cannot be determined, then a majority vote of the members can determine the meaning. Although it is possible and useful to consult an attorney to obtain help in understanding the Bylaws, it is the MEMBERSHIP which makes the determination, not a "legal opinion."

In other words, advice given by a lawyer BEFORE the Bylaw is enacted helps determine the INTENT. A legal opinion AFTER a Bylaw is enacted may be helpful to the members in understanding technical language and relevant legal points, but does not determine the meaning of the unclear bylaw. Only the members can decide this if the intent is not clear. In our case, we may need to look back more than half a century to discern the meaning of any unclear bylaw, which was written when APsaA was incorporated.

2. AMENDING THE BYLAWS - REVISITED

In the January 30 "Civics Lesson #6" I went through a long (and tedious) account of my two weeks of trying to "deconstruct" the incredibly convoluted paragraph in the Bylaws which sets out the rules for amending the Bylaws.

After I figured out what the mechanism is supposed to be (recently we haven't followed it correctly, at least in one instance), I then concluded that the Bylaw got that way because of the 1951 incorporation and the fact that the corporation law does not allow amending the Bylaws by a mail ballot. Some people seemed to feel I was a bit imaginative with my explanation. I conjectured then:

In 1951, APsaA was INCORPORATED in New York State under what was then the "Membership Corporation Law" (The MCL.) To permit this incorporation, the Bylaws had to be changed, and one of the most important changes was a change in the way the Bylaws are amended. This is because, under the MCL (and its 1969 successor, the current N- PCL) it is illegal to ADOPT Bylaw amendments BY A MAIL VOTE (unless every single eligible voter agrees in writing). So in practical terms, Bylaw amendments can ONLY BE ADOPTED at a meeting…

The "clever" change which was made to the APsaA Bylaws in 1951 took advantage of a provision in the MCL which allows the Board of Directors of a Corporation (in our case, the Executive Council) to ADOPT Bylaws on its own. But clearly, the membership was not willing to grant this unfettered power to the Executive Council. So … [etc.]

I can now say that I have been able to determine the INTENT behind that Bylaw's convoluted wording, and it turns out that my conjecture was EXACTLY correct. With the help of the Central Office staff I was able to read the memorandum from the APsaA Counsel who advised the Committee working to revise the Bylaws in anticipation of the 1951 incorporation. It also turns out that the "subtle" change in that particular Bylaw was just one instance of other changes which had to be made for an identical reason, which is that: MAIL BALLOTS ARE NOT ALLOWED IN NEW YORK CORPORATIONS INCLUDING, OF COURSE, FOR THE PURPOSE OF AMENDING THE BYLAWS.

The document I read and quote from here is the 1950 report of the Committee on Incorporation. That report consists entirely of an April 24, 1950 legal memorandum titled "Memorandum of Counsel Regarding Proposed Incorporation under the New York Membership Corporation Law." The 1950 memorandum deals with those changes, which would be have to be made in the 1946 Bylaws in order to comply with the corporation law. The introductory paragraph of the 1950 memorandum clearly states that the INTENT of the proposed amendments is to avoid making any changes in the 1946 Bylaws EXCEPT FOR THOSE WHICH ARE REQUIRED by the act of incorporation:

"It is our understanding that so far as possible it is desired that the present provisions of the by-laws be continued in effect."

In regard to the 1946 section on members voting in a "referendum" [1946 Bylaws term] by mail to take an action (if the Executive Council chooses to follow that route instead of acting itself) the Counsel's memorandum says:

"Subdivision (iii) should be changed to comply with the theory that when the Executive council submits any proposed course of action to the members, the action is taken by the Executive Council subject to approval by the members. (This theory involves a subtle legal distinction. Under New York Law ALTHOUGH THE USE OF A PROXY IS LEGAL, MEMBERS OF A MEMBERSHIP CORPORATION CANNOT VOTE BY MAIL. We believe, however, that it is possible for the Executive Council to take action on a matter, at the same time providing that such action is not to become effective unless and until the written approval of a specified percentage of the members has been obtained; and such written approval could be given by mail. The distinction is between the concept of action taken by the Executive Council, subject to the approval of the members, and action taken by the members, to whom the proposal has been submitted by the Executive Council.)" [emphasis added]

This suggested change is now reflected in both the section on mail voting in general, and the section on amending the Bylaws where in both places the distinction between ADOPTING something (or TAKING and action) and APPROVING something is now clear. These sections are now Article V, Sec. 8, (on mail approval of Council actions in general) and Article XIV, Section 2 (on amending the Bylaws).

3. VOTING (AT MEETINGS)

Based on the understanding that mail votes are not allowed in APsaA because it is a membership corporation, it is now clear why the meeting of members is so important. The meeting of members is the ONLY situation in which each individual member of APsaA is guaranteed by law the right to VOTE on the policies of APsaA. (Most Societies elect their Executive Councilor, but an election is not specifically required in our Bylaws or the N-PCL.)

So, at this point you must be wondering why we have recently elected our officers and Councilors-at-Large (gasp!) by mail ballots.

In the 1946 Bylaws, the election of officers AT MEETINGS was allowed to include ballots submitted by mail. In the 1951 Bylaws, this provision had to be dropped but that meant that members who were not at the meeting couldn't vote for officers. However, the 1951 Bylaws provided for "proxies" at the meetings (see below) so in 1954 a "Committee on Voting Problems" pointed out that proxies for electing officers AT MEETINGS could be used instead and spelled out certain details about such "proxies" which were, in effect, a legal form of "mail ballots." This was the method by which we elected our officers until 1994.

In 1992, A Committee chaired by Charles Brenner, (acting on a charge which came, I am imagining, from someone who didn't understand why our voting was being done as it was) suggested that we abandon the meeting/proxy method of voting and adopt our current mail voting method. This change was enacted as a Bylaw in 1994, but I think it is probably not a legal change. I have no idea whether the APsaA Counsel in 1994, who vets all Bylaws proposals, had a rationale for allowing this change or simply didn't read the law or understood our history.

I believe we must return immediately to the pre-1994 method of electing officers AT OUR MEETINGS OF MEMBERS (with "ballot-like" proxies for those members who can't attend meetings.)(Note 1)

4. PROXIES

Proxies are a continuing source of confusion and trouble and that's why parliamentary authorities recommend against allowing them. However, as you can see from the above, there are certain situations in which an organization may depend on proxies in order to make it possible for members to express themselves.

The history of proxies in APsaA clearly shows a strong inclination either to avoid proxies altogether or sharply to restrict their use.

In the old 1938 APsaA, members were allowed to issue proxies to members to vote for them at meetings, but a member could issue such a proxy only if he/she had attended the previous three meetings. This restriction seemed to be aimed at promoting attendance at the meetings and severely limited the number of proxies which could turn up at any meeting.

In the 1946 Bylaws, ALL PROXIES WERE STRICTLY PROHIBITED, but the 1946 Bylaws provided that for the election of officers at meetings "Ballots sent by mail shall be counted."

In the 1951 Bylaws amendments (for incorporation) proxies were permitted because the old Membership Corporation Law required such a provision. The 1951 bylaw said "Ballots may be cast by proxy subject to the proxy requirements of Article III, Section 2" and this is the legal way we can elect officers today even though this provision was removed when the change to mail voting took place in 1994. (The current law permits, but no longer requires, that proxies be allowed.)

The APsaA Bylaws provision related to proxies causes two problems for us, and now that we know how important the meeting of members is, we can see that these two points are both important as well.

The first question is can a proxy be issued to another member who can then vote any way s/he chooses on behalf of the issuer of the proxy? (Called a general proxy) or can the person issuing the proxy specify that the holder can vote as s/he chooses on a specific category of items such as "new business?" (another form of "general proxy") OR — on the other hand — must a proxy be LIMITED to specific matters and tell the holder exactly how to vote (a limited proxy.)

The wording of the APsaA Bylaws is:

"… no proxy may be voted on any matter other than the matters referred to in the notice of such meeting (unless such other matter is specified in the proxy)." [Article III, Section 2]

Perhaps this wording leaves some "wiggle room" so that one could argue that if a proxy says "any item of new business" and since "new business" is an item in the meeting announcement, a proxy such as the one recently sent out would be allowed. However, again we can look to the INTENT of the Bylaw to understand it and I think I found that intent in the same legal memorandum I cited above. In regard to the addition of a proxy provision to the Bylaws in 1951, the 1950 memo clearly indicates the extent of the concern that the introduction of the use of proxies, which were then forbidden in the Bylaws, should be restricted as much as possible to safeguard "against possible abuses." After explaining the legal necessity of having a proxy provision, the memo continues:

"If it is feared that the use of proxies may be abused, certain conditions my be attached to the use of proxies, e.g.:

(a) Require that the proxy must have been signed not more than thirty (30) days before the meeting and

(b) Require that the proxy must have been filed with the Secretary not later than seven (7) days before the meeting.

"An additional possibility would be to provide that proxies may be voted only on those items of business which were set forth in the notices of the meeting which were sent to all the members, except that the proxy may also be voted on additional items of new business IF THE ADDITIONAL ITEMS ARE SPECIFIED in the proxy. (Such a provision may occasionally lead to a dispute as to the scope of the proxy, but on the whole, it should work out reasonably well.) [emphasis added]

All these suggested provisions are reflected in the actual 1951 amendments, and based on this memorandum I think its fair to conclude that the APsaA Bylaws intend only to allow limited and specific proxies. I also believe that the intent was that such proxies should be sent ONLY to the Secretary and should specify exactly how the Secretary is to count (or vote) them on the specific items they address (i.e., for or against each specific item, just like the proxies which are typically sent to shareholders of mutual funds and business corporations.)

The intent to restrict the use of proxies is also shown in the final report of the Committee on Incorporation, which reads, in this regard:

> "The current By-Laws expressly prohibited proxy voting. Legal counsel advises that under the law it is necessary to permit proxy voting by members at meetings of the members. The new form of this section was agreed upon after careful deliberation by legal counsel and the Executive Council as meeting the requirements of law and also safeguarding against possible abuses of the privilege." [Committees at Work (1951) Bul. Amer. Psychoanal. Assn., 7:26-46] p. 30.

I think that neither the proxies sent out by APsaA in anticipation of our May meeting, nor the substitute proxies, are correct OR VALID.

5. THE QUORUM

Proxies also cause a complication in deciding if there is a quorum at the meeting.

In deciding whether a quorum is present, do proxies count toward the existence of a quorum at a meeting? If they are limited proxies, like ours, do they then allow votes to occur only on issues for which the proxy is valid?

I still don't have an answer to this question, but I can say that the legal memorandum which I cited above says nothing about changing the wording of the quorum bylaw to include proxies in the quorum.

The quorum section of the Bylaws, since 1946, clearly allows counting only members PRESENT at the meeting. Since there are many examples of Bylaws of organizations in which it is desired to count proxies, and on which it is made completely clear that proxies do count toward a quorum, it seems to me that if that were the intent to include proxies in the quorum, our Bylaws would say so as well.

Bylaws or statues where proxies do count toward a quorum usually say that the quorum includes members who are "present or present by proxy" or "present or represented by proxy." The omission of such a suggestion in the 1950 memorandum suggests an INTENT to stay with the 1946 quorum requirement, i.e., count only those PHYSICALLY PRESENT. However, this inference of intent, due to omission of a change in 1951, is a less reliable determination of intent than the affirmative indications of intent, which I cited in regard to the other questions addressed above. It could have been an oversight, although the Counsel's careful analysis of other needed Bylaws changes in the Counsel's memorandum leads me to doubt this.

A 1992 memorandum from the current APsaA legal Counsel (based on "policy" considerations rather than a review of the intent when the Bylaws were written) "tentative[ly]" opined that "valid proxies may be used to satisfy the quorum requirement" but then later adds that proxies may be used "to satisfy the quorum requirement for a vote on this matter" suggesting that limited proxies do not create a quorum for votes on other matters which may come up at the meeting. If one agrees with the premise that limited proxies do at least count toward a quorum on the specific matters in the proxy, it would be absurd to make any other assumption.

For instance, suppose that three members show up at the meeting and that the Secretary has 500 proxies containing a vote on some specific trivial matter which had been announced in advance. Does that mean that once the meeting is convened that the three members PRESENT can then vote, for instance, to reverse any action of the Executive Council that they choose? It seems much more reasonable to assume that, if the proxies count toward a quorum at all, (I don't agree that they do under the current APsaA Bylaws) that the meeting could be convened, a vote taken on the matter referred to in the proxies, and then (unless no one noticed that a quorum was physically present) the meeting would have to adjourn with NO OTHER VOTES.

Since the New York law explicitly leaves the proxy matter to the organization's Bylaws, we can't really look to the law to answer the above question and need to rely on our understanding of the Bylaws' intent. Again, I believe that if the intent were to count the proxies toward a quorum at all, the memorandum and the Bylaws would say so.

As to the May 2002 meeting, since neither of the two proxy forms which were sent out will result in valid proxies, I don't think that any of those proxies can either be counted toward a quorum or voted on any matter. If anyone disagrees with this and the issue comes up, I guess we can vote on it (if a quorum is present!)

—————————

Note 1: Not all States have such a restriction. For example, in Illinois, the law says: "Where directors or officers are to be elected by members, the Bylaws may provide that such elections may be conducted by mail." [805 ILCS 105/107.50]

Date: Wed, 8 May 2002:
Civics Lesson — Part 10 —

Constructive Suggestions for Quorums, Elections, and Proxies
Some possible solutions to the problems of quorums, elections, and proxies

In previous "civics lessons" I have pointed to some big problems in the current governance of APsaA. In this brief note, I'd like to offer some possible solutions to three of these problems. I am in no way suggesting that these proposals are the only ways we can fix the difficulties we find ourselves in, but rather I'm trying to show that these three problems CAN be addressed using common sense.

Others may have different ideas, all of which should have an opportunity to be heard. This is why I strongly object to any attempt to rewrite or revise the bylaws of APsaA, or write a Procedural Code for APsaA, through a secretive process in a small committee, a process which is completely contrary to the open process in a large, broadly representative committee, which both makes sense and is urged in Robert's for such an important purpose.

These three problems and my proposals are intended to restore our governance to lawfulness in a way that (hopefully) members of various "factions" in APsaA can all view as NEUTRAL. Furthermore, I believe these suggestions are all well within the range of options allowed us under the New York Statute:

[1] THE POSSIBLE DIFFICULTY IN HAVING A QUORUM AT THE MEETING OF MEMBERS GIVEN OUR ENLARGED VOTER BASE:

I suggest that we lower the quorum requirement from 10% of the members to 5% (which would presently be about 170 members at a meeting) with the further provision that the minimum number of votes needed to pass a measure requiring a majority must obtain the affirmative votes of at least 5% of all the members eligible to vote. This would establish a situation essentially the same as we have today except that, even with an attendance as small as 5% of the members, items to which no one objects could be passed. The minimum number of votes to pass a measure requiring a 2/3 vote would have the added provision that the minimum required number of affirmative votes would have to be 6 2/3% of the members eligible to vote. (For the truly picky, the majority "minimum" could be set at 5% + 1 to almost exactly duplicate the situation today.)

[2] THE CURRENT ILLEGALITY OF OUR SYSTEM OF MAIL VOTING FOR OFFICERS:

To restore our election of officers to a lawful process (i.e., it must take place at the Fall {Winter?} meeting) we can return to the pre-1994 method of mail voting for officers via proxy/ballots at the meeting. However, the proxies can be changed so that they are IRREVOCABLE. This would allow the votes to be counted before the meeting, as they are today, by an outside firm or the Central Office staff, and the Secretary would cast those proxy votes at the meeting. Anyone who didn't submit a proxy could actually vote at the meeting but the number who would choose to do so would probably be very small. This would address what, based on my inquiries, seems to have been the complaint about the pre-1994 system — the difficulty of counting a large number of votes DURING THE ACTUAL MEETING. (In the pre-1994 system, the votes couldn't be opened until the meeting because each member had the right at the meeting to withdraw her proxy and vote in person, and if the proxy/ballots had been opened before the meeting there would have been no way to associate a particular proxy with the member who submitted it. Making the election proxies irrevocable would obviate that problem.)

[3] THE AMBIGUITY ABOUT THE USE OF PROXIES IN CONSTITUTING A QUORUM AT THE MEETING OF MEMBERS:

In order to eliminate this ambiguity and still allow members who cannot attend meetings to participate in our governance, we might spell out that:

(a) Every proxy, in order to be valid, would have to specify the exact matter(s) on which it is to be voted and the voting intention of the voter on each such item of business. In other words they would be similar to "ballots." All such proxy votes would be cast by the Secretary at the meeting according to the express wishes of the person submitting the proxy. No proxy could be voted on any other matter. (Based on my reading of the historical intent, this is pretty much what the Bylaws appear intended to say today.)

(b) The Bylaws could then spell out clearly that proxies can be used to constitute a quorum to convene a meeting and to conduct votes on the issues for which the proxies are valid. In the absence of a quorum being physically present, however, no other item of business could be conducted at the meeting. (This will prevent a small group from taking action at a meeting which was convened on the basis of a quorum built on proxies submitted for a different purpose.)

I'm offering these in the same spirit that I suggested a "consent agenda" as a way of addressing the fact that the Council cannot legally conduct e-mail votes on routine matters. That suggestion has now been taken up as part of our Council procedures and works trouble-free.

It's really up to all of us to decide how, and to what extent, we wish to revise the APsaA Bylaws. However, we cannot rely on outside professionals to tell us what we want — they can only put into words what we tell them we want to do. While the suggestions above are intended to be neutral, other changes in the Bylaws could turn out to be anything but neutral and could have had major consequences for the balance of "power" in the organization. Such changes cannot be made without getting some group or another seriously agitated and if that group constitutes as many has 1/3 of the voting members the changes will be blocked.

The current secretive process which seems to have been launched, with no actual open discussion in advance, is definitely NOT the way to go, and will almost surely fail.

Date: Wed, 19 Jun 2002:
Civics Lesson — Part 11 —

2002 Election Problems

The Rules Which Govern APsaA Elections and Our Need to Follow Them

For those members who attended the meeting of members in Philadelphia last month, it should have been clear that a significant change had taken place: Outside the meeting hall were three tables at which members entering the meeting could sign in and receive VOTING CARDS. I think that this new symbolic recognition of members' voting rights at meetings is a turning point for APsaA and a dramatic demonstration of the leadership's understanding that we DO have to follow the rules under which APsaA is governed.

While it may seem petty to some that anyone should insist on following such rules, I think the alternative is unnecessary strife in the organization. This is so because APsaA is essentially a democratic organization and belongs to all the members. If we follow the rules of democratic governance, then we are ALL responsible for the policies the organization follows. Attempts to blame policies we dislike on "them" (i.e., the leadership) no longer hold water because in a democratically run organization "them" are all of "us."

In some earlier notes I have pointed to several ways that our current practices are either out of compliance with our bylaws, the New York State N-PCL, and/or Robert's Rules of Order — the very documents which lay out the framework of our democratic governance. In the May 2002 Executive Council, a motion introduced by Mike Gundle to have a Council Task Force look into these issues, and to come up with some possible solutions (but without any specific recommendations) for the Council to consider was tabled — in my opinion, a big error. Shutting the Council out of the process of addressing these issues, so that they can instead by addressed only by the Executive Committee closeted with the Association's counsel, is a VERY poor way to build confidence in our democratic intentions.

Meanwhile, there are some issues which cannot be tabled, which DO need to be addressed, and which cannot wait until our next meeting (in January 2003) because they directly impact the conduct of the coming elections this fall. Since the elections in APsaA have started to become "about something" rather than being the usual mere name recognition and personality contests, it is more important than ever that the elections be conducted according to fair, clear, and specific rules and timetables to minimize divisive arguments about the outcome.

Unfortunately, the current situation is a bit muddled. Here's why:

I. CHANGE IN OUR MEETING SCHEDULES.

Although our meeting schedule was changed for very good reasons, which most of us understood and supported, I have since come to regret the way in which that change was made. I don't think any of us realized at the time that the Bylaws of the Association, our governing document, actually dictate the meeting schedule. Therefore our having changed the schedule, i.e., changing the "fall" December meeting to January, and changing the "Annual" meeting to June, when it could no longer be in conjunction with the APA meeting, WITHOUT CHANGING THE BYLAWS was grossly improper.

Had those changes been made in a lawfully correct way, i.e., by submitting the proposal to change our meeting arrangements to a vote of the membership in the form of a Bylaws amendment (I would have voted in favor), the following problems MIGHT have come to light and MIGHT have been dealt with reasonably at that time.

II. ACCORDING TO THE BY-LAWS, UNTIL 1994, ELECTIONS WERE
SUPPOSED TO TAKE PLACE AT THE "FALL MEETING."
(Because the law requires elections to take place at meetings.)

The procedure for electing officers, which was set up in 1954, provided
for the election of officers at the fall Meeting. In 1994, the long established
and legal procedure for proxy mail voting was changed through a Bylaws
amendment. I have expressed my view that this change was a well meant but
unintentional violation of the New York Not-for-Profit Corporation Law.

Until 1994, the provisions for elections in the Bylaws read:

The election of a [President-Elect, Secretary, Treasurer] shall take
place ... at the Fall meeting of Members. OLD Article 4, Sec. 2(a & b).

and

All elections of officers shall be by written ballot. OLD Article 4,
Sec 2(c)

In 1994, these and the analogous provision for election of Councilors-at-
Large, were changed so that MAIL VOTING was substituted for mailed-in
proxy voting at the Fall Meeting:

The election of a [President-Elect, Secretary, Treasurer] shall be
conducted by mail ballot... Article 4, Sec. 2(a & b).

and

All elections of officers shall be conducted by mail ballot. Art. 4,
Sec 2(c)

Incredibly, when the above changes were made, no one seemed to notice that a number of other provisions in the Bylaws, those which set out the procedures for carrying our elections, are based on the assumption that the elections WILL occur at the "Fall Meeting" and these WERE NOT changed. In particular, some important deadlines for nominations are still expressed in terms of a certain number of "days before the Fall Meeting." (see below)

III. NOMINATIONS OF CANDIDATES FOR OFFICE

In all the recent elections held in APsaA, the nominees have been selected by the Executive Council, acting as a "Nominating Committee" as provided in the Bylaws. Usually there have been two candidates for President, Secretary, or Treasurer and four nominees for the election of two Councilors-at-large. Many members, however, are not aware that the Bylaws do not limit the number of nominees to such numbers and the Executive Council COULD nominate a larger slate of candidates (Note 1):

(d) The Nominating Committee shall nominate AT LEAST two eligible candidates for each office to be filled by election. [emphasis added] Article VII, Section 2(d)

The Secretary is then supposed PROMPTLY (I'm checking my mailbox daily) to MAIL a list of the nominees to all members:

(e) THE SECRETARY OF THE ASSOCIATION SHALL PROMPTLY MAIL A COPY OF THE LIST OF NOMINEES TO EACH MEMBER OF THE ASSOCIATION, together with a notice reminding members of the provisions of Section 3 of this Article VII, and inviting additional eligible nominations by the members thereunder. [emphasis added] Article VII, Section 2(e)

Section 3 of this article importantly expands the democratic rights of the members because under the provision of that section ANY NUMBER OF ADDITIONAL NOMINEES can be added to the election slate by direct nomination petitions from the membership. All it takes is the signatures of 20 members to add ONE OR MORE other nominees for any of the positions up for election. I believe that there WILL BE such nominees in the coming election.

However, the problem caused by the meeting change is this:

The Bylaws deadlines for the additional nominations are stated IN RELATION TO THE DATE OF THE "FALL MEETING" as follows:

SECTION 3. NOMINATIONS BY MEMBERS.

(a) Any twenty voting members of the Association may nominate, in writing, one or more eligible candidates for each office to be filled by election by sending a written communication, signed by such Members, to the Secretary of the Association not later than 60 DAYS PRIOR TO THE FALL MEETING OF MEMBERS AT WHICH THE ELECTIONS ARE TO TAKE PLACE.

(b) In the event of such nominations by members, the Secretary shall not later than ONE MONTH PRIOR TO SUCH FALL MEETING of Members, mail to each member of the Association a list of all candidates for each office to be filled by election, designating those candidates nominated by the Nominating Committee and those candidates nominated by action of the members under this Section 3. No other method of nomination is authorized. [emphases added]

While it would be simple enough to move the deadlines forward so that they are geared to the new "winter Meeting" in January, who is empowered to decide this?

Even worse, if such a change is made, then the 60 day deadline would occur in the middle of November, which could very well be too late for the publication of "position statements" in TAP by SOME of the nominees. Because all nominees in the election have to be treated equally (with one exception, see below) omission from TAP of any position statements of lawfully nominated nominees would be very unfair.

The single exception to the equal treatment of all nominees is the provision that the Secretary must inform the entire membership as to the way in which each person running for office was actually nominated ("… designating those candidates nominated by the Nominating Committee and those candidates nominated by action of the members…") as quoted above in Article VII, Section 3(b).

IV. CONSTRUCTION OF BALLOTS AND METHOD OF COUNTING

In the past few years, we have switched from the previous method of balloting, in which all candidates on the ballot were ranked (if there were more than two nominees), to a simpler system in which one voted only for the number of persons to be elected in such a case. This works well when there are only two nominees for an officership. However, when there are additional nominees, as we may have this year, the use of such a method could easily lead to no candidate's receiving a majority vote. However, the Bylaws specify that no one may be elected without having received a majority vote:

(c) … Every member entitled to vote shall have one vote for each office to be filled by election, and THE PERSON RECEIVING THE

MAJORITY OF VOTES CAST shall be deemed to be elected to such office. [emphasis added] Article IV, Section 2(c)

Because of the need to receive a majority vote, the exact structure of the ballot cannot be determined until the number of nominees is known, and that can't be known for sure until the 60-days-before-the-fall- Meeting deadline passes. The Bylaws wisely provide that the EXECUTIVE COMMITTEE will determine the structure of the ballot as follows:

(vi) The Executive Committee shall determine a form of ballot to ENSURE THAT THE FINAL RESULT SHALL YIELD A MAJORITY FOR EACH ELECTIVE POSITION (e.g., requiring second and third place votes, with successive elimination of the candidate with the lowest number of votes). [emphasis added] Article IV, Section 2(d) (vi)

The Executive Committee (now acting for the Council between Council meetings) will have to PROPOSE (but not IMPOSE) ways to resolve the other problems and it must do so in way, which is perceived to be completely fair. But while changing the TAP publication schedule is a simple step (at least administratively), changing the actual Bylaws deadlines without Bylaws amendments would be another instance of circumventing the Bylaws, a step which I think should be avoided.

Although no one thinks that there is any actual plot to undermine our democratic governance, failure to adhere to the "rules of the game" certainly can create the impression that the rules are not taken seriously.

"Where law ends, tyranny begins."
— William Pitt, Earl of Chatham. (1708–1778) Case of Wilkes. Speech, Jan. 9, 1770.

So what of those who say that we must once again ignore the Bylaws because of some "necessity?" William Pitt's son covered this one as well:

"Necessity is the plea for every infringement of human freedom. It is the argument of tyrants; it is the creed of slaves." — William Pitt (the younger), speech on the India Bill, Nov.1783

In the minutes of the Executive Committee for May 30, 2002, there is the following statement:

"6. MAIL BALLOT VERSUS PROXY BALLOT SYSTEM
"Dr. Fischer outlined the difficult dilemma of the Association in its efforts to follow its rules. Our Bylaws require that we follow Robert's Rules of Order, which forbids email votes; our Bylaws require mail ballots for election of officers; New York State laws for not-for-profit corporations require proxy ballots. In addition, we have established the precedent, since 1994, to conduct mail balloting, along with many other not-for-profit corporations in the state of New York. Finally, our Bylaws have gathered numerous inconsistencies over many years of revision, and a Bylaws Committee is currently hard at work to resolve these issues. After discussion, the ExCom decided to consult our legal counsel for guidance concerning the most reasonable course of action while our Bylaws are reconciled with the law."

Consultation with the APsaA legal counsel is a wise course of action at this point, as long as what is intended is to find a way of dealing with this situation which does not involve simply getting cover for further "fudging."

It should be clear that the Bylaws do not extend to the Executive Committee, the Executive Council, the Officers, or anyone other than the membership as a whole, the power to change Bylaws of the Association. If the only reasonable course of action in the current situation requires that a Bylaw provision be set aside or changed then it seems to me that the obtaining of the consent of the entire membership must be a condition for doing so. I believe that in such a situation a mail vote of the membership would be legal, provided that the VOTE IS UNANIMOUS, because the law allows actions by mail WHEN NO ONE OBJECTS. However, if a single member feels his or her rights are being trampled by whatever change is proposed, then it seems to me that the current Bylaws must be followed.

—————————

Note 1: I am aware that no one is breaking down the doors to run for office!

Wed, 6 Nov 2002:
Civics Lesson — Part 12 —

Analyst Farm?
The Erosion of Democratic Governance Compared with Orwell's "Animal Farm"

In this lesson I recapitulate my construction of how the democratic spirit has eroded from the Association so that now I, and many of you, have absolutely no say as to the standards of the profession of psychoanalysis (as represented by APsaA) despite our being full members:

In 1946, the new APsaA was formed in spirit of openness and democracy. It was a membership organization and each member, anyone who was a member of one of the original Societies, had an equal vote. The 1946 Bylaws are a mix of representative democracy and direct democracy, but the evident suspicion of centralized control shows up in the somewhat anti-democratic

242

fact that there was no requirement that Societies ELECT the Councilors who represent them (still true today.)

From the very start there were factions: those who saw the profession as open to change and exploration of new approaches — and those eager to establish "standards" to keep the profession respectable and medical. The latter began to change the role of the Board of [sic] Professional Standards from its intended role as a "deliberative body for the exchange of ideas between the constituent institutes" into a regulatory body similar in some ways to medical certifying boards. By 1951 it had assumed complete control over which institute graduates could join the Association.

In 1952, the Association became incorporated and as a result of an argument over the role of the Board on[sic] Professional Standards, the Association's legal counsel unambiguously opined that the final authority for ALL matters within APsaA was vested in the Board of Directors — the Executive Council. This opinion was published in the Bulletin, but then ignored.

Control of admissions to the organization had a powerful effect, because it limited new members to those who themselves "bought into" the system (about 2/3 of the new graduates) while the 1/3 who were less conformist were left out in the cold. During the period of very rapid growth, this meant that the Association became filled with members who actually believed that the Board on Professional Standards had the authority it claimed to have and who had no knowledge of its history.

In 1955, an Executive Committee of the Executive Council was formed. The formation of an Executive Committee is a known way of undermining the authority of a Board of Directors in a non-profit, although, with vigilance, it need not be so. However, the addition of the Chairman of the Board on Professional Standards to the Executive Committee was an omen of what was to come and caused a raised eyebrow (in writing) on the part of the Association's legal counsel, because the Chairman was not a member of the

Executive Council. This was eventually remedied by making the Chairman a voting member of the Executive Council (Although his/her status was changed to 'nonvoting' in 2001, both the Chairman and the Secretary seem still to vote in the Executive Committee!) Eventually, the Executive Committee began to complain about the amount of work it had to do in carrying the heavy decision-making burden it had generously assumed. Salaries were even suggested for the officers!

Over the years, the Board on Professional Standards, which is NOT ELECTED, or even chosen by the general membership, extended its power. Almost ALL offices in the Association were held by TA's (and still are to this day). TA's, who were in some way thought to know more about psychoanalysis than other members, were the only ones allowed to serve on the Board on Professional Standards, etc. They had more analytic patients, and higher incomes than general members. Whether due to acceptance of this system, fears of loss of referrals in large cities where TA's controlled most of the analytic referrals, or a failure to work through overidentification with TA status during the required training analysis with (of course) a TA, there was relatively little criticism of these developments.

In 1969, the law under which APsaA was incorporated was repealed and replaced by a new law. Under this new law it was even more explicit that the Board of Directors (the Executive Council) had the FINAL AUTHORITY for all APsaA policies. In fact, the Bylaws provision from 1946, which allowed the membership to vote to overrule the decisions of the Executive Council was no longer valid (even though it is still in the Bylaws.)

As the Association grew, it was clear that there was an implicit a two-class system of membership even after membership was opened to the non-certified. The Executive Council became more ceremonial as the Executive Committee appeared to take over its policy making responsibility. The Council itself deteriorated further as the office of Councilor became something of a parody and Councilors illegally switched places with other members during their terms, so that members, who were not actually Councilors or officially designated Alternates, were sent to meetings and actually (and illegally) cast votes. The carefully constructed bound books of the proceeding of the business meetings were discontinued in the mid-90's so that institutional memory of the reasons for subsequent decision is lost.

The meetings of members (strictly required by law) deteriorated so that no attendance was taken, no quorum was checked, and eventually hardly anyone bothered to show up. In the late 90's these meetings were reconstructed into a kind of parody of business meetings in which awards were handed out and a ceremonial atmosphere of "good feelings" was promoted for PR purposes. No lists of prospective members are circulated to the members in advance of the meetings; no votes are taken on new members (this is required by the bylaws), so they now become eligible to vote without being legal members; Life Members, to whom the bylaws do not accord the right to vote, nonetheless vote in elections; until recently the required mailing of proxies had been discontinued, etc., etc.

And finally, on top of the 70+ "Committees of the Executive Council" (almost all of them illegally constructed because of the presence of non-Councilors on them) were added two additional bureaucratic layers of "Coordinators" and a "Steering Committee," the latter of which eventually shrank in size to a small number of mostly TA's and former officers. Huge amounts of paper are generated in that there are now 4 reports a year from each of these committees flowing to Coordinators who send them on to the Steering Committee which now meets and then reports to the Executive Committee, etc. This created an enormous smoke screen of busyness when, in fact, the changes going on in the real world of psychoanalysis were largely unaddressed. TA's eventually seemed to become the only members who had any patients in analysis is some parts of the country.

Discussion of such timely questions as "Can real (including training) analyses take place at a frequency of three times a week?" (Note 1) seem not to be under serious study in the Board on Professional Standards. In the meantime, the myth that the Board on Professional Standards is empowered to decide who may be "certified" without any oversight from the Executive Council was promoted by the authoritarian minded members. Attempts to address this mythology were met with contempt, shunning or worse. Finally, a Task Force of 20 members, 17 of whom were TAs came within a hair's breadth of trying to change the APsaA Bylaws to establish some kind of "final authority" of the Board over educational and professional standards. (This change would not be legal under the state law even if it had been accomplished.)

So how did we get to this point? Maybe the following meditation on human nature shows that as a group, we are the same as everyone else and that we are subject to the same dark forces.

At just about the time that the creation of the new APsaA was under consideration, in 1943, George Orwell was writing his classic novel "Animal Farm" which was published, ironically, in 1945 and copyrighted in 1946, the year APsaA was actually formed. (Note 2)

Animal Farm is a satirical send-up of the Soviet Union as it existed in the 1940's and tells the story of an idealistic and egalitarian takeover of Manor Farm by the animals, who overthrow their human owners and take over the farm themselves. They rename the farm "Animal Farm." Their disdain for everything human outside the farm was encapsulated in the following seven commandments:

1. Whatever goes upon two legs is an enemy.
2. Whatever goes upon four legs, or has wings, is a friend.
3. No animal shall wear clothes.
4. No animal shall sleep in a bed.

5. No animal shall drink alcohol.
6. No animal shall kill any other animal.
7. ALL ANIMALS ARE EQUAL.

However, the pigs, who were considered to be brighter than the other animals, soon began to assume leadership of the farm, eventually changing the structure of the farm in such a way that they were in controlling and privileged positions. The sheep, due to their limited intelligence, were unable to remember all seven commandments, and instead reduced the entire ideology of "Animalism" to the slogan:

"FOUR LEGS GOOD, TWO LEGS BAD"

which they bleated, over and over, on ceremonial occasions and at times of stress.

Certain passages in Orwell's text, and some features of the history I have recounted above, strike me as similar. Can you match them up?

After the humans are driven from Manor Farm, the Animals have to decide who could be a member of their new organization. It is at first decided that every animal, domestic and wild, is considered an "animal" even though the dogs and cats are inclined, as earlier, to kill rats:

"Comrades," he said, "here is a point that must be settled. The wild creatures, such as rats and rabbits—are they our friends or our enemies? Let us put it to the vote. I propose this question to the meeting: Are rats comrades?"

The vote was taken at once, and it was agreed by an overwhelming majority that rats were comrades. There were only four dissentients, the three dogs and the cat, who afterwards was discovered to have voted on both sides. Major continued:

"I have little more to say. I merely repeat, remember always your duty of enmity towards Man and all his ways. Whatever goes upon two legs is an enemy. Whatever goes upon four legs, or has wings, is a friend."

However, at the weekly meetings, at which anyone can make proposals, only the pigs seem to have any ideas:

"After the hoisting of the flag all the animals trooped into the big barn for a general assembly which was known as the Meeting. Here the work of the coming week was planned out and resolutions were put forward and debated. It was always the pigs who put forward the resolutions. The other animals understood how to vote, but could never think of any resolutions of their own."

Then the pigs organize some committees:

"Snowball [a leading pig] also busied himself with organizing the other animals into what he called Animal Committees. He was indefatigable at this. He formed the Egg Production Committee for the hens, the Clean Tails League for the cows, the Wild Comrades' Re-education Committee (the object of this was to tame the rats and rabbits), the Whiter Wool Movement for the sheep, and various others, besides instituting classes in reading and writing. On the whole, these projects were a failure."

Some of the food on the farm seems to be disappearing, but then it is discovered that the pigs are seizing it:

"The mystery of where the milk went to was soon cleared up. It was mixed every day into the pigs' mash. The early apples were now ripening, and the grass of the orchard was littered with windfalls. The animals had assumed as a matter of course that these would be shared out equally; one day, however, the order went forth that all the windfalls were to be collected and brought to the harness-room for the use of the pigs. At this some of the other animals murmured, but it was no use. All the pigs were in full agreement on this point..."

Eventually, the pigs are empowered to decide all policies of the farm:

"Many meetings were held in the big barn, and the pigs occupied themselves with planning out the work of the coming season. It had come to be accepted that the pigs, who were manifestly cleverer than the other animals, should decide all questions of farm policy, though their decisions had to be ratified by a majority vote..."

Eventually the most dominant pig, Napoleon, cancels all public meetings:

"He announced that from now on the Sunday-morning Meetings would come to an end. They were unnecessary, he said, and wasted time. In future all questions relating to the working of the farm would be settled by a special committee of pigs, presided over by himself. These would meet in private and afterwards communicate their decisions to the others. The animals would still assemble on Sunday mornings to salute the flag, sing Beasts of England, and receive their orders for the week; but there would be no more debates.

Of course, this means a lot of work for the pigs:

"Comrades," he said, "I trust that every animal here appreciates the sacrifice that Comrade Napoleon has made in taking this extra labor upon himself. Do not imagine, comrades, that leadership is a pleasure! On the contrary, it is a deep and heavy responsibility. No one believes more firmly than Comrade Napoleon that all animals are equal. He would be only too happy to let you make your decisions for yourselves. But sometimes you might make the wrong decisions, comrades, and then where should we be?"

Eventually, production on the farm deteriorates, but by controlling the communications, which allowed the facts that there isn't enough food, and that the animals are constantly fighting among themselves, is suppressed because it is bad PR-wise for people to know this outside the farm:

"Starvation seemed to stare them in the face.

"It was vitally necessary to conceal this fact from the outside world. Emboldened by the collapse of the windmill, the human beings were inventing fresh lies about Animal Farm. Once again it was being put about that all the animals were dying of famine and disease, and that they were continually fighting among themselves and had resorted to cannibalism and infanticide. Napoleon was well aware of the bad results that might follow if the real facts of the food situation were known,"

However, the appearance is maintained that the farm has grown richer and the pigs seem to be very busy:

"Much of this work was of a kind that the other animals were too ignorant to understand. For example, Squealer told them that the pigs had to expend enormous labors every day upon mysterious things called "files," "reports," "minutes," and "memoranda." These were large sheets of paper which had to be closely covered with writing, and as soon as they were so covered, they were burnt in the furnace."

Despite all this adversity, the Animals are proud to be part of the farm, even though the pigs now are living in the farmhouse, wearing clothes, and sleeping in beds:

"And yet the animals never gave up hope. More, they never lost, even for an instant, their sense of honor and privilege in being members of Animal Farm. They were still the only farm in the whole county — in all England! — owned and operated by animals."

As everyone knows, at some point, as the pigs gained total control of Animal Farm, and eventually established close relationships with their human neighbors, six of the original seven commandments are erased from the wall of the barn, and only the seventh commandment remains — in modified form. It read:

ALL ANIMALS ARE EQUAL
BUT SOME ANIMALS ARE MORE EQUAL THAN OTHERS

Maybe instead of opening our meetings as we presently do, we should consider having everyone say in unison several times:

"FOUR SESSIONS GOOD, THREE SESSIONS BAD"

So, we can all keep reminding ourselves what we are supposed to believe in.

———————

Note 1: In case anyone cares, I do not favor such a change.

Note 2: Orwell's full text of "Animal Farm" is on line at: https://gutenberg. net.au/ebooks01/0100011h.html

Date: Wed, 21 Sep 2005:

Civics Lesson — Part 13 —

Membership

Three years ago, I began a series of notes on one of our lists, which I called "Civics Lessons." In those notes I shared with other members what I had been learning of the history of the governance problems in APsaA.

Many, but not all, members appreciated that work. Those notes, for anyone interested, are at:

http://mosher.com/apsaastuff/apsaacivics.htm

I was motivated to write this new addition to the "Civics Lessons" by the following passage, which appeared in the minutes of the Executive Committee for June 4, 2005:

"6. MEETING OF MEMBERS PREPARATION Mr. Stein reported that Tina Faison spends about a day and a half preparing lists and proxies for the Meeting of Members. Although the proxies are rarely used to vote on any issue during the meetings, it was agreed that the process must continue. The Executive Committee asked Mr. Stein to outline the high cost of this governance process for publication in TAP."

While it is true that our costs of governance are higher than they would be if APsaA were a typical "nonprofit" corporation, these costs are not excessive. They result from the fact that APsaA is a MEMBERSHIP CORPORATION, not a NON-PROFIT CORPORATION WITH "MEMBERS" (which may be the type of organization that Mr. Stein had in mind in his comments about the meeting of members.)

Confused? In this note I want to explain the difference between these two similar sounding kinds of organizations.

I. WHAT IT MEANS TO BE A "MEMBER"

Although you'd think this is a simple matter, the fact is that most of our APsaA members are unaware (as I was until I read up on this subject) of the actual meaning, in a technical sense, of being a member of APsaA. The confusion on this subject arises from the fact that APsaA is a MEMBERSHIP CORPORATION. This is NOT the same as a typical not-for-profit corporation, WHICH DOES NOT HAVE "real" members — even though there are individuals associated with such nonmembership corporations who are referred to as "members!"

The confusion is caused in part by the fact that APsaA is regulated under the same law, which governs NON-MEMBERSHIP nonprofit corporations.

APsaA was originally incorporated in New York under the old "Membership Corporation Law." That ancient law was replaced in the late 1960's by the more general Not-for-Profit Corporation Law (the N-PCL). Membership corporations, like APsaA were brought under the N-PCL, but the N-PCL also applies to MANY not-for-profit corporations, which are NOT REAL MEMBERSHIP corporations.

However, for corporations which ARE membership corporations, like APsaA, the N-PCL actually strengthened the protections for members' rights in such MEMBERSHIP CORPORATIONS. The law contains special provisions for MEMBERSHIP CORPORATIONS. The concept of "membership" is intimately tied to your right to vote, and your right to vote is intimately tied to the Annual Meeting of Members.

Here's an example of a not-for-profit non-membership corporation of which I am a "member" but which does not actually have MEMBERS in the legal sense, which I am referring to:

> Our local public TV station is organized as a not-for-profit corporation. The Corporation, "WMHT Educational Telecommunications, Inc." collects donations from the TV audience and everyone who contributes is called a "member" and gets a program guide.

However, "members" of this station DO NOT VOTE FOR THE directors (or officers) because this is not a MEMBERSHIP corporation. The corporation, like MOST not-for-profits is managed by the Board of Directors (also sometimes called "Trustees") who ELECT THEIR OWN SUCCESSORS. This arrangement is similar in organization to a religion with a self-perpetuating directorate.

So-called "members" of the TV station have no role in governance. The fact that non-membership corporations of this type AND real membership corporations are governed by the same law seems to be the source of considerable confusion.

In her book on the subject, Victoria Bjorklund puts it this way:

[Under the N-PCL] "Member" refers to one having membership rights in a corporation in accordance with the provisions of its certificate of incorporation and its bylaws.

She goes on:

"This differs from common usage of the word 'member' by nonprofit organizations, which often refers to preferred customer or patron status. This frequent use of the term does not give such contributors or customers the legal rights of membership."

Members also have obligations to follow the rules:

"Joining [as a member] a nonprofit organization means one is bound by its rules and barred from seeking legal redress unless the corporate rule or action contravenes the certificate of incorporation or a strong public policy. VALID BYLAWS ARE PART OF THE CONTRACT OF MEMBERSHIP." [emphasis added]

For "managers" concerned with "efficiency" of operation in nonprofits, having real "members" is a major pain in the keister because the managers cannot simply establish a cozy relationship with the directors and the officers and run the organization in the way they see fit, including hand-picking succeeding board members.

Instead, in a real membership corporation, in which the Board — and perhaps even the officers — are elected by the entire membership, there can be a much wider distribution of political power; member opinion has real teeth because the members (typically) VOTE to elect the Board of Directors.

The N-PCL was written to parallel as much as possible, for membership corporations, the structure of business corporations. In business corporations, unless there are special provisions to modify this (like in Google) each shareholder has one vote for each share s/he owns. In a membership corporation, each MEMBER is conceptualized as owning ONE share of the organization and therefore has ONE vote. This vote is typically exercised at the ANNUAL MEETING OF MEMBERS. The Annual Meeting of Members is required BY LAW.

In many business corporations, the management finds it inconvenient that the shareholders are able to vote and some actually seem to resent such voting rights. In the Google case, the two founders of the company own 1/3 of the shares, but their special shares give them TEN votes per share so the two of them, with 30% of the stock, have 80% of the votes. Many other corporate managers wish that their shareholder also had no effective voting rights, and this can happen with the mangers/officers and the "members" in a not-for-profit corporation, as well.

In fact, in her book on the N-PCL Ms. Bjorklund recommends that when setting up a new not-for-profit, the "membership" form of a corporation should be avoided, presumably if the mission is "efficient" pursuit of an axiomatic goal:

"… counsel should recommend the non-membership form as preferable."

Although the membership form might have some advantages, she goes on:

"[T]he disadvantages of the membership form outweigh its benefits. For larger organizations, it may be difficult to gather a quorum for the [required] annual meeting. The proxy process is expensive, time consuming, and often ignored." …

"Non-membership status avoids many of the housekeeping requirements and expenses such as the annual meeting, where members elect directors and conduct other membership business. Because members may have standing to sue, non-membership status reduces the danger of litigation. It more easily enables a board to execute policy. Despite the dangers of a self-perpetuating board, non-membership corporations may more easily carry out the non-profit's mission."

II. DO WE NEED A MEMBERSHIP CORPORATION?

So given this, why is APsaA organized and incorporated as it is? Beside the fact that the membership structure supports a democratic organization and is therefore a good thing, it is also true that we don't have any choice. The reasons are simple:

(1) The nonmember form of organization is intended for non-profits like charities, certain arts and educational organizations, and for similar organizations in which "fund raising" rather than members' support (expressed through willingness to pay dues) defines the legitimacy of the organization.

(2) APsaA is a professional MEMBERSHIP organization and it would make no sense to have an organization of such "members" who cannot vote and have no membership rights. Being a true membership organization, a MEMBERSHIP CORPORATION best corresponds to what APsaA actually is. I don't know of any professional membership organization that does not have real members.

(3) Finally in order to protect the rights of members in the Constituent Organizations, the bylaws of the IPA REQUIRE all Constituent Organizations

[such as APsaA] to be incorporated as professional membership organizations:

"(9) INCORPORATION. Each Constituent Organization shall be separately INCORPORATED AS A MEMBERSHIP ORGANIZATION OR ASSOCIATION, if possible under the laws of its territory, via organizational instruments that satisfy IPA Criteria. In jurisdictions with laws that distinguish between business and not-for-profit corporations, a Constituent Organization shall be the latter." [second emphasis added] IPA Bylaws, Article IV(A)(9)

I called attention to one aspect of the erosion of members' rights in APsaA in an earlier in February 2002 in Civics Lesson #8:

MEMBERSHIP POWER HAS BEEN ERODED BY IGNORING RULES RELATED TO MEETINGS OF MEMBERS: http://mosher. com/APsaAstuff/APsaAcivics.htm#cl8

Up until that time, the LEGALLY REQUIRED Annual Meeting of MEMBERS had become a sort of PR "dog and pony show" with no attempt to keep track of who was actually at the meetings (many non-members seemed to drift in), to track who might vote should a vote take place, and with failure to send out the required proxies. No attempt was being made to determine if a quorum was present (in person or by proxy)!

Of course, attending to these issues is an inconvenience and a small expense. However, these costs are the overhead of democracy and are part of the protection of members' rights in APsaA. The Annual Meeting is the time we cast our votes (in person or by proxy.) As Representative John Lewis said at the Judge Roberts hearing last week:

"The right to vote is precious, almost sacred. It is the most powerful non- violent tool we have in a democratic society."

As a membership corporation, we have considerable latitude in how we structure our organization and we can even harm ourselves, politically speaking, by making governance changes which vote away or weaken some of our existing members' rights. As we get into a more focused discussion of APsaA governance in the coming months, I'll add some other "Civics Lessons" with my view of what our existing members' rights currently are, and how we might lose them by making unwise changes in our governance structure in the interest of "efficiency."

CHAPTER 16

Introduction: A. A. Brill; Certification

by Arnold D. Richards

The paper on A. A. Brill (1) and the paper about certification (see below) should be read as a pair. A core idea in the second paper is that certification is a consequence of the non-medical exclusion policy propounded by A. A. Brill. In this paper we discuss the history of membership and certification in American psychoanalysis. Paul and I led the fight to end the certification requirement for TA appointments after it was no longer a requirement for membership, running for office, or voting for bylaws. This paper had a positive impact on the controversy. It was followed by the adoption of a local option for the certification requirement and the sunsetting of BoPS, in which it had been enshrined. Inclusion and democratization were a high priority for Paul and I am pleased that I was of help in that effort. One of my best collaborative efforts. It was one of my best collaborative efforts. I appreciated his erudition, his knowledge of history and his attention to detail.

Abraham Arden Brill, 1874–1948

A.A. Brill was one of the most influential American psychiatrists of the past century. His efforts and personal views were major factors in the development of psychiatry, psychotherapy, and psychoanalysis in the United States during the century's first half. Brill left the Eastern European village of his childhood at the age of 14 and came, alone and without resources, to the United States and New York City to seek his fortune. By the time he was 29, he had graduated from the Columbia University College of Physician and Surgeons and then trained in psychiatry and neurology. In 1907, he traveled to Europe to pursue the latest advances in psychiatry and became acquainted with the work of Sigmund Freud. Upon his return to New York City, he began what was the first private practice of psychoanalysis in the United States (1).

Brill became Freud's first English translator, and Brill's translations played a major role in the popularization of psychoanalysis in the United States. In 1911, Brill organized a group of 20 physician colleagues to found the first American psychoanalytic organization, the New York Psychoanalytic Society. Brill thought of himself as the father of American psychoanalysis, writing in 1938:

> Psychoanalysis was unknown in this country until I introduced it in 1908.... [psychoanalytic terminology], some of which I was the first to coin into English expression, can now be found in all standard English dictionaries. Words like abreaction, transference, repression, displacement, unconscious, which I introduced as Freudian concepts, have been adopted and are used to give new meanings, new values to our knowledge of normal and abnormal behavior. (2)

Throughout his career, Brill was unalterably opposed to the practice of psychoanalysis and psychotherapy by nonphysicians and worked diligently to promote psychoanalysis as a subspecialty of psychiatry. In 1931, he helped to found the New York Psychoanalytic Institute, devoted to training physicians in psychoanalysis. As a result of almost a decade of Brill's efforts, the American Psychiatric Association established a Section on Psychoanalysis in 1934 with Brill as its first head.

REFERENCES

Richards A: (199). AA Brill and the politics of exclusion. *Am J Psychoanal* 17:9–28.

_____ *(2005). Psychoanal. Rev., (92)(6):865-894* The History of Membership and Certification in the APsaA: Old Demons, New Debates by Paul Mosher MD and Arnold Richards MD

Freud S: (1938). *The Basic Writings of Sigmund Freud,* trans. by A.A. Brill. New York: Random House.

CHAPTER 17

The History of Membership and Certification in the APsaA: Old Demons, New Debates

by Paul Mosher MD and Arnold Richards MD
Psychoanalytic Review (2005), Vol 92, 6: 865-894

"It is true that in all fields a person may repeat the same mistake for innumerable years and call it experience." —C. P. Oberndorf, A History of Psychoanalysis in America, p. 24:6.

A.A. Brill, "the first American psychoanalyst," can be regarded as the founder of the American Psychoanalytic Association (APsaA), and in today's APsaA the influence of Brill's personality is still visible. Clear traces of the ways questions of status and inclusion determined his outlook on life can still be found in how the issues of certification and membership are framed in the APsaA today.

Historian Paula Fass has linked Brill's professional attitude toward membership and status to the dynamics of his character and his personal history (Fass, 1968). Brill was a poor boy from eastern Europe (Kanczuca, Galicia/Austro-Hungary) who emigrated to America in the late 1880s. When he was fourteen years old he landed in New York alone, with two dollars in his pocket, determined to make a place for himself in society. He studied medicine at Columbia at the dawn of the twentieth century, and trained as a psychiatrist for four years at New York's Central Islip State Hospital. On a trip he made to Europe, to broaden his knowledge of international trends in psychiatry, Brill was captivated by the dynamic psychiatry of Freud. He pursued additional training at the psychoanalytically informed Burgholzli in Switzerland, and paid a visit to Freud himself, in Vienna, who selected Brill to translate his works into English.

After his return to the United States in 1908, while working at Columbia's Vanderbilt Clinic, Brill established a private practice in New York, and thus became the first American psychoanalyst. Brill, who by this time had already joined the exclusive Harmony Club, also displayed his taste for distinction and status by promoting the requirement of a medical degree for membership in the New York Psychoanalytic Society, which he had founded, and this restriction (the exclusion of lay analysts) determined the earliest practices of what—to Freud's chagrin—eventually became the APsaA. Brill was profoundly committed to establishing the legitimacy in the United States of this exotic European import by making it a respectable medical subspecialty within psychiatry.

The New York Psychoanalytic Society began at a meeting with his medical colleagues at Brill's home on February 11, 1911. By 1912, the New York Psychoanalytic Society had 27 members, all physicians. At that period, in its early history, most meetings were attended by only a handful of members, and the Society functioned more as an intimate study group than as an administrative institution.

In the same year as Brill founded his organization, a short-lived "American Psychoanalytic Association" was founded in Baltimore. This group was established at the instigation of Ernest Jones with the blessings of Freud, who had hoped that Brill would form an American Psychoanalytic Association with James Jackson Putnam as its first president. The choice of Putnam reflected Freud's preference for a non-Jew to head the psychoanalytic organization. Brill was invited to join the original "American Psychoanalytic Association" with his own group, and serve as its secretary. Brill did become a member of the Baltimore organization, but, resisting intense pressure from Jones and Freud, he neither became an officer nor worked to merge his New York-based Society with the new organization.

While Brill's collegial and cohesive New York Psychoanalytic Society survived and prospered, the Baltimore-based American Psychoanalytic Association, whose founding members were a mixed group of psychiatrists and psychoanalysts, did not flourish and ultimately was dissolved. Eventually, prominent members of the Baltimore-based Association, such as William Alanson White, floated proposals intended to disband their American Psychoanalytic Association and to merge it into what was later to become the American Psychiatric Association—then called the American Psychopathological Association.

Although Brill's New York group was strongly medical in its orientation and eager to be recognized as a legitimate branch of psychiatry, it was, at the same time, understandably resistant to the prospect of being absorbed into a larger group of psychiatrists, many of whom were openly hostile to psychoanalytic concepts. The conflicting interests, to belong to American psychiatry while not being digested by it, made it impossible for medical analysts over the decades to agree on proposals to establish *board certification* within psychiatry for psychoanalysis.

I. "CERTIFICATION" ATTESTS TO PSYCHOANALYTIC TRAINING

In the 1920s, before standardized rules for the training of psychoanalysts had been established in the United States, people who wished to become psychoanalysts—whether or not they had medical degrees—traveled to Europe to be trained by established psychoanalysts there. When they returned to the United States with a *certificate* from their teacher documenting that they were now trained as analysts, they expected to be admitted to the New York Psychoanalytic Society. In other words, the certificate attested to their *training;* it was not a recognition of the postgraduation competence of these individuals. But although at first the New York Psychoanalytic Society accepted such people as members, it changed its position as it became ever more strongly committed to limiting the practice of psychoanalysis to physicians. In 1934 it reached an agreement with the International Psychoanalytical Association (IPA) providing that analysts "who had been trained in Europe and *were so certified* but who in other respects did not meet the requirements of the Society to which they applied could be refused admission" (Oberndorf, 1953, p. 196).

Brill's medically oriented New York Psychoanalytic Society survived through the succeeding decades, and by the end of the 1920s somewhat similar analytic societies had been founded in Washington-Baltimore, Chicago, and Boston. In 1932, those four societies confederated to form a new American Psychoanalytic Association, the forerunner of today's APsaA. Each of these societies had or was forming a training institute, and these training institutes were not in any sense a function of the APsaA or any outside organization; each training institute was administered by its respective society.

Between 1932 and 1946, the APsaA was a confederation with two classes of members: individual members and member societies. An individual member of a component society was automatically accorded individual membership in the APsaA as well. There was no central control over eligibility for individual membership in the Association. Some issues were determined by votes of individual members, but other issues were voted on by societies: that is, each member society had one vote. The Council on Professional Training could make recommendations, but no change in the official recommendations of the Association regarding training and standards could be made without the *unanimous* approval of all the member societies. The Pre-1946 Bylaws said very clearly that *the Authority of the Council on Professional Training shall be limited to making recommendations.*

The Association was dealing in the 1930s with several intertwined questions: the absorption of the refugee psychoanalysts, the enduring question of lay analysis, and the controversial proposal to establish a psychoanalytic credential and subspecialty within the American Psychiatric Association. There was serious concern about a shortage of analytic patients in New York; it was feared that the influx of European analysts (some of whom were not physicians) would make the shortage worse. It is not unlikely that the influx of nonphysician analysts from Europe contributed to the interest in making psychoanalysis "medical." In 1938, the Association introduced a new rule stating that only physicians who had completed a psychiatric residency at an approved institution could become members (Hale, 1995, p. 128). This rule was part of a larger effort that reflected the aspiration of Brill and others to make psychoanalysis a medical discipline, and found expression in proposals to create a *board certification* in psychoanalysis. Board certification in medicine is the traditional way legitimacy is achieved for practitioners of new specialties and subspecialties, and to some extent it limits the ability of non-certified physicians to compete in the practice of their specialty.

II. Certification In Psychoanalysis as a Subspecialty of Psychiatry

Brill and his colleagues believed that achieving such *medical board certification* would legitimize psychoanalysis as a medical discipline, and, in the United States, *certification in psychoanalysis* initially referred to the possibility of establishing psychoanalysis as a medical specialty. The New York Psychoanalytic Society, accordingly, passed a resolution in 1941 urging the APsaA, the national organization, to advocate such a certification within the American Board of Psychiatry and Neurology. However, the APsaA leadership rejected this proposal on the grounds that the proportion of psychoanalysts within psychiatry was not yet sufficient to give the APsaA adequate influence on the certifying board. As an alternative, the leadership of the 1932-1946 APsaA declared that, for the time being, an APsaA membership card would constitute *official certification in psychoanalysis* (Knight, 1953). So, while "medical board certification" attests to the postgraduate assessment of a professional, the "certification" that Knight and the APsaA leadership instituted was simply an affirmation of the fact of training—because *completion of training* was the only criterion for eligibility to join the APsaA at that time.

The young APsaA's response to the problems created by the influx of European analysts escaping the Nazis was the cause of serious disagreement with the IPA on the issue of lay analysis— Brill's *bete noire*. Brill had succeeded in establishing the M.D. degree as a requirement for membership, first in the New York Psychoanalytic Society and then in the APsaA. But this position was not universally supported. When a group of psychoanalysts formed the new San Francisco Psychoanalytic Society, which joined the APsaA in 1942, the new Society was told by the APsaA that it could not retain as full members the distinguished lay analysts Anna Maenchen, Erik Erikson, and Siegfried Bernfeld. The San Francisco Psychoanalytic Society capitulated reluctantly, giving their lay analysts affiliate membership status in their Society, since giving them full membership would have meant that they were also automatically full members of the APsaA.

Even the New York Psychoanalytic Society had offered a second-class membership status to such New York lay analysts as Theodore Reik, Erich Fromm, and Ernst Kris. But Brill staunchly resisted the inclusion of psychologists as full society members, and Brill's exclusionary views held sway in the APsaA for decades. In fact, as late as 1954 the American Psychoanalytic Association, the American Psychiatric Association, and the American Medical Association published a joint resolution holding that *all psychotherapy* was a medical procedure and so should be practiced only by physicians.

Other than in a few exceptional places and times in history, psycho-analysts have always been keenly aware of the limited demand for their services, the controversy over psychoanalytic practice by nonphysicians has a long and troubled history going back at least to 1912 in Europe. According to Schroter (2004) Carl Jung wrote to Freud in 1912 complaining about a potential nonmedical psychoanalyst, saying, "There are just enough patients for ourselves" (p. 161). Schroter comments in a footnote: "It can be safely assumed that *economic concerns,* as expressed by Jung in the above quotation, played a critical role in most stages of the controversy over lay analysis. *Since, however, they were rarely admitted openly but rather tended to be veiled by statements of principle,* their impact is difficult to assess" (p. 161, emphasis added).

Tensions in the profession increased in the early 1940s, with emotional disagreements between those who advocated a Freudian orthodoxy and those who advocated academic pluralism and the freedom to challenge the basic Freudian tenets. In April 1941, Karen Horney was demoted from training analyst to lecturer by a majority of those voting (but not a majority of those present, because many abstained) at a meeting of the New York Psychoanalytic Society. After the vote was announced, Horney, Clara Thompson, and three younger members of the New York Psychoanalytic Society (Kellman, Robbins, and Efron) walked out of the meeting and, later, resigned from the society (Hale, 1995, p. 143). The story, apocryphal perhaps, is that they stood outside the building on West 86th Street singing "Let My People Go," and then walked to the bar at the Tip Toe Inn on Broadway, where they discussed founding a new Society. Later in 1941, Karen Horney and her associates founded the American Association for the Advancement of Psychoanalysis (AAAP), whose very title infuriated the New York Psychoanalytic Society. The AAAP itself evolved into several other groups (in part because of the lay-analyst/medical-affiliation issue), among them the William Alanson White Institute and the New York Medical College group.

271

The William Alanson White Institute was founded by Clara Thompson and Eric Fromm, who felt that Horney had marginalized them by not assigning them new candidates for analysis and supervision. The name was probably chosen by Harry Stack Sullivan in honor of his mentor William Alanson White, who was also one of the founding members of the APsaA in 1911.

The New York Psychoanalytic Society had formed an Educational Committee in 1923 and an institute in 1932. Sander Rado was the Society's first director of training. But he was removed from his position as Education Director of the New York Psychoanalytic Society in 1941 due to perceived deviations from orthodoxy in his teaching. In 1942, Rado, David Levy (a former president of the APsaA), George Daniels, Abraham Kardiner, and Carl Binger left the New York Psychoanalytic Institute and started a new psychoanalytic society in New York, the Association for Psychoanalytic Medicine; they also went on to found a new training institute associated with the College of Physicians and Surgeons of Columbia University. However, the bylaws of the APsaA, which allowed only one society in each city, prohibited the affiliation of this new society with the APsaA. The Rado group, who wanted a psychoanalytic society affiliated with a university, applied for recognition by the APsaA in 1942, and the group's members threatened to resign from the APsaA if the new society was not recognized. A proposal to amend the APsaA bylaws, which still prohibited more than one institute per city, was defeated. Rado threatened to create a new national organization unless a way could be found to include the Association for Psychoanalytic Medicine within the APsaA.

These splits might not have had any impact on the APsaA, except that the William Alanson White group, which included Erich Fromm and Clara Thompson, had been designated as the New York branch of the Washington School of Psychiatry, which was a part of the Baltimore-Washington Psychoanalytic Society and Institute. This in turn was an affiliate of the APsaA. Candidates trained at William Alanson White, therefore, were eligible to become members of the APsaA. But that situation changed when the Baltimore Society ended its association with the Washington School, and eventually the William Alanson White Institute analysts who were still members of the APsaA sought independent-affiliate status for their institute in the APsaA. A committee was formed to consider their application. The deliberations were drawn out, to say the least, and they ended when the William Alanson White members realized that they never would be accepted because of their heretical interpersonal point of view. The situation also changed because after the Baltimore and Washington institutes split, the Washington School of Psychiatry was divorced from the Washington Psychoanalytic Institute and could no longer maintain its accreditation in the APsaA (Gray, personal communication, April 14, 2004).

In 1946, following contentious years of negotiation and partly as a result of the fallout from the Columbia Institute controversy, the American Psychoanalytic Association that had been founded in 1932 was disbanded, and a new American Psychoanalytic Association—the one we have today—was formed. The founding principles of the new Association represented a compromise between those who demanded diversity and those who insisted on "standards" and central control. Under the new organization, societies and institutes were now completely independent. The rule that only one society could exist in a given geographic area was abolished. These were major changes that favored those pressing for diversity, and that threatened those who feared that new competing institutes would deviate from the traditional training standards—that is, a frequency of at least four sessions per week for training analyses and control cases and four years of academic courses.

By the time the APsaA was reorganized in 1946, Rado's new Columbia Institute was an "approved institute" and the new Society was an "affiliate society," but the White Institute was unaffiliated and not APsaA approved. We have taken note of this early history at some length because of our belief

273

that the resolution of the William Alanson White issue and the admission of Rado's institute had important consequences for the character and the later history of the APsaA.

III. APsaA Membership "Equivalent" to Medical Board Certification

In the new APsaA, in its 1946 incarnation (which marks the beginning of the current Association), the Board on Professional Standards was required by the new bylaws to certify in writing that each individual applicant for membership met its ethical and professional standards. This certifying process thus became an additional criterion for membership and was carried out by a membership committee of the Board on Professional Standards in an increasingly controversial and rigorous manner. The 1946 bylaws did not explain clearly whether what was being certified to was *the fact of training* or the result of a *post-training evaluation of the applicant* by a body outside the applicant's institute. This ambiguity was at the crux of what would become a fifty-year-long dispute in the APsaA. Until 1977, a prospective Active Member applied for *membership* in the APsaA through the certifying process of the membership committee; that post-1946 membership process was not formally called "certification" until 1977.

Even though it was not explicitly called "certification" before 1977, from 1946 forward, characterizing membership in the APsaA as the equivalent of a certifying medical credential took the place of the unattainable further step of gaining a board certification of psychoanalysts as practitioners of a subspecialty of psychiatry. It served further to reinforce the exclusion of non-physicians from the profession. These two trends—exclusion of nonphysicians from psychoanalytic training and practice, and use of a medical specialty-like certification process for medical psychoanalysts—

took root only in the United States. One may rightly ask, therefore, what it was about the historical development of the profession in the United States that led to this unique situation.

Certainly there is no simple explanation of this phenomenon. We have already referred to A.A. Brill s personal inclination toward exclusivity. Other writers have remarked on psycho-dynamic factors that might be important. Wallerstein thought that the issue of identity in the profession was an important determinant. Is psychoanalysis a branch of general psychology, as Freud believed, or is psychoanalysis a part of medicine—a sub-specialty within the specialty of psychiatry as Brill believed it must be? Levine (2003) has explored additional possible dynamic determinants.

Furthermore, Brill himself was strongly influenced in his support of board certification and the exclusion of analysts without M.D.'s by the times in which he lived—times in which the structure of medicine and psychiatry in the United States was changing dramatically.

"The problem of lay analysis" was the cause of such extreme contention between the European IPA and the APsaA that it threatened to fracture the international psychoanalytic movement and was, ultimately, put to rest only by a truce in the form of a makeshift resolution. A full understanding of this issue is impossible without an understanding of the social environment in the United States during the 1920s and 1930s, the two decades in which the U.S. position hardened. It was in the 1920s (the anything-goes Roaring Twenties) that American psychoanalysts took the first official steps to limit psychoanalytic practice to physicians. And it was during the difficult and dreary days of the late 1930s (the depth of the Great Depression) that the proposal to add the requirement of board certification in psychoanalysis first surfaced. The restriction of access to professional practice in the healing arts was deeply imbedded in the *Weltanschauung* of this entire era.

In 1929, an APA Committee endorsed the creation of a set of qualifications for a practitioner to be seriously regarded as a psychiatrist (APA, 1929).

The movement for special qualifications in the medical professions gained momentum in 1933 when the existing four certifying boards combined to form the Advisory Board of Medical Specialties (Starr, 1982, p. 357). The movement to limit the practice of specialties through certification of specialists was intensified by the severely competitive environment for practice of the Great Depression (Starr, 1982, p. 356).

The Flexner Report, which was published in 1910, just two years after Brill established his practice, pushed for restricting the training of physicians to university-based programs. Prior to that time, physicians were trained in proprietary medical schools (some of which were known to be diploma mills), and by being apprenticed to practicing physicians. Over the 1920s and 1930s the last of these schools closed down as the Flexner Report's recommendations were implemented. Furthermore, while the Flexner Report signaled the beginning of closer regulation of the healing professions, it addressed mainly *institutions* claiming to train physicians. The issues relating to the regulation of individual practitioners were addressed through legislative methods.

In 1912, accreditation of medical colleges by a federation of state boards began (Beck, 2004). But it was not until 1926 that the New York Legislature passed the Webb-Lomis bill, which lead to the New York Medical Practice Act. This Act required the *licensing* of physicians by the state. The aim of this law was to eliminate practitioners who were either outright frauds or who had been trained in obsolete or inadequate programs, all loosely referred to as *quacks*.

The principal targets of this bill were chiropractors. According to Wallerstein (1998, p. 29), the Europeans believed that Brill was behind this law, and that its intention was to declare lay analysis illegal, but we have found nothing in the historical record to support this belief.

It is not well remembered today that in the very earliest part of the twentieth century, psychiatry was almost completely limited to hospital practice. The American Psychiatric Association was founded in 1844 by thirteen superintendents of asylums. Outpatient treatment of patients with nonpsychotic disorders such as hysteria was carried out mostly by *neurologists,* some of whom used elementary psychotherapeutic approaches such as persuasion combined with physical approaches.

It is the advent of psychoanalysis in the United States in the period after Brill established his practice *that began the transformation of American psychiatry from a purely inpatient discipline to one in which outpatient treatment was feasible.* Between 1922 and 1932, membership in the American Psychiatric Association increased by 40 percent. From an organization in which all but a negligible proportion had been engaged exclusively in hospital practice, by 1932 only 54 percent of its members fit this description! (Russell, 1932). Much of the growth during the Roaring Twenties had come from practitioners who were practicing analysis or other outpatient therapies based on the ideas that psychoanalysis had brought to this country. This transformation in the APsaA, related to the influx of psychoanalysts and other psychiatrist-psychotherapists, appears to have caused something of a culture shock among the old guard of hospital superintendents.

These changes highlighted the fact that there was at that time no formal definition of "psychiatrist." Although there had been a movement to define special qualifications for practice in certain subfields of medicine (the "specialties") starting in 1917, there was no certification or other special qualification in psychiatry. In 1928, Adolph Meyer, in his Presidential Address to the APA, urged the creation of a diploma in psychiatry. "The fate of progress depends on minimal standards," he said.

Psychiatry had resisted such certification for the prior two decades partly because the old-guard psychiatrists thought of themselves not as specialists, but rather as experts in the complete medical care of hospitalized patients with chronic mental disorders. However, the situation had changed drastically by the 1930s. As noted earlier, the new-guard psychiatrists, largely analytically influenced outpatient practitioners, had now come to comprise half of the membership of the organization. In 1933, James B. May, in his presidential address to the APA, urged the creation of a board certification in psychiatry (Russell, 1932). He spoke of the invasion of the field of psychiatry—first by neurologists and then by psychologists, and blamed the second invasion on the advent of psychoanalysis. He wrote:

The next great invasion of the field of psychiatry was directly attributable to the psychologists. This was probably due to the productivity of Freud and other well-known exponents of the psychoanalytical school. The astonishing activity of these writers finally attracted the attention of psychologists who had never been aware of psychiatry up to that time. It was not very long before they began publication of articles, magazines, books, contributions of all sorts, on the subject of abnormal psychiatry, which is psychiatry pure and simple, and does not belong within the domain of psychology.... The psychologists soon invaded the clinical field and are now laying down rules intended to guide those who are interested in the actual treatment of the abnormal. (p. 4)

In that same year, 1933, a special section on psychoanalysis was established within the American Psychiatric Association with A. A. Brill as its chairman. Brill clearly saw himself as the father of American psychoanalysis. In 1938 he wrote:

Psychoanalysis was unknown in this country until I introduced it in 1908. [Psychoanalytic terminology] some of which I was the first to coin into English expressions, can now be found in all standard English dictionaries. Words like abreaction, transference, repression, displacement, unconscious, which I introduced as Freudian concepts,

have been adopted and used to give new meanings, new values to our
knowledge of normal and abnormal behavior. (Brill, 1938, p. 3)

Brill was a dogged proponent of a close tie between psychoanalysis and the
American Psychiatric Association and remained unalterably committed to
the limitation of clinical psychoanalysis to physicians. He wrote:

The American Psychiatric Association, which is the largest psychiatric
organization in the world, has always been fair-minded and kindly
disposed toward psychoanalysis; although some of the members were
naturally critical, I always found there a sympathetic forum. Since
1926 I had worked hard to establish a Section on Psychoanalysis in this
organization and…the council of this association finally recommended
that a Section on Psychoanalysis be formed. (Brill, 1938, p. 30).

He was still unbending on the issue of lay analysis: "I have always felt that
psychoanalysis as a therapy belonged to the medical profession, to psychiatry,
and what I have learned during all these years has not changed my opinion"
(Brill, 1938, p. 29).

Three years later, summing up his career, Brill (1942) wrote (note here
his echoing of May's use of the concept of invasion):

This leads me to the non-medical practitioners, to the so-called lay-
analysts who began to invade this field of psychotherapy about twenty
years ago. Despite the fact that I have known some highly educated lay-
analysts, conscientious men and women, whose theoretical knowledge
of psychoanalysis leaves nothing to be desired, I feel that as the problem
now stands they should not be allowed to practice psychoanalysis or for
that matter, any other form of psychotherapy (p. 546).

The American Board of Psychiatry and Neurology was established in 1942, and immediately a movement began, certainly promoted by Brill, to establish a subspecialty board for psychoanalysis within that new board. In that year, Brill's New York Psychoanalytic Society passed a resolution urging the APsaA to press for the establishment of such a board, but in a recapitulation of an earlier dynamic, this proposal was not acceptable to other APsaA societies, evidently concerned about losing control to a board composed of mostly nonpsychoanalysts. Instead, as noted, the officers of APsaA declared that for the time being a membership card issued by their organization would constitute official certification. Finally, in the reorganization of the APsaA in 1946, the Board on Professional Standards was given jurisdiction over the admission of individual applicants for membership. Soon the membership process was aping the procedure of board certification in medical specialties. Until the 1946 reorganization, membership in the APsaA had been automatic for all graduates of APsaA-affiliated institutes. The 1946 reorganization had the following fateful consequences:

The determination of who could become an individual member of the national organization was taken away from the societies and transferred to the central organization.

Within that central organization, the specific determination of who could become a member of the national organization was placed in the hands of the training analyst members of the Board on Professional Standards, an entity that represented only the faculty members in the approved institutes, and which did not represent the overall membership throughout the affiliate societies!

Clara Thompson, one of the founding members of the William Alanson White Institute and a member of APsaA, maintained that the 1946 rule was implemented to screen out applications from the deviant Washington School/William Alanson White Institute/Baltimore-Washington group. She wrote that after the rule was put into place, one of her people (Ed

Tauber) told her that he was given a hard time. But others contend (Charles Brenner, personal communication to A. Richards, 2003) that the reason for the new membership procedure was concern that Sandor Rado's new Columbia Center for Psychoanalytic Medicine would institute a three-times-per-week training requirement for training analysis and control cases. The APsaA authorities feared that Rado's graduates would automatically become members unless there was a membership procedure that specifically stipulated a four-times-per-week requirement. (Needless to say, Rado saw the handwriting on the wall and went along with the higher frequency.)

Under the new arrangement, the Board on Professional Standards, the successor to the advice-only Council on Professional Training of the 1932-1946 organization, had to certify in writing the eligibility (as to ethical and professional standards) of each individual applicant. The new bylaws, however, failed to state exactly what was being certified. *Was the power to certify intended to be a simple review of the applicant's training in an approved institute, as in the analogous situation of a professional applying for membership in a professional organization? Or was this certification intended to be a detailed, separate postgraduate evaluation of the applicant's competence, corresponding to examination by a medical specialty board? Out of this ambiguity, the new power to certify eventually morphed into a rigorous oversight and credentialing that in the 1970s was actually renamed* certification.

During this early period of the new APsaA, from 1946 through the 1950s, training functions dominated the activities of the Association. But the small organization was growing at a breakneck pace, and for a while it was not apparent to many that the Board on Professional Standards, which represented only the approved institutes, would over the succeeding decades become less and less representative of the overall APsaA membership. In 1932 the APsaA had 32 members; In 1940 it had 192 members, but by

1960 there were 1,000. There were twice as many candidates in the training programs as there were actual members in the Association!

Less than five years after the 1946 reorganization the control of eligibility for individual membership had become a flash point. Enough applications were being held up by the new membership committee of the Board on Professional Standards that in 1951 an investigation committee, instigated by a motion floated by some of the earlier dissidents, was appointed by the APsaA president, Robert Knight, to review the membership procedures. The investigation committee's report generally supported the Board's procedures, and the committee's report was for the most part accepted by the Executive Council. However, the investigation committee's recommendation that there be a mandatory due-process review of any application for membership that was rejected or deferred was ignored by the Executive Council, and so the membership committee of the Board on Professional Standards and its "process" gained complete control over who could become a member of APsaA.

We should also note at this point that in 1951-1952, the APsaA was incorporated under the New York membership corporation law. The APsaA Executive Council, which consists of the nationally elected officers, the elected society representatives, and the nationally elected councilors-at-large, was designated as the Board of Directors of the new corporation, so the Executive Council had final authority over APsaA policies. In theory, this clarified the lines of power in the APsaA and intentionally placed it under some degree of state/public scrutiny (a fact that went largely ignored until the late 1990s). But a myth that the APsaA was governed by a bicameral legislature—with a "Senate" (the Board on Professional Standards), representing only the "approved" training facilities, coequal with a "House of Representatives" (the Executive Council representing the societies)—persisted for forty years. The fact is that the Executive Council is the Board of Directors of the APsaA and the legal status of the Board on Professional Standards is unclear.

Over the next twenty years, the membership process became more and more arduous, and growing numbers of graduates of approved institutes chose not to apply for membership/ certification. Many of these psychoanalysts, already senior board-certified psychiatrists, felt the entire membership procedure to be demeaning. So while most graduates of the approved institutes joined their local affiliate societies, it appeared increasingly more likely that they would forever be denied membership in the national organization. It is difficult to overstate the bitterness and hostility this engendered.

Many of these analysts became negative ambassadors for the APsaA among a much wider group of mental health professionals, which served only to heighten the hostility toward the APsaA already felt by other mental health professionals in response to its exclusionary policies.

(It is a tribute to the wish for professionals to be part of a national organization of peers that a very large percentage of such approved institute graduates actually did join the APsaA when they were finally offered the opportunity, albeit with a kind of second-class status. However, they still refused to subject themselves to any individual vetting, as we will see later. And many brought with them into the APsaA a lingering bitterness stemming from their earlier exclusion.)

As the growth of the APsaA and profession, which had at first been very rapid, eventually moved at a slower pace, a smaller proportion of new institute graduates were required to function as teachers in institutes and as training analysts. A curious fact, as yet unexplained, is that despite the slowing growth in the APsaA, with the accompanying decrease in the relative importance of training as an activity, political dominance in the Association has remained vested in those members who are designated as training analysts. In the half-century since the APsaA was reorganized as a professional membership organization, all of its officers, with the exception of two presidents and two treasurers, have been training analysts. No person who was not a training analyst has *ever* served as secretary of the Association!

The stark and irrefutable fact that training analysts have so completely dominated APsaA political offices for half a century also raises questions about the effect of the Training Analyst system on the direction the APsaA has taken. The first training analyst, Hans Sachs, believed that a training analyst should withdraw from all offices in the institute and society (Bernfeld, 1962). How far in the exact opposite direction have we gone? Can the peculiar fact of the domination of APsaA elective offices by training analysts be related to unanalyzed and thus unresolved idealizations in the minds of all the voters in APsaA, all of whom, of course, have had an important analytic relationship with a training analyst? Is there, in fact, a false organizational self in APsaA, analogous to the false self that some have suggested is fostered in individual members by our training system? (See Berman, 2000.)

The proceedings of the Board on Professional Standards, and the recorded farewell addresses of the board's chairs, yield the impression that the APsaA's main raison d'etre has been gatekeeping. Has this gatekeeping been sheltered under the administrative euphemism "maintenance of standards"? Unauthorized training, lay analysis, certification—in each case the result of the Board's actions has been to keep people out. This spirit of exclusion has permeated the APsaA since its inception. In fact, the section on membership of the 1946 bylaws, which is still on the books, begins with this unusual negative and exclusionary description of eligibility for APsaA membership: "No person shall be eligible for election as an Active Member unless...."

In 1972, in the face of a Nixon-era initiative for a national health plan, many analysts came to believe that board certification for psychoanalysts would be the key to obtaining third-party payments under any such plan. A committee was set up to consider the possibility of establishing a board outside APsaA to carry out such certification, but the opinion of the societies, as it had been in the past, was distinctly negative.

So, as an alternative, in 1977 the APsaA membership process was renamed *certification* and the membership committee was renamed the *certification committee;* all current members of the APsaA were declared certified, and *certification* became the lynchpin criterion for eligibility for membership. After 1977, a prospective Active Member applied for certification and, once certified, could then apply for active membership.

IV. "Certification" as the Principal Criterion For "Membership" Eligibility

In 1976, in a paper devoted to this membership problem, Anton Kris wrote that "some 800 eligible psychoanalysts, graduates of Association-approved institutes, have not applied for active membership, many explicitly because of the application requirements. This number is more than one-half the roughly 1400 active members of the Association" (p. 22). This means that of 2,200 graduates, only 1,400 (64%) applied for membership between the 1950s and the mid-1970s.

The widespread resentment of and antagonism toward the membership application process, and the consequent refusal to pursue Association membership by large numbers of graduates, led to concern among the leadership about the moral and financial health of the APsaA. Still, those in control of the application process stoutly defended its methodology and rationale. They felt that certification was a valid postgraduate requirement for would-be members of the APsaA. They passionately believed that allowing graduates of member societies to join the Association as individual members without any further review—that is to say, without having to go through a qualification process overseen by the Board on Professional Standards— would eventually lead to an erosion of the very standards that it was the purpose of the Board to maintain.

But others saw the membership application procedure as a way for the Board on Professional Standards to impose its otherwise dubious control over the member institutes and their training programs. Indeed, Kris (1976) concluded that the Board on Professional Standards was using its control over the professional fate of individual graduates as a hold over the approved institutes. Even though the Board conducted quality-control site visits of all member institutes, it had no practical mechanism for enforcing its recommendations within the institutes other than by pressure exerted through its examination of individual graduates and the threat of their applications being rejected. As Stein (1990) wrote:

It is argued that the board can exert influence to improve the educational work of the various teaching organizations through its Committee on Institutes. Its impact is, however, severely limited since the only effective sanction the Board can recommend for an institute that is failing in its duty toward its candidates is tantamount to suspension. The Board is understandably reluctant to take such extreme action, which would affect adversely every member of the affected institute and all its candidates in training whatever their qualifications. It is inevitably a move of last resort. For all practical purposes the Board is left with only one way to exert effective influence on psychoanalytic education: by requiring graduates who apply for active membership to provide evidence of competence in the practice of psychoanalysis—that is certification.

In 1974, one outside observer of the APsaA wrote:

> *...it is not possible to do without rules and regulations in psychoanalytic education and certification, but the growth of them makes one wonder, "Why the fear?" For example, a recent issue of the Journal of the American Psychoanalytic Association contains page upon page of rules, regulations, discussions of rules, ad hoc and post hoc committees, so that one wonders when these people have time for work, leisure, or the aesthetics of the process. It is as though the claim to complication were a way of arriving at absolute Truth and Perfection. (Lefer, 1974)*

It is not surprising that the membership issue continued to be a bone of contention in the APsaA. Those responsible for the overall financial health of the Association, including the treasurers, called attention to the lack of membership growth and the aging of the membership into non-dues-paying status. Others, concerned about developing more diversity and openness in the APsaA, joined them, gladly adding their voices to those urging changes in membership policies.

During the 1970s a series of modifications (essentially, attempted compromises) in the APsaA's membership structure were grudgingly instituted to address this perceived membership problem. Each successive change helped the Association's coffers, but otherwise served only to highlight further the continuing problems caused by the restrictive membership policy and the second-class status experienced by the large group of noncertified but fully trained psychoanalysts.

The first modification, put into effect in 1973, was the creation of a dues-paying, nonvoting, time-limited Associate Member category open to all graduates of approved institutes. This measure was intended to entice noncertified graduates into applying for membership/certification. Immediately, 225 new members joined the APsaA (40 percent of those invited); still, even though the three-year limited time period was extended for some, it became clear that most would not apply for certification leading to Active Membership and so would have to be dropped—but by that time the Association had become dependent on their dues. A decision was made to send each of these members a letter asking for an expression of intent to apply for certification. Those so indicating would not be dropped, even though the time limit of their Associate Membership had passed.

V. Certification as Criterion of Voting Membership in the APSAA

By the early 1980s, few Associate Members had actually applied, so another membership category, Extended Associate Member, with no voting rights or right to hold office, was proposed in a 1983 bylaw amendment and was adopted by an overwhelming vote of 661 to 44. This new category was not time-limited, and was open only to those who were in the third year of their three-year Associate Member sojourn. In addition, as an ingathering gesture through a one-time waiver, an application deadline of December 1984 was established for graduates who were not already Associate Members. Almost all of those initially accepting this new permanent membership (120 out of 1,200 invited) were already Associate Members, and only 10% of eligible nonmembers applied. By 1987, there were 1,576 Active Members, but there were also 568 Extended Associate Members, and an additional 174 Associate Members—the result of the transition of previous Associate Members who did not apply for certification to Extended Associate member status. A financial crisis still loomed, unless the post-1984 application rate of new graduates could be increased.

In the 1980s, therefore, as new classes of nonvoting membership were created that did not require certification, certification effectively became a prerequisite for *voting* membership in the APsaA, for holding office, for being a member of committees or of the Board on Professional Standards, and for being appointed as a training analyst.

In 1989, The Los Angeles Psychoanalytic Society and Institute conducted a survey of the APsaA Active Membership on the requirement of certification for (full) Active Membership. As reported to the Board on Professional Standards, this survey resulted in a strong expression of preference for dropping the requirement (77.5 percent vs. 22.5 percent, with a 50 percent response rate).

Pressure was thus mounting to dispense with the membership-certification link altogether, and to grant some kind of permanent Active Membership to noncertified institute graduates. At that time, Arnold Richards was editor of *The American Psychoanalyst* (TAP), the newsletter of APsaA. In 1990, Richards proposed that TAP put out a special issue dealing with the possibility of the separation of membership from certification, which was then called *delinkage,* and proponents from both sides of the issue were invited to submit statements for publication.

Although many felt that the weight of logic and practicality was on the side of delinkage, a bylaw amendment did not muster the two thirds majority of the voting (i.e., certified) members required for passage. The number of members concerned that the standards of the APsaA's training programs would be in jeopardy if noncertified graduates became voting members was large enough to prevent the vote in favor of the amendment from reaching the necessary two thirds majority. Of course, the (noncertified) Associate Members could not vote. But the vote of the certified voting members was close enough to warrant another attempt. This time a compromise proposal was put forth that conferred permanent "Active Membership" on noncertified graduates, but created a new kind of division within the category of "Active Members" based on the Member's certification status. Noncertified Active Members were granted *limited* voting rights (such as voting for officers), but were barred from voting on any *bylaw amendments*. Finally, a new provision, titled *"Certification Requirement"* was added to the bylaws as part of the compromise with the explicit intention of "protecting" the Board on Professional Standards. This provision stated that only a certified Active Member could become an officer, an Executive Councilor, or a training or supervising analyst; furthermore, only a certified Active Member could serve as a Fellow of the Board, or could be appointed a member of any committee of the Board. (In retrospect, this was probably an illegal arrangement under state law. It created classes of voting members with different voting rights, but without the necessary formalities required under corporation law to assure the preservation of the rights of each such membership class.)

This compromise proposal *did* receive the two thirds majority necessary for passage, and the bylaws were amended in 1992. As a result of this delinkage, the Associate and Extended Associate membership categories were abolished and all such members became *second-class* full members instead.

However, this change finally put to rest the earlier contention that Active Membership in the APsaA was somehow equivalent to *certification* in a medical subspecialty. Instead, certification now had become a category serving a political function in the *internal governance* of the APsaA.

The settlement of the lawsuit that enabled admission of nonmedical applicants to APsaA institutes, and the delinkage of certification from membership, saved the APsaA from fiscal and other significant problems, but these changes did not resolve the political difficulties within the organization. To wit: Eliminating the certification requirement for full membership was a step in the direction of a real professional membership organization, but a two-tiered membership situation was created in which a large number of Active Members were barred from any leadership positions and were granted only limited voting rights.

In the meantime, psychoanalysis in the United States was undergoing major changes that would eventually affect the APsaA from without. The first of these was the collapse of third-party reimbursement for psychoanalysis, which very sharply reduced the pool of potential private psychoanalytic patients during the 1980s and 1990s. The second was the development of training programs for psychoanalysts in institutes entirely independent of the American Psychoanalytic Association; these programs trained nonphysician mental health professionals (e.g., psychologists and social workers) as psychoanalysts. Many of these new psychoanalysts had little love for the APsaA because of its long history of exclusionary policies. Third, the prestige of psychoanalysis in the United States was rapidly diminishing. The large number of psychiatry chairs in medical schools held by psychoanalysts in the 1960s and 1970s were now being occupied by medically oriented psychiatrists. In the early 1990s the Association's monopoly on training psychoanalysts eligible for IPA membership in the United States was lost as the IPA began directly to accredit institutes not approved by the APsaA. (The APsaA agreed to make some graduates of such institutes eligible membership , subject to individual scrutiny by the Board on Professional Standards.) Finally, in 2002, the State of New York enacted legislation creating a *profession of psychoanalysis* with statutory training requirements and professional licensure. The new profession will be a master's level mental health discipline similar to social work in the extent of prerequisite mental health training.

In 2001, there was a partial undoing of the two-tier membership arrangement. A bylaw amendment granted noncertified Active Members full voting rights, including the right to vote on bylaw amendments and to serve as officers and Executive Councilors. However, parts of the early 1990s "Certification Requirement" remained in place, in bylaws stating that a noncertified Active Member may not be appointed a training or supervising analyst, and may not serve as a Fellow of the Board on Professional Standards or a member of any Board committee. These restrictions remain in the bylaws of the Association today, and cannot be changed without the affirmative vote of two thirds of the members who vote on such proposals.

VI. Certification as an Indicator of "Clinical Competence"

In the late 1990s a new definition of the role of "certification" began to emerge. Previously, certification had served principally as an evaluation of the training of applicants for membership. However, with certification now principally determining eligibility for a training analyst appointment, supporters of the process started to claim that certification is necessary as a "national indicator of clinical competence" (Eric Neutzal, personal communication to A. Richards, 2003), and that such an indicator is necessary to assure that the analysis of new trainees will be in the hands only of analysts whose "competence" has been confirmed. This proposition seems to harken back to the paper in which Anton Kris (1976) had pointed out that the mechanism and entire enterprise of "certification" was maintained in order to exercise control over the member institutes; the vetting, and the possibility of rejecting graduates of member institutes was the only way, short of the threat of suspension, for the Board on Professional Standards to enforce its policies and regulations on institutes.

The "Educational Standards" of the Board on Professional Standards make it clear that the development and assessment of professional competence for graduation is supposed to be the responsibility of the individual institutes. The word "competence" appears seventeen times in the "Educational Standards." Clearly it is the responsibility of the Board, in its oversight of institutes, to assure that this competence-determining function as carried out *by the institutes* is authoritative:

The primary goal of psychoanalytic education is to facilitate the development of psychoanalytic competence and a core psychoanalytic identity.

The candidate should have psychoanalytic experience with a number and variety of types of patients in order to develop the competence needed to conduct psychoanalysis independently.

Graduation shall be construed as an indication that the Institute has adequately and carefully evaluated the candidate and considers the candidate competent to undertake independent psychoanalytic work. (Educational Standards, Board on Professional Standards, emphasis added)

However, the document also contains this somewhat contradictory statement:

The capacity to independently conduct competent psychoanalysis is a standard that should be anticipated with confidence at the time of graduation but is more clearly demonstrable upon certification by the Board on Professional Standards. (Educational Standards, Board on Professional Standards)

Certification Today: The Restructuring of the APsaA and A Final "Delinkage"?

To understand where the APsaA is today we have to turn the clock back to 1995. The settlement of the lawsuit brought by four members of Division 39 against the APsaA for restraint of trade in regard to training psychologists meant that members of the IPA who did not train at APsaA institutes (including those trained at the New York Freudian Society or the Institute for Psychoanalytic Training and Research) were now eligible to apply for membership. Two of the new members, Gail Reed and Arlene Kramer Richards, also applied for certification. Reed's application was accepted but Richards's application was deferred. Although Richards was told that the Committee would understand if she decided to withdraw her application, she decided to persist and was passed by the second committee. Her experience heightened the awareness of one of us (Richards) about how the test does and does not work, and he decided to moderate a discussion on the *Openline,* an APsaA members' listserv. A lively and spirited discussion ensued with many participants from the pro- and anti-certification camps weighing in. It appeared that although views differed on the validity, reliability, and relevance of the test, there was widespread agreement that making certification a requirement for voting for educational bylaws or for running for office was neither rational nor adaptive for the APsaA.

A "Task Force on Education and Membership" (TFEM) was convened by the officers of the APsaA. It recommended that the bylaws should be changed to allow all members to vote for everything and run for everything. Many of us were pleasantly surprised by this outcome, although we did wonder if there would be a catch. There turned out to be one in another recommendation, this one for a "Procedural Code," proposed as a sort of "pseudo-bylaw" that would not require approval by two thirds of the membership. This "Procedural Code" would codify a relationship between the Board of Professional Standards and the Executive Council in a form that guaranteed the Board's independence of the ExecutiveCouncil. In addition, the intention was to enact this part of the "plan" by the Executive Council and the Board on Professional Standards in such a way that it could only be rescinded with the agreement of *both bodies.* This arrangement would have had the effect of etching in stone the bicameral structure of the APsaA that had in fact already been in place since the 1946 reorganization. Paul Mosher posted a series of "civics lessons" on the *Openline* that called our attention to the possibility that the structure the TFEM had proposed was not in accordance with New York State *Not-for-Profit Corporation Law*, because the law both designated the Board of Directors of the APsaA as the *final authority* for the Corporation's policies, and forbade the Board of Directors from transferring this authority to any other body.

A group of us who had been communicating on a private "delinkage" listserv raised a small amount of money to hire a legal expert to confirm Mosher' assertions. That attorney advised us that our concerns were well founded, and that the proposed "Procedural Code" was not in accord with New York State Not-for-Profit Corporation Law which, at a minimum, would have required such an arrangement to be enacted as an actual bylaw (and would therefore have required a vote by the membership).

The APsaA's officers, apparently not convinced that our attorney was correct, hired Victoria Bjorkland, the leading legal authority on New York's Not-for-Profit Corporation Laws, and author of the definitive textbook on the subject. Ms. Bjorkland confirmed what Mosher and our lawyer had asserted. A bicameral structure with the Board of Professional Standards and the actual Board of Directors as coequal governing bodies was not legal. Ms. Bjorklund used the bombshell term "legal nullity" (that is, lacking any legal basis to assert any role in APsaA governance) in describing the current status of the Board. The officers then took the step of appointing, with the membership's endorsement, a "Restructuring Task Force" to recommend a new set of bylaws to "cure" the illegal status of the structure of the Association, including the relationship between the Executive Council and the Board.

These events provide the backdrop for what we have called the "third delinkage"—removing certification as a requirement for training and supervising analysts—a requirement that is unique to the APsaA in world psychoanalysis and is based on the conviction among some analysts that a "national test of clinical competence" is essential to assure the best training for its candidates and for the overall integrity of psychoanalysis as a discipline.

In 2003, a group of members proposed two bylaw amendments intended to address the relationship between the membership and the training that the APsaA "approves." The first would have made it clear that the Board of Professional Standards was subordinate to the Executive Council and that the latter was responsible for overseeing all Board decisions. The second would have permitted the Board to dispense with the requirement of certification for the training analyst appointment if it chose to do so. These bylaw amendments were opposed by both the Board of Professional Standards and the Executive Council; nevertheless, they respectively received the support of 48 percent and 42 percent of the voting membership—substantially short of the two thirds required to pass a bylaw amendment, but certainly an indication of substantial support in the face of disapproval by the APsaA leadership.

In 2004, 105 members signed a members' petition for another bylaw amendment that would transfer the authority to require certification as a prerequisite for training analysts from the Board on Professional Standards to the individual approved institutes (the so-called "local option"). This amendment was considered by the Board and the Executive Council in June 2005, and voted on by the members in the summer of 2005. It did not pass, but more than 40 percent of the members voted yes.

Although "certification" now plays no role in most activities within the APsaA, the fact that certification is required for a training analyst appointment and for Fellowship on the Board of Professional Standards or membership on any Board committee means that certification continues, through those remaining bylaw provisions, to be the basis of a two-tiered membership structure in the APsaA.

A pragmatic issue remains as well, in that some institutes are hobbled by the certification requirement. It prevents them from accepting as candidates mental health professionals who are in analysis with their own noncertified analysts and who are not willing to interrupt an analysis in order to apply for admission. Passing the *local option* would facilitate the "approval" of institutes such as the New York Freudian Institute (of the New York Freudian Society).

To sum up, we have traced the way in which the issues of certification, membership, the exclusion of nonmedical psychoanalysts, and internal political power have been intertwined in the history of psychoanalysis in the United States and especially in the history of the American Psychoanalytic Association over the past half century. Over the years, the changing ways in which certification in the APsaA have been employed, or rationalized, seem to indicate that certification in psychoanalysis, aside from what intrinsic value it may have in principle, has mostly served a changing set of discriminatory and exclusionary goals. Such an exclusionary attitude is deeply embedded in the history of American psychoanalysis, beginning with A. A. Brill's ironclad conviction that only medically trained psychoanalysts should be allowed to treat patients in the United States.

REFERENCES

American Psychiatric Association. (1929). Proceedings of societies: Report of the Committee on Medical Services. *Am. J Psychiatry*, 86: *417–422.*

Beck, A. H. (2004). The Flexner report and the standardization of American medical education. *JAMA*, 291: *21–39.*

Berman, E. (2000). The utopian fantasy of a New Person and the danger of a false analytic self. *Psychoanal. Psychol.,* 17:38–60.

Bernfeld, S. (1962). On psychoanalytic training. *Psychoanal. Q.,* 31:453–482.

Brill, A. A. (1938). *The basic writings of Sigmund Freud.* New York: Modern Library.

Bernfeld, S. (1942). A psychoanalyst scans his past. *J. Nerv. Ment. Dis.* 95 (5): 537–549.

Fass, P. (1968). A.A. Brill: Pioneer and prophet. New York: unpublished master's dissertation, Columbia University.

Hale, N. G. (1995). *The rise and crisis of psychoanalysis in the United States: Freud and the Americans, 1917–1985.* Oxford: Oxford University Press.

Kris, A. O. (1976). The problem of membership in the American Psychoanalytic Association. *J. Philadelphia Assoc. for Psychoanal.* 3 (1&2): 22–36.

Levine, F. (2003). The forbidden quest and the slippery slope: Roots of authoritarianism in psychoanalysis. *J. Amer. Psychoanal. Assn.* 51 (suppl.): 203–45.

Obendorf, C. (1953). A history of psychoanalysis in America. New York: Grune & Stratton.

Russell, W. L. (1932). Presidential address: The place of the American Psychiatric Association in modern psychiatric organization and progress. *Am. J. Psychiatry* 12:1–18.

Schroter, M. (2004). The early history of lay analysis, especially in Vienna, Berlin, and London: Aspects of an unfolding controversy (1906-24). *Int. J. Psycho-Anal.* 85: 159--178.

Starr, P. (1982). *The social transformation of American medicine.* New York: Basic Books.

Stein, M. (1990). *TAP.* Special Supplement.

Wallerstein, R. (1998). *Lay analysis: Life inside the controversy.* Hillsdale, NJ: Analytic Press.

CHAPTER 18

Comments on the proposal for a Personal Analyst System

by Ralph Fishkin and Paul Mosher

The PPP Proposal (i.e., the one presented by Rick Perlman, Warren Procci, and Bob Pyles; see Perlman, 2021, pp. 380-381) has changed several times since it was introduced. In order for people to understand and to comment on what PPP are advocating, they need to have it at hand. According to his [Perlman's] post in the Members List of the *American Psychoanalytic Association* (APsaA) of June 18, 2021, the proposal for a Personal Analyst system seems to have been reduced to a single sentence and we question whether it is misleading to call such a focal proposal a system:

> *A National Personal Analyst System:* Candidates at approved training institutes of the American Psychoanalytic Association shall have the right to undertake personal psychoanalysis in fulfillment of requirements for psychoanalytic training with any graduate psychoanalyst, regardless of institute affiliation or membership, subject only to the conditions that the analyst (a) shall be a member in good standing of the American Psychoanalytic Association, (b) shall have no ethical violations, and (c) shall have a minimum of five years of psychoanalytic experience following graduation from training» (see Perlman, 2021, p. 381).

Furthermore, the proposal is internally contradictory where it states, regardless of institute affiliation or membership, subject only to the conditions that the analyst (a) shall be a member in good standing of the American Psychoanalytic Association [emphasis added].

The Training Analyst system is like ground cover, not a discrete plant. It has local roots (APsaA's Approved Institutes), national roots (APsaA, *Confederation of Independent Psychoanalytic Societies* [CIPS]) and international roots (*International Psychoanalytic Association* [IPA] and its other Constituent Societies across the world.) As such, a national remedy will not eliminate a system that exists beyond APsaA's jurisdiction. In their understandable motivation to end the Training Analysis (TA) system, PPP's plan does not address the futility of abolishing it in APsaA, because it will remain in effect in other local national, and international organizations. Certainly, one can understand their dissatisfaction that, while the local option that APsaA now accords to its Institutes would facilitate some of them to eliminate the TA, it immunizes others to maintain their TA policies.

The reader should keep in mind the difference between "allowing" institutes to abandon the TA system directly (or indirectly, as in the Contemporary Freudian Society's TA appointment process) or "banning" the TA system from being used by institutes individually or in splinter groups of institutes (the *American Association for Psychoanalytic Education* [AAPE]) that still maintain their Approved Institute status in APsaA. This is an important problem that local option has not solved, even as it has permitted progress in some places. The PPP Proposal would put in place a ban on TA appointment in institutes that would want to continue it.

What PPP cannot account for is that there is no remedy at the national level that will entirely eliminate the TA system. If APsaA banned the appointment of TAs, it might cause institutes that want to retain the TA to defy or withdraw from APsaA and to affiliate exclusively with AAPE. We think it is better to facilitate the overall withering of the TA system in local institutes where local option would permit it, rather than to risk losing institutes and members that are not yet ready to eliminate it, or to risk reinstitution of coercion into the national system of Standards that someday could impose rigid regulations for appointing the analysts of candidates.

It is important to recognize that the TA system, at least in APsaA, is, historically, really two things:

1. An exclusive franchise to analyze candidates for credit in the institute training program,
2. A system that permitted almost total domination by TAs of all administrative positions in APsaA and the local institutes. In 2000, the election of Paul Mosher and Elise Snyder as Councilors at Large marked the first time in APsaA history that any non-TA was elected to that position. In addition, in all of APsaA history up until that time, there had been only two Presidents and no Secretaries elected nationally who were not TAs.

In other words, the TA "class" abused their titles by using them as a kind of bonding signal which allowed them to dominate positions that had nothing to do with training analyses. This domination, as Rick Perlman points out, has been partially resolved and now non-TAs are regularly elected to national positions.

We do not think it is widely appreciated that local option and the gradual evolution of APsaA's Educational Standards is made possible by its designation as the IPA's only Regional Association (RA), a designation that allows APsaA to set its own Standards independently. Because of this prerogative, APsaA is envied and resented by many who do not have it. There is a danger that IPA members could vote to change its rules to eliminate the RA. This would be disastrous for APsaA, the IPA, and psychoanalysis, but it could happen through the failure of discussions in the IPA about ways to provide parity with APsaA for all IPA Societies through local option. PPP's call for the abolishment of the TA system in this revision of the APsaA Educational Standards could, if enacted, increase the divide between APsaA and the IPA.

What APsaA could do, and what we wish PPP would advocate for, is to provide options in its Standards to institutes that address the well-documented problems with the TA system by approving an institute and its model of education that does not require TAs [*Note: This was accomplished in 2022*]. Such a model exists at the *New York University* (NYU) *Postdoctoral Program*, where candidates may choose any analyst whose training is equivalent to the NYU Postdoc's educational standards. This model is substantially equivalent to APsaA's model in the rigor and quality of its educational program. In contrast to the PPP Proposal, the analyst does not have to be on the faculty of the NYU Postdoctoral Program or a member of any institute or professional organization. There is no TA appointment within the program. Instead, emphasis is placed on the qualifications of its Supervising Analysts and Faculty.

We would like to provide our recollections, as participants, of certain events in Dr. Perlman's excellent account of the conflict within APsaA. Our version differs in minor ways, but we are providing it because we think the written record should be as accurate as possible.

Toward the end of the *Board of Professional Standards* (BoPS) regime, and due to the efforts of the late Lee Jaffe, at that time a BoPS Fellow, the BoPS, after being prevented by the BoPS leadership from the opportunity to vote on it for several years, passed his motion allowing one representative from each approved institute to be a non-TA. This led to a relaxation by the BoPS of some rules over the objection of the BoPS leadership, but it also led to their increasing feeling that an era was about to come to an end. As institutes began to adopt their own policies that were not permitted by the BoPS standards, a BoPS officer stated that the "compact" between the BoPS and the Approved Institutes had broken down. This led the BoPS leaders to propose and ultimately to preserve the BoPS educational model by pursuing the creation of external certifying and accrediting bodies (*American Board of Psychoanalysis* [ABP] and AAPE). They proposed that APsaA would support and endorse this plan. In the subsequent discussions in the Executive Committee, such support was not forthcoming, but they proceeded anyway. The post externalization shape of APsaA, which came to be known as the 6 Point Plan, took several years to be formulated and negotiated. It benefitted from very helpful consultation from an organizational consultant with experience in dealing with emotional issues in organizational leadership.

As Dr. Perlman writes, a major conflict about the TA system crystallized around the issue of certification. It is important to add to his account that Mosher and Richards (2005) wrote a very influential paper explaining how the certification credential served as a way of keeping graduates out of APsaA. Perlman attributes this crystallization to "a coalition of analysts calling themselves the 'Alliance.'" Actually, the Alliance was preceded by the Wednesday Group, whose major concern was the deficiencies in democratic governance in APsaA and the power given to the BOPS in APsaA's governance. The Wednesday Group morphed into the Delinkage Group that fought for passage of the local option and delinkage bylaws, both of which failed to achieve the two-thirds majority that would have enabled certification to be delinked from TA appointment in institutes that chose not to require it. Following those defeats, and at the onset of the 21st Century, the analysts in these groups formed Alliance 21, a private Listserve, where a more comprehensive set of democratic changes in APsaA's governance could be discussed and planned. To belong to its Listserve, Alliance subscribers were asked to endorse the "A Simple Alternative Program" (ASAP) Principles. They can be found on the web at www.asapforapsaa.org. As the web page states, "ASAP for APsaA is a set of proposals intended to ensure that all APsaA members have an effective voice in the organization's governance, and to assure APsaA, Inc.'s compliance with the New York State *Not-for-Profit Corporation Law* (N-PCL) which protects the rights of APsaA Members."

Of its five proposals for changes in governance, four were achieved and one was partly achieved. These achievements have led to additional changes in APsaA governance, including the 6 Point Plan, which was worked out in the Executive Committee, discussed thoroughly at the Executive Council and ultimately approved by it. These changes and the bylaw that established the Executive Council as responsible for all of APsaA's affairs (including education) have markedly transformed its governance in a democratic direction. Thus, hopefully the reader will recognize that it was a series of major democratic changes in governance that enabled the progressive changes in educational policy to proceed.

In his discussion of the *Institute Requirements and Review Committee* (IRRC), Dr. Perlman (2021) glosses over the Personal Analyst Waiver that permitted candidates in ongoing productive analyses with non-TAs to continue those analyses without being required to interrupt them to switch to a TA. In the Philadelphia institute, approximately six candidates have received these personal analyst waivers and three have already graduated. It is hard to know exactly how many have received these waivers, since these personal analyses are private. This waiver established the principle that an *effective* analyst, not one whose appointment conferred status, was a significant essential in the formation of a psychoanalyst.

A final comment has to do with the need for democratic governance in approved institutes. Just as in the governance of APsaA, democratic change, defined as the right to decide major educational policies in Approved Institutes by a majority vote of the Faculty or members of an institute, will reduce conflict and discontent and is essential to the health and vigor of the institute. The standards revision being contemplated by the IRRC will contain such a provision.

We conclude our communication by reproducing an email that one of us (Paul Mosher) sent on July 30, 2008, and appeared also on p. 262 of the 2009 edition of Kirsner's 2000 book *Unfree Associations*:

"It's starting to look to me as if the tide around the world is turning on the issue of the "Training Analyst System," and that the entire hierarchical set-up it promotes of having a cadre of **Über**-Analysts, who are somehow better qualified than the rest of us to conduct the analysis of candidates, is finally starting to collapse.

The evidence for this assertion is as follows:

(1) Numerous authors (e.g., Arlow, Bernfeld) have pointed out for many years the detrimental effect of having such a distinction among the members of our profession.

(2) More recently Jurgen Reeder (2004), in his book *Hate and Love in Psychoanalytical Institutions: The Dilemma of a Profession*, has attributed much of the animosity and warfare in our "institutions" to this arrangement in which some kind of offensive "official" stamp of "better analyst" is awarded to some colleagues.

(3) In the *International Psychoanalytic Association* there are now three different so-called "training models," two of which entirely lack any explicit Training Analyst designation.[9]

(4) The current President of our Association was elected to office on a platform which *explicitly* included the replacement of the Training Analyst system by the so-called "Personal Analyst" system.

---

9   The "Training Analyst" title was abolished in Uruguay in 1974. Analysts who analyze candidates are now "members of a group with training functions," which a member may join by presenting an application to the Group and with a decision *based on objective and transparent criteria* made by the entire Group. There are two other such "Groups:" Supervisors and Professors. Any member may apply to join any of the three Groups. I'm not certain as to whether one may belong to more than one group (See Bernardi, 2008, p. 236).

(5) The *New York Freudian Institute*, an IPA component, has instituted a selection process for TA's which, in effect, actualizes the Personal Analyst system, but does so within the IPA constraints which prevail in the United States.

(6) The New York licensing law for psychoanalysts contains an explicit training requirement for "a minimum of 300 hours of personal analysis" but contains no concept of a "Training Analyst."

(7) Finally, in a lovely "Letter from Geneva" in issue no. 3, 2008, of the *International Journal of Psychoanalysis* (Quinodoz, 2008) we read of yet a fourth "training system" now in place in the French-speaking part of Switzerland. This system sounds similar to what has been called the "French" model. The training system in Geneva, called the "Independent Model," is based on a personal analysis followed by a system of training in which many members of the Society participate in a program of seminars and supervision. The article says:

"The Swiss Society delegates considerable responsibility for training to its members. It no longer requires candidates to have been analyzed exclusively by training members of the Society, as previously; analysis by other members of the Swiss Society is also acceptable. Similarly, in order to attract more associate members, the Society accepts that one of the two obligatory supervised cases be based on three-sessions-per-week analysis, with the other having four such sessions. (…) The question then arises: is any form of training better than another? When we compare our system with those adopted in other Societies throughout the world, our conclusion is that when candidates complete their training, i.e., when they become members of the Society, the level of expertise acquired through our model is at least equivalent to that of more structured institutional designs. Each system has its pros and cons; as things stand at present, however, we have seen nothing that would persuade us to adopt the institutional model." (Quinodoz, 2008, pp. 477-478).

Don't all these changes taking place in the rest of the world make our continuing in APsaA to squabble over the remnants of our TA system (with it's fading companion, certification) seem a bit last-century? Why do we keep doing this instead of looking forward?"

Original Italian edition: Commenti sulla proposta di un sistema nazionale di analisti personali.
Psicoterapia e Scienze Umane, 2021, 55 (3): 391-396. DOI: 10.3280/PU2021-003001.
© Copyright *Psicoterapia e Scienze Umane* ("Psychotherapy and the Human Sciences"),
www.psicoterapiaescienzeumane.it/english.htm, ISSN 0394-2864, published with permission.

REFERENCES

Bernardi R. (2008). Letter from Uruguay. *International Journal of Psychoanalysis*, 89, 2: 233-240. DOI: 10.1111/j.1745-8315.2008.00024.x.

Kirsner D. (2000). *Unfree Associations: Inside Psychoanalytic Institutes*. London: Process Press (Updated edition: 2009).

Mosher P.W. & Richards A.D. (2005). The history of membership and certification in the APsaA: Old demons, new debates. *Psychoanalytic Review*, 92, 6: 865-894. DOI: 10.1521/prev.2005.92.6.865.

Perlman F.T. (2021). Cronache psicoanalitiche: il dibattito sull'analisi didattica all'interno dell'*American Psychoanalytic Association* [Psychoanalytic chronicles: The critical debate on training analysis within the *American Psychoanalytic Association*]. *Psicoterapia e Scienze Umane*, 55, 3: 363-424. DOI: 10.3280/PU2021-003001.

Quinodoz J.-M. (2008). Letter from Geneva. *International Journal of Psychoanalysis*, 89, 3: 475-479. DOI: 10.1111/j.1745-8315.2008.00060.x.

Reeder J. (2004). *Hate and Love in Psychoanalytical Institutions: The Dilemma of a Profession*. New York: Other Press.

CHAPTER 19

Introduction; Report of the Investment Advisory Committee

by Jonah Schein

I wrote my Report for the Board in July after our Committee finished its work. When Tom Newman told me of Paul's passing I was quite shocked and very much saddened. Tom suggested I might want to re-write my report. I decided not to do that. The Report, which Paul had seen and helped edit, is below.

The first time I met Paul was when we were both on the Executive Council of the American. Paul was outspoken in his perception that the policies and structure of the American needed to change. He helped bring those changes about. I later got to observe his absolute brilliance with technology when I was appointed as a PEP Trustee. And then of course I got to work with him on the Investment Advisory Committee.

The Investment Advisory Committee came into existence because of Paul. When Bill Glover asked me to join the Committee he told me that Paul had, in a sense, been badgering the ExCom about the need to examine our investment policy and strategy. The word "badger" is mine. I use it with great respect and even greater affection, because if you knew Paul, you knew that he approached things that he believed in with a combination of passion, integrity and incredible tenacity. Paul's interest in our finances was not just because he had an interest in money. He had an interest in the welfare of the American that included its finances, but went far beyond that. He understood that for APsaA to be able to fulfill its various missions today and into the future, it had to have the right governance and the right structures in place.

Even before our Committee actually began to meet Paul would send me multiple emails that outlined his position. Those emails came with charts, many of which he had created, that reinforced whatever point he was making. In the end, after our committee voted unanimously to endorse the advice of our Consultant, we basically arrived at the position Paul had advocated from the beginning. I knew he was pleased. I remember that one thought I had was, "Well, no more emails." Of course there were more emails. Paul wanted us to move forward faster by moving our money immediately because that would mean we would save the fees that the Association was paying its current advisors.

I do hope that after reading the Report and the material that accompanies it, including charts provided by Paul, you will vote to endorse the various items in the report. Yes, in doing so you will be doing what Paul wanted and what he thought was right. I hope you will do so not because of Paul's recent death, but because it is about doing a small but important thing that will help ensure that the American can continue to fulfill its mission.

REPORT of the INVESTMENT ADVISORY COMMITTEE
SEPTEMBER 26, 2021

Dear Members of the Board,

Since Time is Money, I will try to make this brief, but it will be longer than I would wish in the hope of making the report clear and the process involved transparent.

For a number of years, the money held by APsaA in its Reserve Fund (approx. 7 million dollars) and in its Defined Benefits Pension Plan* (approx.

310

2 million dollars) has been managed by an outside Money Management firm. I am attaching the results for the past 5 years of the returns on our money. (Nonprofit organizations generally adhere to a strategy that allows for having roughly 60% of their money in equities and 40% in fixed income assets. The theory is basically to allow for growth while maintaining a fair degree of safety.) Those investments were supposed to be overseen by an Investment Committee of APsaA. That Committee's mission was to review the performance of our money manager to make sure they were meeting our needs in terms of market performance and conforming to the Investment Guidelines of our organization. Unfortunately, that committee had for years not been functioning.

Thanks largely to the efforts and at the urging of Paul Mosher, who has been a member of APsaA's Finance Committee and has had an interest in following our investment results on his own, a new Investment Advisory Committee was appointed in the late Spring of 2021. Paul has long advocated that we move to what is called a Passive Money Management approach that would allow our performance to mirror that of the market and do so at a significantly lower cost.

The committee appointed by Bill Glover consisted of myself, Paul Mosher, Julio Calderon, Craig Lichtman and Tom Newman. We felt our mission was not only to review our current investments but also to take a look at both our investment strategy and our Investment Policy Guidelines, which were last approved in 2011. Maybe most importantly our mission was to re-establish the Investment Advisory Committee as a functioning and effective body.

When we met via Zoom, it was clear that while we all had some reservations about the performance of our current Managers, it was not clear about what to do next. Paul was quite strong in his opinion that we would be better off moving to a low cost balanced index fund which would immediately eliminate most of the cost of having our money managed, while matching the overall performance of the markets. If you know Paul you can imagine that he came prepared. He sent us numerous charts about performance of active v. passively managed funds. (Some are attached.) It was pretty quickly clear that the rest of us on the Committee could use some outside advice.

As a committee, we unanimously agreed to hire a consultant to review our Investment Guidelines as well as help educate us about what might work best for our organization's investment strategy and advice that would allow us to fulfill our fiduciary responsibilities. I interviewed two potential consultants and decided to recommend we hire Doug MacGray, who leads a small money management firm, Stonecrop Wealth Advisors based in Chadds Ford, PA. Stonecrop has a number of non-profits as clients. Doug is both a lawyer and a Certified Financial Planner. In his proposal to be a consultant Doug agreed that neither he nor his firm would be considered as possible Money Managers for APsaA.

Doug met with the Committee and listened to our investment history, our concerns as a committee and as an organization. After that meeting we sent him our Investment Guidelines as well as a number of other documents including reports from our current managers.

After reviewing all of those he met with us again. He provided us with a proposed updated Investment Guidelines document as well as a Memo with his thoughts about how we might proceed – both are attached.

I think there are two main takeaways:

1. We needed to re-establish an active Investment Advisory Committee that would meet regularly to review our investments and establish protocols for conducting those reviews. He felt that until such a committee had established itself, it made sense to move our money to a low cost balanced index fund. One of the largest and the one with the lowest costs is run by Vanguard. **The immediate effect would be to save us about $40,000.00/year in costs — .50 %**

Colony v .07% latest Vanguard fee. The Committee might at some point recommend moving to an actively managed funds or even some combination of active and passive funds, but until such time as the Committee had had a chance to establish itself we were best off moving to the lowest cost Balance Index fund we could find.

2. The Treasurer, who will be a member of the Investment Committee, should report to the Board on the status of our investments on a biannual basis. The Board should expect that such a report be given in a manner that is lively, informative and transparent. That report should require it to be voted on by the Board. While we might choose to invest in "passively managed funds" we cannot afford to be "passive investors".

I have heard that there are some who have raised concerns about our having investments in companies that are not considered to be socially responsible. We did discuss this as an issue. We think that investing in a fund like the Vanguard Balanced Index Fund (VBAIX), which has investments in over 3000 different entities should not and could not be considered as an endorsement of any of those companies. Should APsaA's investments move to a more active style, being invested in a manner that is socially responsible will be a part of that strategy.

As mentioned we are attaching a number of documents including some of Paul's charts that are intended to show the performance of index fund investing and a Five Year summary of our current investment advisors five year performance.

We are asking you to approve four items:

1. The revised Investment Guidelines.
2. The newly written Investment Committee Charter.

3. An updated Reserve Funds Use Statement in which the Executive Council is changed to Board to reflect our current structure.
4. The transfer of our investments from our current manager to the Vanguard Balanced Index Fund.

We welcome your questions and comments.

Respectfully submitted,
Jonah Schein

APsaA no longer offers a Defined Benefits Pension Plan.

This graph shows the behavior of a family of mutual funds from Fidelity, which utilize an asset allocation strategy.

The period covered is 12/21/2007 - to yesterday, so it includes both the 2008 financial collapse and the more recent 2020 market decline.

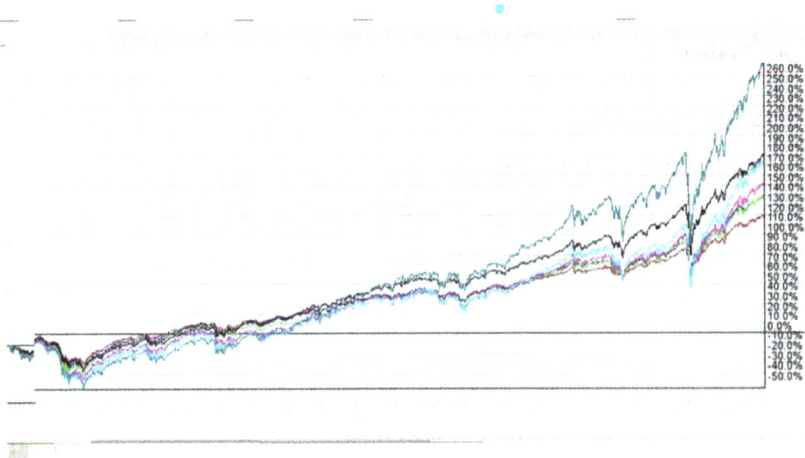

(red) FFANX – 40% Stocks, 60% fixed income, (blue) FASMX – 50% "50%", (green) FASNX – 60% "40%", (purple) FASGX – 70% "30%" (teal) FAMRX – 85% "15%", In addition, the graph includes:(black) VBINX – 60% Stocks, 40% fixed income (the fund I suggest we use) (gray) SPY – A 100% stock S&P500 Index ETF.

During the financial collapse in 2007-2012, this is what happened:

1. The S&P plunged by as much as 53%. In other words, a portfolio of just stocks could have dropped by half.
2. It took 4 years in this example for the S&P to recover.

Such a great "black swan" event can happen any time. Imagine the anxiety this would cause in the leadership who would feel the pressing need to "do something." The 60% balanced fund declined about 35%.

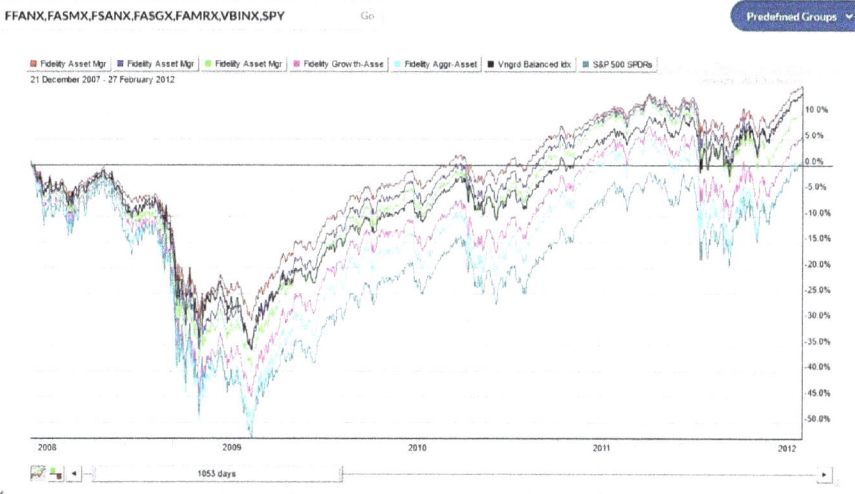

This 33% decline in 2020 was much shorter in duration. But again you see how the 60% fund (in black) declined about 21% and recovered fairly quickly. It took an additional month for the S&P to recover.

![Stonecrop Wealth Advisors logo]

TO: American Psychoanalytic Association Investment Committee

FROM: Douglas R. MacGray, JD, CFP*

DATE: July 20, 2021

RE: <u>Compare/Contrast Active Consulting vs. Passive Vanguard</u>
            <u>Approach</u>

INTRODUCTION

You are considering a very inexpensive and simple approach to managing your two portfolios. Specifically, you are considering putting all the money in the Vanguard Balanced Index Fund.

The contrasting approach would be to develop a traditional relationship with an investment advisor to manage the portfolio with a diverse portfolio of funds and other investment vehicles.

PASSIVE FUNDS

All mutual funds and exchange traded funds (ETFs) have internal costs. These costs include marketing costs as well as the costs to compensate the individuals who choose which stocks or bonds to hold in the portfolio. These costs are referred to as "expense ratios", and thus are measured by a percentage, for example 1.0%.

With a passive approach, the fund generally chooses an index (e.g., S&P 500, MSCI EAFE, Russell 2000, etc.), and then essentially buys stock in all the companies in that index. The goal is to achieve the return of the index, minus the expense ratio. Because the fund need not pay expensive talent to choose which stocks to buy and not to buy, its personnel costs tend to be significantly lower, and its expense ratio can be lower.

The appeals to a passive approach are:

- The costs are lower.
- You dependably obtain the return of the index, and
- It is simple to understand and execute.

With active mutual funds, the fund buys less stocks, and only those in companies which the fund managers believe will outperform the relevant index. As a result, the fund needs to hire individuals on staff who are experts at analyzing companies and how to effectively trade in and out of such funds. This increases the costs of managing such funds, and thus their expense ratios are higher.

THE VANGUARD BALANCED FUND

There are a variety of balanced funds you could use, but for purposes of this memorandum, we are going to focus on the Vanguard Balanced Fund. Vanguard is the most well-known family of index funds, and always seeks to be among the lowest cost providers.

The ticker for this fund is VBINX.

VBINX is a balanced fund that maintains a fixed, U.S.-only 60% stock/40% bond portfolio. There are no international stocks or bonds in the fund.

For the stock portion of the portfolio (60%), the fund tracks the CRSP U.S. Total Stock Market Index. This is an index maintained by the Center for Research in Security Prices, a University of Chicago entity. In the index are nearly 4,000 company stocks across mega, large, small, and micro capitalizations, representing nearly 100% of the U.S. investable equity market.

The bond portion tracks the Bloomberg Barclays U.S. Aggregate Bond Index, representing the U.S. investment-grade taxable-bond market.

The managers ensure the fund remains within 1% of its 60% equity and 40% bond allocation targets. The expense ratio is 0.18%.

VBINX was launched in 1992. The current equity portfolio managers (there are two) began working in the fund in 2016, and the fixed income portfolio manager started in 2013.

Below is a table showing the relative return between the Vanguard Balanced Index Fund (VBINX) and a weighted index of 60% FTSE Global All Cap Equity Index and 40% Bloomberg Barclays U.S. Aggregate Bond Index.[10] In each year, we shaded in green the fund that had the higher return. VBINX had the higher return in five of the 15 years. Other than 2011 and 2008, the returns were very close to one another.

The FTSE Global All Cap Index is a market-capitalization weighted index representing the performance of large, mid and small cap companies in Developed and Emerging markets. The index is part of the FTSE Global Equity Index Series (GEIS), and covers over 7,400 securities in 47 different countries, capturing 98% of the world's investable market capitalization.

---

10 Most investment advisors would recommend and likely deliver a diversified portfolio that would include international stocks. Therefore, I thought it most appropriate to compare how this fund has done versus that kind of traditional approach, i.e., a globally diversified stock index and a U.S. based bond index.

	YTD to 7/12/21	2020	2019	2018	2017	2016	2015	2014	2013	2012	2011	2010	2009	2008	2007
Vanguard Balanced Index (VBINX)	9.47%	16.26%	21.67%	2.97%	13.75%	8.63%	0.37%	9.84%	17.91%	11.33%	4.14%	13.13%	20.05%	22.21%	6.16%
FTSE Global All Cap (60%)/Blmbg Barc US Agg Bond (40%)	10.11%	14.04%	22.38%	2.63%	14.52%	8.23%	1.05%	10.60%	18.62%	11.29%	1.45%	14.00%	17.83%	17.58%	6.29%

Below is return data compared to the S&P 500:

Periodic Return

Data as of July 19, 2021

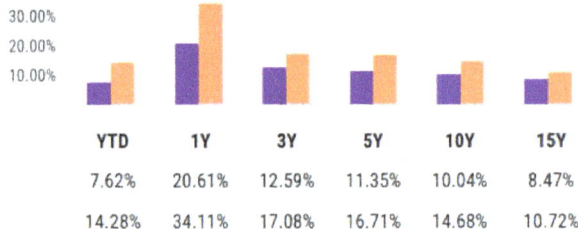

	YTD	1Y	3Y	5Y	10Y	15Y
VBINX	7.62%	20.61%	12.59%	11.35%	10.04%	8.47%
Benchmark	14.28%	34.11%	17.08%	16.71%	14.68%	10.72%

Performance data quoted presents past performance; past performance does not guarantee future results; the investment return and principal value of an investment will fluctuate; an investor's shares, when redeemed, may be worth more or less than their original cost; current performance may be lower or higher than quoted performance data and can be accessed at https://go.ycharts.com/fund_contact_info

Stonecrop

Annual Return

Data as of July 19, 2021

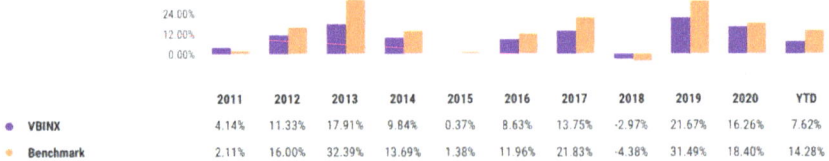

	2011	2012	2013	2014	2015	2016	2017	2018	2019	2020	YTD
VBINX	4.14%	11.33%	17.91%	9.84%	0.37%	8.63%	13.75%	-2.97%	21.67%	16.26%	7.62%
Benchmark	2.11%	16.00%	32.39%	13.69%	1.38%	11.96%	21.83%	-4.38%	31.49%	18.40%	14.28%

Performance data quoted presents past performance; past performance does not guarantee future results; the investment return and principal value of an investment will fluctuate; an investor's shares, when redeemed, may be worth more or less than their original cost; current performance may be lower or higher than quoted performance data and can be accessed at https://go.ycharts.com/fund_contact_info

A Traditional Approach with an Investment Advisor/Consultant

There are a variety of reasons why you should consider using an investment advisor. [Be aware that your current perception is likely skewed by the fact that the Committee has not been paying close attention, and your current investment advisor has not been proactive in serving your needs.] Note that each one of these items below needs to be ferreted out by you in the RFP process if you go that route.

1. Provides a resource and a shield to the trustees.

Trustees owe fiduciary duties of loyalty and care to the entity. As such, if anything negative occurs with the investments, someone could target the trustees claiming negligent exercise of the duty of care. This is especially so if you do not hire an expert to manage the portfolio. Hiring a consultant and doing your appropriate due diligence before hiring the consultant, shows that you are exercising due care by hiring a professional to perform investment functions. You can appropriately exercise your duty of care doing it yourself, but hiring an expert creates a stronger case. In addition, if something negative happens with the account, you have a company, and its assets, and its insurance coverage to go to as a deep pocket to protect the entity and its trustees from liability.

The counterpoint is that VBINX states that it will proactively keep the portfolio always within 1% of the 60/40 allocation, and their history indicates that they will reliably do this. So the VBINX approach limits the possibilities of any surprises or negative things occurring beyond normal market gyrations.

2. Having a Relationship with an Investment Advisor Smoothes Trustee Transitions

Having an investment advisor helps as the board transitions from year to year. One year you may have one or more people on the Investment Committee with investment acumen, but another iteration of the committee in the future may not. Having an investment consultant in place can provide greater continuity and stability in the long term.

3. Proactive Investment Advice and Service

With an investment consultant in place, you always have an individual and an entity watching out for the portfolio. Performance is not guaranteed, but attention can be. An investment consultant will be paying attention to the portfolio, the investment cycle, whether the asset allocation has drifted, performance in between trustees' meetings, and news about fund managers, etc.

4. Customized Performance Reporting

We have found that many institutions do not have a good handle on how their assets have been performing. Monthly statements do not provide enough information. With money going in and out, it can be a difficult process to determine the actual total return of the portfolio, how it is currently invested, whether volatility is picking up, whether the allocation has moved dangerously in the wrong direction, etc. Trustees need a cogent, consistent report that allows them to quickly get up-to-speed on how the portfolio is doing and whether the allocation and performance are within the parameters of the investment policy statement.

A competent investment advisor should provide customized performance reporting digitally, in hard copy and online to make this as effective as possible.

The counterpoint to this factor is that it is fairly easy to track the performance of one fund (i.e., VBINX). However, you will likely find it difficult to get a timeweighted, dollar-weighted report that shows how your actual portfolio is doing taking capital flows into account. But you can get close.

5. Keeping the Investment Policy Statement Up to Date
You should always have an up-to-date Investment Policy Statement. A good investment advisor can help you update what you currently have and keep it current.

6. Running Projections and Analyses
If you need analyses to show how long the assets last under a various assumption, an investment consultant can run these projections to assist you in decision making.

CONCLUSIONS

The last ten years has been a fairly extraordinary time period for stock markets because of the long recovery from one of the worst stock markets in the history of the U.S. stock market (the "Great Recession"). Over the last ten years, the S&P 500 has produced average annual returns of 14.68%. If we go back over longer periods, the average annual return is significantly lower, and what you should plan on going forward.

From 1970 to today, the S&P 500 has averaged 8.256% returns. From 1960 to today, it has averaged 7.392%. From 1950 to today, it has averaged 8.081%.

Therefore, although VBINX has been averaging 10.04% over the last ten years, and 8.47% over the last fifteen, the next ten years are likely to be closer to the average, so closer to 6% to 8%, still enough to achieve the purposes of your portfolios.

A proactive investment advisor can provide significant value over time for all the reasons stated above, but the Investment Committee must be committed to holding any investment advisor it hires accountable for some fairly simple tasks:

1. Regular meetings with understandable presentations and generous Q&A.
2. Cogent performance reports.
3. Constant availability.
4. Willingness to educate new committee members.

Some investment advisors are appropriate when hired, but through changes of personnel or other factors no longer provide the services needed, and the Investment Committee must be committed to keeping the investment advisor on a short leash.

My advice is to move to VBINX now, and all at once while the Investment Committee commits to regular meetings and processes. While the money is in VBINX, you can take your time in determining whether to hire an investment advisor, and the process you will use to choose such an advisor. If you do hire an advisor, you will have developed a cadence of regular meetings before the new advisor comes on board.

The Colony Group

PERFORMANCE BY ASSET CLASS

Discounted Cash Flow Method Net of Fees

APSAA Inc Composite

5 Year Review

Year	APSA Equities	Benchmark S&P 500	APSA Fixed Income	Benchmark Aggregate Bond Index	APSA Total Portfolio	Mgt Fee
Annualized	12.73	15.2	2.41	4.35	7.91	0.53%
2020	18.68%	16.26%	2.75%	7.42%	10.98%	0.48%
2019	30.70%	28.88%	4.17%	8.68%	16.12%	0.50%
2018	−6.77%	−6.24%	1.19%	−0.05%	−3.28%	0.56%
2017	15.97%	19.42%	2.30%	3.53%	10.45%	0.54%
2016	8.89%	9.54%	1.12%	2.56%	5.65%	0.56%

APsaA

A M E R I C A N

PSYCHOANALYTIC

A S S O C I A T I O N

APsaA Reserve Fund Investment Policy Approved by Board of Directors

———————

(date)

The Board of Directors of the American Psychoanalytic Association (the "Association") has adopted this Investment Policy for the purpose of setting forth a framework for the management and oversight of the Reserve Fund of the Association.

Compliance

In managing its Reserve Fund, the Association shall comply at all times with applicable laws and regulations (including but not limited to the New York Prudent Management of Institutional Funds Act (as the same may be amended from time to time, "NYPMIFA")), its Amended and Restated By-laws (as the same may be further amended from time to time, the "By-laws"), and its Conflict of Interest Policy. This Investment Policy shall remain in full force and effect until amended, changed, or repealed at any time by majority vote of the Executive Council.

Statement of Purpose

The Association invests its Reserve Funds to allow for growth in order to fund future special projects supported by its Board of Directors as well as provide funds to the annual budget of the Association. The purpose of this

Investment Policy is to define the investment policies for their supervision, management, and oversight. This document sets forth:

- Delegation of responsibilities for the oversight and management of the asset.
- Investment objectives and policies.
- Strategies to achieve the investment objectives.
- Due diligence criteria for selecting funds or investment managers.
- Criteria for monitoring and evaluating investment results for individual investment managers.
- Criteria for evaluating the overall success in meeting investment objectives.

The Investment Committee of the Finance Committee is responsible for this Investment Policy. The Investment Committee will be responsible for ratifying all changes to this Investment Policy, subject to approval by the Association's Finance Committee and Board of Directors.

Reserve Fund Objectives

The primary mission of the Association in establishing these investments is to provide a funding vehicle to carry out the programs of the Association. The mission of the Investment Committee is to establish an investment process for the assets that is prudent and appropriate. The Investment Committee will consider the following factors in managing the Reserve Funds of the Association: to the extent relevant, the following factors mandated by Section 552(e)(1) of NYPMIFA:

(A) General economic conditions.

(B) The possible effect of inflation or deflation.

(C) The expected tax consequences, if any, of investment decisions or strategies.

(D) The role that each investment or course of action plays within the overall investment portfolio of the Association.

(E) The expected total return from income and the appreciation of investments.

(F) Other resources of the Association.

G) The needs of the Association and any applicable investment fund to make distributions and to preserve capital.

(H) An asset's special relationship or special value, if any, to the purposes of the Association. It is agreed that the investments be managed at all times in compliance with the laws of the State of New York and other applicable laws and regulations.

Responsibilities

Responsibilities for the oversight and management of the Reserve Fund's assets are delineated as follows:

Investment Committee

The Association's Board of Directors through its Finance Committee has delegated primary fiduciary responsibility for protecting the assets of the Reserve Fund to the Investment Committee. In carrying out its responsibilities, the Investment Committee is authorized to:

1. Establish investment policies.
2. Determine prudent asset class strategies.
3. Make prudent asset allocation decisions.

4. Retain investment managers, as needed, to implement asset allocation and asset class strategy decisions.

5. Control and account for all expenses associated with the Reserve Fund.

6. Monitor and supervise all service vendors and investment options.

7. Take corrective action by replacing an investment manager at any time deemed appropriate.

8. Ensure that proper internal controls are developed to safeguard the assets of the Reserve Fund.

The Investment Committee has the right to delegate duties to other parties and to establish suitable oversight procedures so that it always retains ultimate responsibility for the investment outcomes.

Investment Consultant or Advisor

The Investment Committee may retain an objective, third-party investment consultant or advisor ("Investment Consultant") to assist the Investment Committee in managing the overall investment process. The Investment Committee will establish written instructions and guidelines for the Investment Consultant to help ensure that the Investment Consultant performs in a manner consistent with applicable laws and regulations and this Investment Policy Statement.

Investment Managers

The Investment Committee or the Investment Consultant may retain one or more independent investment managers ("Investment Managers") to invest Plan assets, through collective investment funds (including mutual funds and exchange traded funds) or separately managed accounts, in a manner consistent with applicable laws and regulations, this Investment Policy, and other governing documents of the Reserve Funds. The Investment

Committee or the Investment Consultant will provide current copies of this Investment Policy and any investment guidelines to each Investment Manager. The Investment Committee or the Investment Consultant will instruct each Investment Manager to review this Investment Policy and notify the Investment Committee of any inconsistencies between these policies and the agreements, investment guidelines or other documents that govern the Investment Manager's services to the Reserve Fund.

Custodians

The Association's Investment Committee will appoint one or more custodians (the "Custodians") responsible for the safekeeping and reporting of the Reserve Fund's assets. A matrix describing decision-making responsibilities for all involved parties is attached to this Investment Policy Statement as Attachment A.

TYPES OF SECURITIES

The investment guidelines in this Investment Policy are a framework to help the Association achieve for the Reserve Funds the investment objectives at a level of risk deemed acceptable. The Reserve Funds will be diversified both by asset class and within asset classes. Within each asset class, securities will be further diversified among economic sector, industry, quality, and size. The purpose of diversification is to provide reasonable assurance that no single security or class of securities will have a disproportionate impact on the performance of the total fund. As a result, the risk level associated with the portfolio investment is reduced.

Equity Securities

The purpose of equity investments, both domestic and international, in the Reserve Funds is to provide capital appreciation, growth of income, and current income. This asset class carries the assumption of greater market volatility and increased risk of loss, but also provides a traditional approach to meeting portfolio total return goals.

Within this category, the Investment Committee and/or Investment Consultant may employ the use of managers who engage in strategies to hedge risks such as long and short positions, use of options, if these are within the structure of a mutual fund or exchange traded fund, or other fund registered under the Investment Company Act of 1940.

Fixed Income Securities

Fixed income investments provide diversification and a dependable source of current income. Diversification within fixed income investments will be flexibly allocated among maturities of different lengths according to interest rate prospects and the goals of the Reserve Funds. Fixed income instruments should reduce the overall volatility of the Reserve Fund assets, and provide a deflation or inflation hedge, where appropriate.

Within this category, the Investment Committee and/or the Investment Consultant may employ the use of managers who engage in strategies to hedge risks such as long and short positions, use of options, if these are within the structure of a mutual fund or exchange traded fund, or other fund registered under the Investment Company Act of 1940.

Cash and Equivalents

Cash and cash equivalents include investments in the highest quality commercial paper, repurchase agreements, Treasury Bills, certificates of deposit, and money market funds to provide income, liquidity for expense payments, and preservation of the Reserve Fund's principal value. No more than 5% of the Reserve Fund's total market value may be invested in the obligations of a single issuer, with the exception of the U.S. Government and its agencies.

Alternatives

This category includes investments in vehicles that are not in the category of equities, fixed income or cash and includes such areas as real estate, commodities, managed futures, merger arbitrage, and hedge fund replication vehicles. The purpose of alternatives investments in the portfolios is to provide greater diversification to the entire portfolios in which they are part, and thus to reduce overall portfolio volatility and risk. Therefore, finding investment vehicles with correlation data that indicate they do not move in the same manner and in the same cycles as equity investments, and yet have higher, long term, historical, average returns than bonds are what the Investment Committee wants to target as alternative investments in the portfolio. Any such investments shall be within the structure of a mutual fund or exchange traded fund, or other fund registered under the Investment Company Act of 1940.

STRATEGIC ASSET ALLOCATION

The primary investment objective of the Investment Committee is to have the assets invested to outperform inflation by the rate of liability growth (spending policy amount, see below) within reasonable risk levels, including any value added from active management. Strategic asset allocation is the principal method for achieving that objective, while maintaining an appropriate level of risk. The Investment Committee has selected the below asset allocation policy as appropriate, pending the next review.

The Plan's asset allocation policy targets and ranges ("Policy Portfolio") are as follows:

Asset Class	Lower Range (%)	Strategic Allocation (%)	Upper Range (%)	Evaluation Benchmark
Equities	48	60	72	FTSE Global All Cap Index[11]
Fixed Income	24	30	42	Bloomberg Barclays U.S. Aggregate Bond Index
Alternatives	0	9	15	Bloomberg Barclays U.S. Aggregate Bond Index
Cash Equivalents	0.5	1	10	Bloomberg Barclays U.S. Treasury Bills 1-3 Month

The Policy Portfolio return is developed by weighting the passive investment allocation alternatives by the policy target allocations. The asset allocation policy will be reviewed by the Investment Committee at least annually. However, more frequent reviews may be engaged if significant changes occur affecting the Association's financial position or the Reserve Fund's financial position.

---

11   The FTSE Global All Cap Index is a market-capitalization weighted index representing the performance of large, mid and small cap companies in Developed and Emerging markets. The index is part of the FTSE Global Equity Index Series (GEIS), and covers over 7,400 securities in 47 different countries, capturing 98% of the world's investable market capitalization.

Rebalancing Policy

The actual asset allocation will be monitored at least quarterly relative to established policy targets and ranges. However, more frequent review may occur at the discretion of the Investment Committee. If any asset goes beyond the upper or lower ends of the specified range of the policy target, the accounts will be rebalanced back to the strategic allocation target. When necessary and/or available, cash inflows and outflows will be deployed in a manner consistent with the strategic asset allocation to rebalance toward targets.

Investment Performance

The Investment Committee's performance objective is for the Reserve Fund's assets to outperform inflation by the rate of liability growth within reasonable risk levels, including any value added from active management. This performance objective is expected to be achieved over the long term and will be measured over rolling three-, five- and ten-year time periods.

The Reserve Fund performance shall always be reviewed as compared to a hypothetical portfolio invested 60% in the FTSE Global All Cap Index and 40% in the Bloomberg Barclays U.S. Aggregate Bond Index. Equites will be measured against this globally diversified index. Bonds and alternatives will be measured against the Bloomberg Barclays U.S. Aggregate Bond Index. We measure alternatives against that index because the goal of alternatives is to provide diversification and risk reduction. However, bonds do both of these things, and the Investment Committee does not want to be in alternative investments that cannot consistently obtain long-term total returns that are better than bond returns.

The benchmark for added value from active management will be peer relative performance. Each Investment Manager's fund performance will be evaluated against its peer group's median manager return and the applicable category index returns over rolling three-, five- and ten-year time periods.

Every quarter, an investment performance report will be prepared by the Investment Committee or the Investment Consultant, and the report shall include at least the following as of the most recent quarter-end:

- Balance
- Asset allocation
- Prior Quarter, Year-to-date, One Year, Three Year, and Five Year Total Return compared to the weighted index.
- Total management and custodial costs for the year to date and prior year.
- Capital flows in and out year-to-date and for the prior year.
- Total investment gain (or loss) in dollars for the year-to-date, prior year, and prior three years.

Risk Tolerance

The Investment Committee recognizes the difficulty of achieving investment objectives considering the uncertainties and complexities of the investment markets. The Investment Committee also recognizes some risk must be assumed to achieve the long-term investment objectives for the Reserve Funds. In establishing the risk tolerance of the Investment Policy Statement, factors affecting risk tolerance and risk objectives were considered:

The Investment Committee has determined that the Association can tolerate some interim fluctuations in market value and rates of return to achieve long-term objectives.

Time Horizon

The Investment Committee utilizes two time horizons in determining its asset allocation policy:

1. A long-term planning horizon (ten years).
2. A shorter-term investment monitoring horizon (one to three years).

The overall strategic asset allocation policy is based on the long-term perspective. The investment guidelines are based upon an investment horizon of a minimum of ten years. Investment horizons for individual investments, like alternatives, may vary from this stated horizon. The Investment Committee will view interim fluctuations with appropriate perspective, dependent on the asset class.

Investment Manager Selection

The Investment Committee will apply the following due diligence criteria in selecting each Investment Manager:

1. Each Investment Manager must be a regulated bank, an insurance company, a mutual fund organization or other fund registered under the Investment Company Act of 1940, or a registered investment adviser.
2. The investment product of such Investment Manager must be correlated to the asset class of the investment option.
3. Each Investment Manager's fund performance must be evaluated against the appropriate market index.

4. Each Investment Manager's fund performance must be evaluated against its peer group's median manager return over rolling three-, five- and ten-year time periods.

5. Each Investment Manager's holdings should be consistent with style.

6. Expense ratios/fees of the Investment Manager should be appropriate for the specific asset class and peer group.

7. Such qualitative selection criteria as determined by the Investment Committee and the Investment Consultant (i.e., manager tenure, organizational stability, etc.).

Monitoring and Control

The investment structure will be monitored and controlled as follows:

- The overall investments will be monitored quarterly to assess the impact of the global economy and global financial markets on the value of assets and the effectiveness of the investment strategy.

- Actual results will be compared to the Policy Portfolio and the appropriate benchmark return on a quarterly basis, to assess the impact of both passively and actively managed strategies on the value of Reserve Fund assets.

- Periodically, the Investment Committee will undertake a detailed review and assessment of the Reserve Fund's strategy and Investment Managers. This review will cover all aspects of the Reserve Fund's strategy, including the performance and stability of individual investment products or Investment Manager assignments. This detailed review will be performed no less frequently than annually. Any change to this Investment Policy will be communicated in writing on a timely basis to all interested parties.

MEASURING COSTS

At least annually, the Investment Committee will review all costs associated with the management of the Plan's investment program, including:

- Expense ratios or fees of each investment product against the appropriate peer group.
- Consulting and administrative expenses.
- Trust/Trading/Custodial fees.

SPENDING POLICY

It is the policy of the Association's Board of Directors to distribute annually four percent (4%) of the total value of the portfolio as December 31 of the year before.

STANDARDS OF CONDUCT

The Association's Reserve Fund assets shall be managed in good faith and with the care an ordinarily prudent person in a like position would exercise under similar circumstances and considering the factors outlined in Section 552(e) of NYPMIFA, if relevant, and the other factors set forth in this Investment Policy. In addition, the Association may incur only those costs that are appropriate and reasonable in relation to the assets, the purposes of the Reserve Funds and the skills available to the Association and must make a reasonable effort to verify facts relevant to the management and investment of the assets of the Reserve Fund.

Appendix A to Reserve Fund Investment Policy Statement
Governance Matrix

	Setting Strategy		Implementing		Operating			Educating
	Asset Allocation	Rebalancing	Manager Selection Structure & Benchmarks	Portfolio Holdings	Investment Operations	Administrative Operations	Performance Reports	IC Education
Investment Committee	Decides & Oversees	Establishes ranges and agrees to overall timing	Decides & Oversees	Oversees	Oversees	Oversees	Sets policy for what is in the reports, and reviews	—
Staff	—	Implements (If no Investment Consultant)	—	—	—	Implements & Manages	—	—
Investment Consultant	Prepares Studies	Implements	Researche s & Recom- mends	Advises & Over- sees	Imple- ments & Monitors	—	Provides	Provides
Investment Manager	—	—	—	Decides	—	—	Provides	Provides
Custodian	—	—	—	—	Imple- ments	—	Provides	—

339

CHARTER OF THE INVESTMENT COMMITTEE OF
The American Psychoanalytic Association (APsaA)

INTRODUCTION:

The Investment Committee is a standing Committee of the Finance Committee of APsaA and is therefore designated as a Committee of the Corporation. This Charter outlines the responsibilities of the Committee with respect to the duties of individual members. The Committee is responsible for the investments of APsaA and those investments shall collectively be referred to as the Portfolio.

PURPOSE OF THE INVESTMENT COMMITTEE:

The Investment Committee has overall responsibility for the operation and administration of the Portfolio. The members of the Investment Committee are fiduciaries of the Portfolio with respect to responsibilities allocated to them. The members will discharge their duties solely on behalf of APsaA's mission and in accordance with APsaA Reserve Fund Policy Guidelines

COMMITTEE MEMBERSHIP:

The Committee shall consist of the APsaA Treasurer, and also include (at the discretion of the Executive Committee of APsaA) independent volunteers with a background and experience in investment and/or financial management. The number and selection of members appointed to the Committee shall be decided upon by the President of APsaA, who shall also designate a Committee Chair. Each membership shall be acknowledged in writing and retained in APsaA's official records.

Members shall serve at the pleasure of APsaA's Board, and membership is a non-compensable position. The Committee shall hold quarterly meetings or meet more frequently if they determine circumstances require. The Committee shall keep minutes of the meetings and provide annual reports to the Finance Committee of APsaA and to its Board of Directors. The Chair shall, in consultation with other Committee members, set the agenda for and preside at the meetings. A quorum for the transaction of business at any meeting of the Committee shall consist of a majority of Committee members. Decisions shall be made by a majority of those present at the meeting. The Committee shall work in tandem with senior leaders of APsaA and may obtain advice and assistance from internal staff for administrative support, as noted below.

AUTHORITY AND RESPONSIBILITIES:

A. Investment duties

1. Understanding and helping set APsaA's investment goals; and ensuring they are aligned with and support APsaA's mission.
2. Periodically reviewing, and revising an Investment Policy statement that will be submitted to the Board for its approval.
3. Monitoring the performance of investment funds and investment managers in accordance with the Investment Policy statement.
4. Retaining or replacing investment managers and/or investment funds for the Portfolio.
5. Deciding if third-party advisors, such as consultants and other providers of Portfolio services are necessary and selecting/monitoring/replacing accordingly.

341

6. Reviewing the backgrounds of Investment Committee members and staff to ensure no conflicts of interest exist.

B. **Administrative duties (to be performed by APsaA staff in support, and at the direction of the Committee)**

1. Furnishing notices and reports to all Investment Committee members and others including the Finance Committee, the ExCom and Board of Directors.
2. Reviewing all fees incurred by or on behalf of the Portfolio for reasonableness.
3. Ensuring preparing and filing such forms as may be required by government entities.
4. Maintaining records for the administration of the Portfolio and the actions of the Committee.
5. Preparing amendments to the Portfolio for changes in design or applicable laws and regulations.

Representations by APsaA:

APsaA staff shall provide the Committee with such information as is necessary or desirable to fulfill its responsibilities. APsaA may furnish the Committee with such clerical and other assistance, as the Committee may need to perform its duties. APsaA shall be responsible for any reasonable costs or expenses incurred in the Portfolio's operation or administration. However, any duly authorized Portfolio expenses may be paid by or reimbursed from the Portfolio.

The Policies and Procedures Committee proposed and the Board approved that the funds currently designated as the Board Designated Capital Fund be merged with the remaining unrestricted and undesignated funds within APsaA's net assets and retitled the "APsaA Reserve Fund."

APsaA RESERVE FUND USE POLICY
Approved by Board

_____

(date)

Purpose of the Reserve Fund

The purpose of the American Psychoanalytic Association's Reserve Fund is to provide funds when and if the operating expenses of the Association exceed the operating budget in a given year or for a special project approved outside of the operating budget. Funds may be used for these specific projects or purposes to be determined and approved at the discretion of Executive Council.

Investment of the Fund

The Fund shall be invested in accordance with APSA's Reserve Fund Investment Policy

Approval of Expenditure from the Fund

Expenditure from the Reserve Fund may be for approved projects authorized by the Board. This includes specific projects approved as part of the annual budget for which designated funding from the Reserve Fund is also part of the approved budget. For projects and other purposes, which fall outside the annual budget, appropriations from the Reserve Fund require specific approval by the Executive Council.

Withdrawal from the Reserve Fund

Withdrawals from the Reserve Fund may only be made for expenditures related to pre-approved projects or purposes. Upon authorization from the Board, these withdrawals may be made by the Executive Director.

CHAPTER 20

Paul Mosher And His Photography

by Jon K. Meyer

I knew Paul for many years through our work in the American Psychoanalytic Association. During those times, there were many dividing lines in our Association, and it is conceivable that Paul and I may have been on the opposite side of all of them. All except for one.

I believed that there was artistry in the souls of our members, otherwise we would not have been psychoanalysts, and established a place on the program where members could show their art. Paul and I both showed our photography and found common interest and shared passion.

I have had the chance to look again at two of his images, "Utica Union Station" and "Twilight Baseball – July 4." Both brought back fond memories because they are quintessentially Paul. Both are technically superb, as Paul always was. The verticals in the images are near perfect (not an easy task); the lighting and the colors are true to life never overcooked; the depth of field is impeccable so that near and far are in focus; none of the brights are blown out to a blinding white; and none of the darks have disappeared into featureless blackness. But most importantly, both are Americana celebrating upper New York State where Paul was born and spent his life. They are not only among his finest images but, in a sense, they are home.

Paul showed his creativity in many ways, perhaps most notably in bringing us the PEP Web so our literature became available in ways once unimaginable. For me, however, Paul's photographic art, like all art, was the most personal side of that creativity. It is fitting that his images will be memorialized as testimony to the multi-talented, multi-faceted, gifted man he was.

Twilight Baseball – July 4

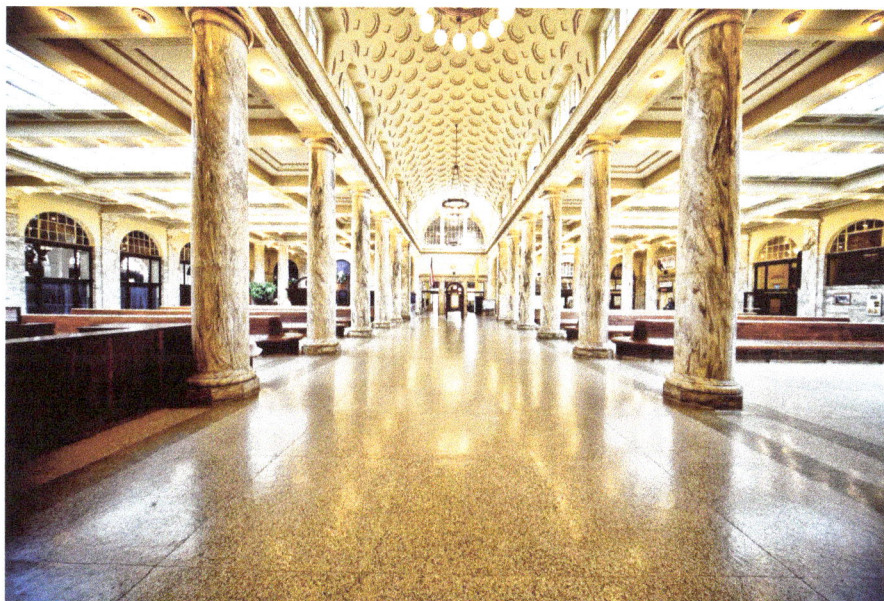

Utica Union Station (Utica New York)

THE IMPACT

CHAPTER 21

Paul Mosher: Scholar, Champion of Privacy and Confidentiality, Parliamentarian, Friend

by Norman Andrew Clemens

I was somewhat in awe of Paul Mosher before I ever met him personally. How could a practicing psychoanalyst, on his own, assemble a database of international scientific literature that could enrich worldwide psychoanalytic studies by orders of magnitude?

The worth of Paul's efforts continues to be demonstrated as the PEP-Web project has evolved a solid organizational structure and powerful software for search and retrieval of content.

I first saw Paul in action at a meeting of the "Wednesday Group" at an APsaA meeting. I had slipped in to see what all the fuss was about. The group was vigorously challenging the staid, hierarchical organizational structure of APsaA, in which the power of the Board on Professional Standards was viewed as detrimental to the interests of the members and of the psychoanalytic societies, as well as an impediment to progress in the field. In the stormy atmosphere, Paul's voice cut like a knife—precise, focused, sometimes sharp, but constructive. I didn't agree with everything I heard that day, but Paul made points that had to be considered thoughtfully.

Paul obviously was a wizard with computers. I had been using them since the mid-1970's, just to share an interest with my then teen-aged son and to learn word-processing and programming in Basic. Paul shared his expertise generously, along with Lee Brauer and Sheila Hafter

Gray, at 7 a.m. on the Fridays of APsaA meetings, with a strong focus on safeguarding privacy, security, and integrity of data. We enjoyed the coffee they provided along with the camaraderie of learning new skills. A generation of nervous computer-using psychoanalysts grew in proficiency under Paul's instruction.

In 1986 I was appointed to APsaA's Committee on Government Relations and Insurance (CGRI), serving as Chair until 1994. Activism on such environmental matters was new to APsaA, sometimes hotly contested in the then-existing Executive Council as a threat to the integrity of psychoanalytic work and the transference relationship. It was also controversial to be interested in supporting psychodynamic psychotherapy along with psychoanalysis *per se*. I brought to the CGRI my American Psychiatric Association experience that had led up to being Speaker of the Assembly in 1994-95, followed by serving six years as Area IV Trustee of APA. As Speaker, I had found strong support among the regional psychiatric leaders for my theme of "Keeping the Psyche in Psychiatry", with psychodynamic psychotherapy as the major paradigm. This led ultimately to being on the APA Committee on Universal Access to Health Care. I was part of a subgroup headed by Susan Lazar, M.D., an APsaA member, who made a presentation to Hillary Clinton's task force on proposed national health care, advocating for the inclusion of psychotherapy in national health insurance. I had previously started local and then national APA programs of outreach to employers to encourage stronger mental health benefits that explicitly included psychotherapy. This activity had led to my chairing the Committee on APA/Business Relationships from 2000 to 2006. I regularly discussed these activities with the CGRI of APsaA and with Paul Mosher in view of the concerns for psychodynamic psychotherapy and psychoanalysis.

If one is going to advocate for the inclusion of psychotherapy or psychoanalytic services in an employer healthcare benefit package or a government-funded health care system, one must meet multiple stiff challenges. Some challenges have to do with the hard-nosed skepticism of the entities that would provide the money, some are with your own professional organization leaders, and some relate to one's own standards. Are psychodynamic psychotherapy and psychoanalysis effective? How do they stack up with medications, cognitive-behavioral therapy, or other forms of psychotherapy? Are they cost-effective? Are they safe? Under conditions of third-party coverage, will they be effective, and can continuity and strict confidentiality be maintained? Paul Mosher helped us in reviewing the increasingly well-designed studies that demonstrated the effectiveness of psychotherapy in general. Eventually, a well-controlled study over a period of years demonstrated that the benefits of psychodynamic therapy were more long-lasting than other forms of psychotherapy.

The components of APsaA charged with the tasks of making the case for coverage and advocating for it were the Committee on Government Relations and Insurance and the Task Force on Economic and Scientific Information (both of which I chaired from 1988 on into the '90s,) The Joint Committee on Confidentiality chaired by Sheila Hafter Gray addressed issues of confidentiality, with Paul Mosher's substantial contribution in relation to privacy of psychotherapy records. The Task Force on Scientific Activities, which Paul Mosher chaired, was especially concerned with the quality of the research on efficacy and outcomes of psychotherapy. All three of those committee chairs, as well as Lee Brauer's committee on Public Information, formed an interactive working group to communicate and coordinate our respective efforts. The advocacy of many mental health organizations achieved success in including coverage for mental health services, including psychotherapy, in Medicare and Obama's Affordable Health Care Act of 2010.

With third-party coverage comes the challenge of maintaining the total confidentiality of sensitive personal information that is revealed in psychotherapy. This historic principle is affirmed in the Hippocratic Oath.

The U.S. Supreme Court's 1996 decision in *Jaffee v. Redmond* (*Jaffee v. Redmond [1996], United States Supreme Court, 95-266*) affirmed an *absolute* privilege of the sensitive personal information disclosed in psychotherapy to any professional "counselor." Paul Mosher led us in closely examining the case, the judicial process, and the implications of this decision. The hero was Karen Beyer, a social worker who resisted breaching the confidence of her psychotherapy client, Mary Lu Redmond. Ms. Redmond was a rookie policewoman who had shot a suspect (Ricky Allen), who was resisting arrest and running after a man with a butcher knife in an apparent intent to stab him. She had subsequently sought therapy because of her horror at having killed someone. Acting as administrator for Ricky Allen's estate, Jaffee filed suit against Redmond and the city that employed her. The plaintiffs demanded Ms. Beyer's psychotherapy notes to bring into evidence the defendant's disclosures about the shooting.

In deciding in favor of the defendant, the Supreme Court established an *absolute* privilege for the personal information disclosed in a "counseling" relationship. The privilege is not subject to a balance test, weighing the prohibition against other considerations. In its favor in the deliberations of the Court, all 50 states have statutes protecting information disclosed to a psychotherapist in psychotherapy; the Supreme Court's decision makes the protection more secure and not debatable.

Paul and I were then leading a Discussion Group during an APsaA national meeting. Karen Beyer was honored at an APsaA meeting for her courage and resilience in defending the psychotherapist-client privilege. Paul invited her and her initial attorney to meet with our Discussion Group; we were inspired by their unpretentious professional dedication to this essential element of trust in a therapeutic relationship.

Paul and I both advocated vigorously for this protection to be explicitly built into the legal system, medical records systems, and third-party payment systems. The focal point became the HIPAA Privacy Rule. The CGRI and

APsaA's attorneys lobbied the U.S. Department of Health and Human Services to respect this ruling as it developed the HIPAA Privacy Rule. As the HIPAA Privacy Rule evolved, Paul and I both wrote extensively on this subject, frequently conferring together and reviewing each other's drafts. Paul and a cousin who is an attorney published a definitive article in an authoritative psychiatry journal (*Mosher PS and Swire PP. The ethical and legal implications of Jaffee v. Redmond and the HIPAA medical privacy rule for psychotherapy and general psychiatry. Psychiatr Clin North Am. 2001; 25:575-584).* From 2000 until 2015, I was the Psychotherapy column editor for the *Journal of Psychiatric Practice* and published many columns on privacy issues and documentation of psychotherapy. I also wrote a *TAP* article for the APsaA membership and several encyclopedia chapters on documentation of psychotherapy and privacy issues.

The HIPAA Privacy Rule was finalized in 2000. With four narrowly defined exceptions, all sensitive personal information recorded in psychotherapy notes is protected from disclosure. The exceptions are 1) for intervention to prevent imminent harm, 2) after suicide of the patient, 3) for professional oversight and training, and 4) for defense in a malpractice action brought in relation to the case.

Maintaining strict protection has been a challenge as highly developed electronic record systems have evolved. Practitioners who are not sensitive to privacy issues may be careless or incautious in segregating sensitive personal disclosures from the objectively observed and factual clinical data that are necessary to support diagnoses or treatment plans. The latter belong in the general clinical record, and subjective, sensitive disclosures belong in psychotherapy notes. Paul and I put much effort into our joint discussion groups and individual activities to make therapists aware of the distinction between the clinical record and psychotherapy notes, especially as the therapists use complicated and intrusive electronic medical records in organized systems of care.

Stimulated by *Jaffee v. Redmond,* Paul dove deeply into cases of egregious violations of professional confidence and trust. As he gathered cases for a monograph in collaboration with Jeffrey Berman, I and others reviewed drafts for chapters, and Paul presented them to our discussion group. Prominent psychoanalysts were among the miscreants, whose stories all ended with tragic consequences. Paul wrote and shared other historical studies as well.

Apart from our privacy interests, Paul Mosher and I both served on the APsaA's Committee on Bylaws, to which I was appointed in 2002 serving as chair from 2006 to 2017. Paul was on the committee most of that time. His growing interest in law, professional ethics, and correct process was of great service to the committee, especially as he had completed the process of being a parliamentarian. He contributed precision in writing, knowledge of parliamentary process, and detailed familiarity with Robert's Rules of Order. Other members of the committee brought their expertise and various points of view as we hammered out amendments. Proposed amendments were also reviewed by the Association's legal counsel.

The first two decades of the century saw enormous changes in the structure and focus of the American Psychoanalytic Association. The bylaws went through many modifications as conflict between membership interests and the psychoanalytic educators was gradually resolved by moving regulation of psychoanalytic education to other bodies. The Committee on Bylaws held to the principle that its role was to implement the will of the Executive Council, later Board of Directors, through clear and unambiguous language that would support effective and fair processes of decision-making and governance. We did not initiate changes except to clarify procedure and to correct identified flaws.

As time went on, Paul's and my personal relationship deepened. We planned ahead to have dinner together during APsaA meeting. We sometimes discussed personal matters as his health problems arose-- a painful hip problem that interfered with walking until it was finally corrected surgically, and later a cardiac issue. Paul was an excellent photographer and made sure that I saw his current display at the meetings. For holiday cards, he and Paula shared striking photographs from their travels. I sensed that Paul's and Paula's family relationships were deep and loving.

At times, I felt that I was playing Dr. Watson to Paul's Sherlock Holmes. His brilliance and a bit of arrogance could be intimidating, but they always seemed dedicated to high principles, to science, and to authenticity. Paul was a good friend personally, a great partner in advocacy, and a servant of scientific integrity in psychoanalysis. I am sad that he has left us.

CHAPTER 22

American Psychoanalytic Association Amici Brief: Jaffee v. Redmond

---

No. 95-266

In The

Supreme Court of the United States

October Term, 1995

Carrie Jaffee as Special Administrator for

Ricky Allen, Sr., Deceased, Petitioner,

v.

Marylu Redmond, Hoffman Estates Police Officer

and Village of Hoffman Estates, Illinois, Respondents.

On Writ of Certiorari to the United States

Court of Appeals for the Seventh Circuit

BRIEF OF THE
AMERICAN PSYCHOANALYTIC ASSOCIATION,
DIVISION OF PSYCHOANALYSIS (39)
OF THE AMERICAN PSYCHOLOGICAL ASSOCIATION,
THE NATIONAL MEMBERSHIP COMMITTEE
ON PSYCHOANALYSIS IN CLINICAL SOCIAL WORK,
THE AMERICAN ACADEMY OF PSYCHOANALYSIS
AS *AMICI CURIAE* IN SUPPORT OF RESPONDENTS

——————————————————

Rex E. Lee
Carter G. Phillips*
Joseph R. Guerra
Dennis D. Hirsch
Sidley & Austin
1722 Eye Street, N.W.
Washington, D.C. 20006
(202)736-8000
Counsel for the Amici Curiae

January 2, 1996   * Counsel of Record

HTML Rendition by Paul W. Mosher, M.D.

QUESTION PRESENTED

Amici will address the following question:

1. Whether federal courts in a civil action should treat as privileged confidential communications made by a patient to a licensed clinical social worker in the course of psychotherapeutic treatment.

TABLE OF CONTENTS

E. Failure to recognize a psychotherapist-patient privilege would raise "difficult and sensitive" constitutional questions concerning patient privacy

CONCLUSION

ENDNOTES

APPENDIX A (STATE STATUTES RECOGNIZING A PSYCHOTHERAPIST-PATIENT PRIVILEGE) NOT INCLUDED HERE

APPENDIX B (STATE STATUTES RECOGNIZING A SOCIAL WORKER-PATIENT PRIVILEGE) NOT INCLUDED HERE

TABLE OF AUTHORITIES NOT INCLUDED HERE

INTEREST OF *ICI CURIAE*

Amici are a consortium of organizations whose members are psychiatrists, psychologists, social workers and others who practice psychoanalysis and/or psychoanalytic psychotherapy, insight-based psychotherapies grounded in the principles and techniques first expounded by Sigmund Freud and developed and advanced over more than 75 years of clinical research by numerous psychoanalytic scholars. The American Psychoanalytic Association («APsaA») is a professional organization of psychoanalysts throughout the United States. The Association is comprised of 40 affiliate societies and 29 training institutes in many cities and has about 3000 individual members. It is a regional association of the International Psychoanalytical Association. The Division of Psychoanalysis (39) is one of 49 divisions of the American Psychological Association. The greater than 3600 full members (not including student members) of Division 39 are psychologists interested in psychoanalysis, the overwhelming majority of whom practice psychoanalysis or psychoanalytic psychotherapy. The National Membership Committee on Psychoanalysis in Clinical Social Work («NMCOP») is comprised of 500 clinical social workers who practice psychoanalysis and/or psychoanalytic psychotherapy. There are 13 area branches of the NMCOP in the United States. The NMCOP is affiliated with the National Federation of Societies for Clinical Social Work. The American Academy of Psychoanalysis is an organization of more than 800 psychiatrists (and some others who do not possess an M.D.) who have undergone extensive psychoanalytic training and practice psychoanalysis and psychoanalytic psychotherapy.

As a direct result of their extensive scholarly and clinical work in the areas of psychoanalysis and psychoanalytic psychotherapy, *Amici's* members strongly believe that confidentiality is critical to the success of psychotherapeutic treatment. The recognition of a psychotherapist-patient privilege is, accordingly, of the utmost importance to *Amici's* members› ability successfully and ethically to practice their profession, and to the welfare of their patients. *Amici* therefore wish to present their views to assist the Court in deciding the present case.[1]

BACKGROUND

Effective psychotherapy requires that the communications between a psychotherapist and a patient remain confidential. Petitioner mistakenly maintains that there is no need for such confidentiality. Indeed, petitioner

---

1   Pursuant to Rule 37.3 of the Rules of this Court, the parties have consented to the filing of this brief. The parties' letters of consent have been filed with the Clerk of the Court.

asserts that disclosure of these communications results in "therapeutic benefits." Pet. Br. 29. Petitioner deems the asserted need for confidentiality a "'counseling folklore.'" *Id.* at 26 (citation omitted).

Petitioner simply ignores the three ways in which confidentiality is critical to effective psychotherapy: (1) it enables individuals to obtain help in dealing with problems or feelings they may consider too shameful, troubling or socially embarrassing to share with family or friends; (2) it is critical to building the patient's trust in the psychotherapist and thereby fosters the "therapeutic alliance"; and (3) it is a critical prerequisite to full disclosure (or "free association"), the fundamental technique by which psychoanalysis and psychoanalytic psychotherapy accomplish their goals.

Petitioner's lack of understanding of psychotherapy leads her not only to denigrate the importance of confidentiality, but to overestimate the importance of patient-psychotherapist communications to the truth-seeking process of litigation. The full disclosure employed in psychoanalysis and psychoanalytic psychotherapy is not a process of identifying objective facts, but a technique designed to explore (through dreams, fantasies, etc.) unconscious factors that shape conscious thoughts or behavior. Psychoanalytic therapy thus gives rise to an extraordinarily intimate relationship in which patients divulge thoughts, feelings, dreams and fantasies that may have little correspondence to external reality. A fuller understanding of psychoanalysis and psychoanalytic psychotherapy, and the crucial importance of confidentiality to them, is essential to the Court's privilege analysis and to its analysis of patients' privacy rights.

1. Confidentiality enables individuals to obtain needed psychotherapy.

People generally seek out psychotherapy for help in dealing with those problems they experience as too shameful or troubling to be shared comfortably with family members, friends or co-workers. For example, a person who experienced unwanted sexual desires, or a law enforcement officer who experienced strong fears in the aftermath of a violent incident and did not want to disclose this to colleagues, might seek out psychotherapy for assistance in dealing with these concerns. In either of these instances and the myriad others that motivate people to seek such assistance, the public disclosure in court of the contents of the therapy would be embarrassing or even job-threatening. Indeed, given the social stigma still attached to the need for psychotherapy, public disclosure of the very fact that the individual had sought treatment might well prove detrimental.[2] See *Parham v. J.R.*, 442 U.S. 584, 600 (1979) (recognizing stigma associated with child who "has received psychiatric care"). In the absence of a privilege, many individuals will be deterred from seeking psychotherapy who currently do or might benefit from it. Thus, "[c]onfidentiality is essential for successful psychiatric treatment [for] [w]ithout it, patients would be hesitant to enter into a meaningful psychotherapeutic relationship." *Psychiatric Peer Review: Prelude and Promise* 175 (J. Hamilton ed., 1985).

2. Confidentiality is essential to the establishment of the "therapeutic alliance".

An important initial step in psychoanalysis and psychoanalytic psychotherapy is the establishment of a "therapeutic alliance." This consists of a positive working relationship between patient and therapist in which both commit

---

2   For example, 55 percent of supervisors surveyed indicated that they would have a negative attitude towards an employee who had seen a psychiatrist. See *Psychiatric Peer Review: Prelude and Promise* 179 (J. Hamilton ed., 1985). The social stigma that attaches to those who seek psychotherapy is further evidenced by the fact that some patients forgo insurance coverage of their treatment rather than risk their employers finding out about it. See *Statement of the American Psychiatric Association* (by Jerome S. Beigler, M.D.) Before the Subcommittee on Government Information and Individual Rights of the Committee on Government Operations (Apr. 9, 1979).

to the common goal of furthering understanding of the patient's problems and conflicts. In a sound therapeutic alliance, the patient experiences trust, hopefulness with regard to the outcome of the treatment, and a willingness to cooperate with the rigors of therapeutic work. See 1 H. Kaplan & B. Sadock, *Comprehensive Textbook of Psychiatry* 470 (6th ed. 1995) (*"Textbook of Psychiatry"*). "No analysis can proceed without the formation of a rational, trusting therapeutic alliance." *Id.* at 1775.

Confidentiality is part of the core foundation for the building of the therapeutic alliance. Through it, the therapist demonstrates trustworthiness and concern first and foremost with the patient's well-being. Confidentiality is, accordingly, "a cornerstone of therapy; it is essential to the therapeutic alliance and setting which fosters the unfolding of the patient's problems and fantasies on every level." 1 R. Langs, *The Technique of Psychoanalytic Psychotherapy* 193 (1973). The possibility that a therapist might reveal in a court of law a patient›s most troubling inner secrets would stand as a permanent obstacle to development of the necessary degree of patient trust in the therapist, and would pose a significant, and for many patients an insurmountable, barrier to effective treatment.

3. Without confidentiality psychotherapy would lose much of its efficacy.

A basic tenet of psychoanalytic therapy is that the patient should reveal to the therapist any thoughts, feelings, dreams, fantasies or sensations that come to mind during a treatment session, no matter how shameful or troubling the patient may find them to be. Thus, confidentiality is also essential to psychoanalytic therapy because it enables patients fully to disclose their thoughts or feelings without fear of public disclosure.

Petitioner concedes this point with respect to "psychoanalysis," Pet. Br. at 27, acknowledging that psychoanalysts "require 'uncensored access to all of their patient's thoughts and feelings,'" and that confidentiality is accordingly essential to this discipline. *Id.* (quoting Shuman, Weiner & Pinard, *The Privilege Study (Part III): Psychotherapist-Patient Communications in Canada*, 9 Int'l J. of L. & Psychol. 393, 416 (1986)). Petitioner appears to believe, however, that such imperatives are not "common" in the field of psychotherapy, and that they apply in "'relatively few cases.'" *Id.*

Petitioner fundamentally misunderstands the field of psychotherapy. For the same reasons that classical psychoanalysis requires confidentiality, other, more widely-practiced forms of psychotherapy that also rely substantially on psychoanalytic principles and technique—generally termed "psychoanalytic psychotherapy"—likewise require it.[3] According to a recent survey, psychoanalytic psychotherapy "is the most common form of treatment among mental health professionals and is a highly valued form of treatment." L. Luborsky *et al.*, Preface in *Psychodynamic Treatment Research: A Handbook for Clinical Practice* (N. Miller *et al.* eds., 1993).[4] *Amici* have extensive experience in the clinical practice of both classical psychoanalysis

---

3　Psychoanalytic psychotherapy "is based on fundamental dynamic formulations and techniques that derive from psychoanalysis." 2 H. Kaplan & B. Sadock, *Comprehensive Textbook of Psychiatry* 1783 (6th ed. 1995); accord I.H. Paul, The Form and Technique of Psychotherapy 9 (1978). However, in contrast to classical psychoanalysis in which the patient generally lies on a couch and sees the analyst for four to five 50-minute sessions per week, the patient and therapist in psychoanalytic psychotherapy generally sit face-to-face (although the couch may, at times, be used), and usually meet for one to three 45- to 50- minute sessions per week. Id. at 1779. Psychoanalytic psychotherapies are also more likely to draw, not only on classical psychoanalytic theory, but on other well-established theories as well. See A. Bergin & S. Garfield, *Handbook of Psychotherapy and Behavior Change* 181 (4th ed. 1994); 2 H. Kaplan & B. Sadock, *Comprehensive Textbook of Psychiatry* 1770 (6th ed. 1995).

4　Officer Redmond appears to have participated in an insight-based form of psychotherapy such as psychoanalytic psychotherapy. Ms. Beyer testified that her principal training was in "psychodynamic" psychotherapy. Dep. of Karen Beyer 61 (July 13, 1992). "Psychodynamic" therapies operate from the premise that "psychopathology is a consequence of repression and a lack and/or avoidance of self-knowledge about how one's mind works.... Accordingly, all psychodynamic therapists attempt to help their patients recover and reintegrate those parts of the patient that were lost to the unconscious and attempt to achieve some degree of insight.... [A]ll psychodynamic therapists presuppose that people have the capacity to change if they can achieve meaningful mental insight." T. Paolino, *Psychoanalytic Psychotherapy* 17 (1981).

and psychoanalytic psychotherapy (collectively, «psychoanalytic therapy»). For the reasons that follow, full disclosure, and hence confidentiality, is an essential ingredient of all psychoanalytic therapy.

Psychoanalytic therapy starts from the premise that the human mind operates on both conscious and unconscious levels. The "conscious" mind consists of those thoughts and feelings of which we are aware. The "unconscious" encompasses those parts of our minds of which we are not aware. Psychoanalytic theory assumes that the conscious concerns and symptoms (*e.g.*, fear, anxiety, depression) that bring a person into psychotherapy are caused, at least in part, by unconscious factors.[5] See C. Brenner, *An Elementary Textbook of Psychoanalysis* 9 (1973) (Freud discovered that "not only hysterical symptoms but also many other normal and pathological aspects of behavior and thinking were the result of what was going on unconsciously in the mind of the individual who exhibited them").

Stated simply, the central goal of psychoanalytic therapy is to help individuals become aware of and/or rework the unconscious factors that (unbeknownst to them) are shaping the way that they think, feel, act or react to a given situation. See D. Louisell, *The Psychologist in Today's Legal World: Part II*, 41 Minn. L. Rev. 731, 746-47 n.56 (1957) ("the very art of successful psychotherapy seems to consist in helping the patient learn for himself the causes of his conduct and the methods of correction").[6] Once this is done,

---

5   While such difficulties or symptoms might be provoked by a traumatic event such as the shooting incident in which Officer Redmond was involved, psychoanalytic therapy nonetheless assumes that a given individual's reaction to such an event (and individuals may react differently, with some being more troubled than others) largely reflects that person's conscious and unconscious psychological make-up. Thus, a psychoanalytic therapist assisting someone such as Officer Redmond would address both the conscious and unconscious factors that inform her response to the shooting. Such a treatment would likely employ full disclosure as well as the other techniques and principles discussed in this section.

6   The Illinois legislature has recognized that licensed clinical social workers such as Ms. Beyer utilize this principle in their work. Illinois law defines a licensed clinical social worker as one who provides "mental health services for the evaluation, treatment, and prevention

the individual is able to use the abilities of the conscious mind—reason, understanding, intention—to deal better with the unconscious aspects of the mind that were causing the distressing symptoms, behaviors or reactions. In this way, psychoanalytic therapy uses insight to alleviate symptoms. "If a [symptom] can be traced back to the elements in the patient's mental life from which it originated, it simultaneously crumbles away and the patient is freed from it." S. Freud, *The Interpretation of Dreams, in* 4 *Standard Edition of the Complete Psychological Works of Sigmund Freud* 100 (1958) («*Standard Edition*»). Thus it might be said that "the healing power of psychoanalysis lies... in the hoary dictum 'Know thyself.'" J. Kovel, *A Complete Guide to Therapy* 75 (1976).

The central challenge of psychoanalytically-based psychotherapy lies in the fact that it is not easy to bring into conscious awareness that which is unconscious. Generally, emotions, thoughts or experiences remain out of consciousness because they are shameful, frightening or otherwise "not acceptable to the patient." American Psychoanalytic Association, *Psychoanalytic Terms and Concepts* 44 (1990); see H. Etchegoyen, *The Fundamentals of Psychoanalytic Technique* 9 (1991) («things are forgotten if one does not wish to remember them, because they are painful, ugly and disagreeable, contrary to ethics and/or aesthetics»). Individuals develop strong unconscious defenses or «resistances» which function to keep knowledge of these disconcerting thoughts and feelings from becoming conscious. *Id*. To further patients' understanding, the psychoanalytic therapist helps them to overcome these "resistances" using techniques whose prerequisite is a safe, confidential treatment situation. See 1 *Psychiatry: the Personality Disorders and Neuroses* 2 (1985).

---

of mental and emotional disorders... based on knowledge and theory of psychosocial development, behavior, psychopathology, *unconscious motivation*, interpersonal relationships, and environmental stress." Ill. Rev. Stat. ch. 225, para. 20/3 (1994) (emphasis added).

Full disclosure (or "free association")—a technique in which the patient is encouraged to say whatever comes to mind no matter how embarrassing, frightening, disturbing or irrelevant it may seem—is the principal method by which the patient and the therapist see beyond the patient's defenses and bring unconscious material into the light of consciousness. It is an essential component of both classical psychoanalysis and psychoanalytic psychotherapy. See *Psychoanalytic Terms and Concepts* at 78 («[t]he basic procedure of psychoanalysis and psychoanalytic psychotherapy... [is that the patient should] express in words all thoughts, feelings, wishes, sensations, images and memories without reservation, as they spontaneously occur.... [T]he patient must often overcome conscious feelings of embarrassment, fear, shame, and guilt"). The purpose of full disclosure is *not* to ascertain objective facts or to establish the actual events surrounding a traumatic experience. Rather, the relaxing of the mind›s internal editing allows unconscious material to emerge and to be observed by the psychotherapist and patient.

The reason for the great value of having the patient relinquish conscious control of his thoughts is this: what the patient thinks and says under those circumstances is determined by *unconscious* thoughts and motives. Thus Freud, by listening to the patient›s «free» associations—which were after all free only from *conscious* control—was able to get a picture, by inference, of what was going on unconsciously in his patient›s mind.

C. Brenner, *An Elementary Textbook of Psychoanalysis* 9 (1973).[7] The patient›s obligation to engage in full disclosure is referred to as the «fundamental rule» of psychoanalytic therapy. *Psychoanalytic Terms and Concepts* at 78.

---

7   The unique window onto the unconscious that full disclosure provides has led some to equate this technique with the microscope or telescope. C. Brenner, *An Elementary Textbook of Psychoanalysis* 8 (1973). Like these other instruments, the patient's free association allows the observer (psychotherapist and patient) to see past the surface to the more profound realities that lie beyond.

A threat to the confidentiality of the psychotherapist-patient relationship, such as that which would result from the absence of a privilege, would profoundly impair the ability of a patient to disclose fully the thoughts that come to mind. As mentioned above, the patient must feel free to discuss *anything* with *no* exceptions. Thus, ideas that the patient experiences as shameful or disturbing, even the confidences of third parties, must be shared if they come to mind during the course of the analytic session.[8] Indeed, given the oftentimes troubling content of unconscious material (which is, in part, why it remains unconscious), it is precisely the most embarrassing, shameful and displeasing thoughts that a patient *should* express in a psychoanalytic therapy.

"[C]onfidentiality of the material... is a prerequisite for free association. No analysand succeeds in divesting himself of all defenses or controls unless he can be certain that the derivatives of his id will not become known beyond the confines of the analytic situation." 4 A. Freud, *The Writings of Anna Freud* 417 (1968); see S.H. Gray, *Quality Assurance and Utilization Review of Individual Medical Psychotherapies, in Manual of Psychiatric Quality Assurance Review* 159-66 (1992) (field data demonstrate that full disclosure depends on confidentiality). Confidentiality is, accordingly, critical to the effective practice of any psychoanalytic therapy. Without it, patients would be reluctant to disclose all that comes to mind and psychoanalytic technique would be severely impaired.

---

8   The failure to disclose any of these thoughts can serve as a defense against knowledge of the unconscious.

It is very remarkable how the whole task becomes impossible if a reservation is allowed at any single place. But we have only to reflect what would happen if the right of asylum existed at any one point in a town; how long would it be before all the riff-raff of the town had collected there?

S. Freud, *Further Recommendations on Technique*, in 12 *Standard Edition* 135-36 n.1

SUMMARY OF THE ARGUMENT

The five factors that the Court should consider in determining whether to recognize a privilege under Fed. R. Evid. 501 decidedly favor recognition of the psychotherapist-patient privilege.

1. Although the widespread adoption of state statutes recognizing the psychotherapist-patient privilege stunted the development of judicial common law dealing with psychotherapist-patient communications, most courts to consider the matter have found that "inviolability of confidence is essential to the achievement of the psychotherapeutic goal," *Allred* v. *State*, 554 P.2d 411, 417 (Alaska 1976), and have accordingly recognized the psychotherapist-patient privilege.

2. "Reason and experience" show that confidentiality is essential to effective psychoanalytic therapy and that the societal benefits of such treatments outweigh any adverse impact the recognition of a psychotherapist-patient privilege might have on the truth-seeking function of litigation. Over the past few decades, more and more Americans have sought the documented benefits of psychotherapy. In particular, psychoanalytic therapy can help police officers such as Officer Redmond to face and learn to accept unavoidable violent encounters rather than dealing with them through emotional numbing.

 The failure to recognize a psychotherapist-patient privilege would prove disastrous for the effective practice of psychoanalytic therapy. Many who could benefit from psychoanalytic therapy, including police officers, would be deterred from seeking it due to the fear of disclosure in court. Moreover, the threat of disclosure would severely undermine the "therapeutic alliance"— the collaborative relationship between therapist and patient that is essential to any successful psychoanalytic therapy. Finally, the central technique of all psychoanalytic therapy is premised on the patient's willingness to disclose to the therapist all thoughts, feelings, fantasies and dreams that come to mind. The lack of a privilege would destroy the protected atmosphere that makes such communications possible and would, accordingly, seriously impair the efficacy of psychoanalytic therapy.

By contrast, the benefits to litigation from the absence of a privilege are minimal. In most cases parties will have other means (*e.g.,* deposition, trial testimony) of obtaining the patient's version of the facts. Moreover, the patient's disclosures to the therapist are inherently unreliable as evidence since psychoanalytic therapy focuses not on reconstructing objective facts, but on furthering understanding of the patient's internal reality through fantasies, dreams and imaginings.

3. Every State in the nation recognizes a psychotherapist-patient privilege by statute. See Appendix A. Comity accordingly favors federal recognition of the privilege. To do otherwise would create the risk of inequitable administration of laws and incentives for unseemly "forum shopping" that this Court condemned in *Erie R.R.* v. *Tompkins,* 304 U.S. 64 (1938).

4. Proposed Rule of Evidence 504, promulgated by the Court in 1972, contained a psychotherapist-patient privilege. While Congress substituted Rule 501 in place of the Court's proposals, these proposals nonetheless serve as guidance and favor recognition of the privilege.

5. Psychoanalytic therapy requires patients to reveal their conscious and unconscious thoughts, feelings, dreams and fantasies no matter how shameful or troubling. Psychoanalytic therapy accordingly implicates the patient's privacy to a greater degree than almost any other human relationship. The Court has consistently construed acts of Congress to avoid raising "difficult and sensitive" constitutional questions. *NLRB* v. *Catholic Bishop*, 440 U.S.

490, 507 (1979). The Court should construe Rule 501 to require recognition of the psychotherapist-patient privilege so as to avoid implicating Officer Redmond's privacy rights. See *Whalen* v. *Roe*, 429 U.S. 589, 599 (1977); *Doe* v. *City of New York*, 15 F.3d 264 (2d Cir. 1994); *United States* v. *Westinghouse Elec. Corp.*, 638 F.2d 570, 577 (3d Cir. 1980).

ARGUMENT

THE COURT SHOULD RECOGNIZE A PSYCHO- THERAPIST-PATIENT PRIVILEGE UNDER FEDERAL RULE OF EVIDENCE 501.

Federal Rule of Evidence 501, which governs federal evidentiary privileges, provides that:

[e]xcept as otherwise required by the Constitution of the United States or provided by Act of Congress or in rules proscribed by the Supreme Court pursuant to statutory authority, the privilege of a witness... shall be governed by the principles of the common law as they may be interpreted by the courts of the United States in the light of reason and experience.

Fed. R. Evid. 501.

In applying Rule 501, this Court should consider five factors. First, it should look to "common law" privilege doctrines. *Id.* Second, it should seek to build on these doctrines «in the light of reason and experience."[9] *Id.* Third, "a strong policy of comity" requires federal courts to recognize the privileges

---

[9]   Congress expressly did not intend Rule 501 to "freeze the law of privilege. Its purpose rather was to 'provide the courts with the flexibility to develop rules of privilege on a case-by-case basis,' and to leave the door open to change." *United States v. Trammel*, 445 U.S. 40, 47 (1980) (quoting 120 Cong. Rec. 40891 (1974) (Statement of Rep. Hungate); H.R. Rep. No. 93-650 at 8 (1973)).

established by state law "where this can be accomplished at no substantial cost to federal substantive and procedural policy." *United States* v. *King*, 73 F.R.D. 103, 105 (E.D.N.Y. 1976); see also *United States* v. *Gillock*, 445 U.S. 360, 368 n.8 (1980). Fourth, the proposed privilege rules that this Court promulgated in 1972 but that Congress replaced with the current Rule 501 provide guidance concerning the scope of federal privileges. See *In re Grand Jury Investigation*, 918 F.2d 374, 380 (3d Cir. 1990). Finally, the Court should construe Rule 501 so as to avoid raising "difficult and sensitive" constitutional questions. See *NLRB*, 440 U.S. at 507. In the present case, all five of these factors decidedly favor recognition of the psychotherapist-patient privilege as a matter of federal law.[10]

A. Common law courts have recognized a psychotherapist-patient privilege.

The common law traditionally held as privileged confidential communications between husband and wife, and between attorney and client, on the grounds that the need for frank communication in these relationships outweighed the litigation need for disclosure. See *McCormick on Evidence* 180, 201 (3d ed. 1984).

Judicial development of a comparable common law privilege for psychotherapist-patient communications has largely been truncated by the widespread adoption of State statutes extending privileged status to such communications. See Appendix A. Nevertheless, prior to these State legislative activities, several courts applied the logic underlying the attorney-client and marital privileges and recognized a psychotherapist-patient privilege as a matter of common law.

---

10   *Amici* will not focus on the second question presented, regarding the extension of this privilege to licensed clinical social workers, since several other amici are doing so. *Amici* favor Respondents' position as to both questions presented.

For example, in *Allred* v. *State*, 554 P.2d 411 (Alaska 1976), the Supreme Court of Alaska considered whether to extend a privilege to defendant's in-custody communications to his drug program coordinator and counselor. The court found that the relationship between a patient and his therapist "is unquestionably one which should be fostered." *Id*. at 417. It further found that confidentiality is essential to the success of psychotherapeutic treatment because "[i]n therapy the patient must often lay bare his entire inner life, including his fantasies, his past behavior, and his feelings of guilt or shame." *Id*. The Court accordingly concluded that the damage to the psychotherapeutic relationship from fear of disclosure "heavily" outweighed the competing litigation interest in full information. *Id*. at 418. It recognized a psychotherapist-patient privilege as a matter of State common law. *Id*.[11] Other State courts have done the same. See *State* v. *Evans*, 454 P.2d 976 (Ariz. 1969); *Binder* v. *Ruvell*, No. 52-C-2535 (Cir. Ct., Cook Cty., Ill. June 24, 1952), *reported in* 150 J.A.M.A. 1241 (1952) (unpublished decision). Petitioner has cited no countervailing common law authority. The common law favors recognition of the psychotherapist-patient privilege.

In applying the "reason and experience" prong of Rule 501, courts have relied on four factors enunciated by Dean Wigmore. See, *e.g., United States* v. *Friedman*, 636 F. Supp. 462 (S.D.N.Y. 1986) (adopting Wigmore's formulation). These are:

1. The communications must originate in a confidence that they will not be disclosed.

2. This element of confidentiality must be essential to the full and satisfactory maintenance of the relation between the parties.

---

11 The court, however, declined to apply the privilege on the facts before it because the communications at issue did not occur during psychotherapy and the drug program coordinator to whom the defendant had spoken was not a psychotherapist. *Allred v. State*, 554 P.2d 411, 418-22 (Alaska 1976).

3. The relation must be one which in the opinion of the community ought to be sedulously fostered.

4. The injury that would inure to the relation by the disclosure of the communications must be greater than the benefit thereby gained for the correct disposal of litigation. (emphasis omitted).

All four of these factors weigh heavily in favor of recognizing a psycho-therapist-patient privilege.

1. As explained above, psychotherapy requires patients to reveal to the therapist the most troubling, unpleasant and shameful aspects of their inner lives. "'The... patient confides more utterly than anyone else in the world.... [H]e lays bare his entire self, his dreams, his fantasies, his sins, and his shame." *Taylor* v. *United States*, 222 F.2d 398, 401 (D.C. Cir. 1955) (quoting M. Guttmacher & H. Weihofen, *Psychiatry and the Law* 272 (1952)). Patients make these intimate disclosures with the expectation that they will be held in confidence; indeed, without such an expectation the disclosures would not occur.

Recognizing that such disclosure can only take place in an atmosphere of complete trust and confidentiality, psychotherapists have made it their professional duty to keep the confidences shared with them. For example, the American Psychoanalytic Association's code of professional ethics requires that

Except as required by law, a psychoanalyst may not reveal the confidences entrusted to him in the course of his professional work, or the particularities that he may observe in the characters of patients. Should he be required by a court of law to give testimony relating to the confidences of his patient, he should make use of all legal means to safeguard his patient's right to confidentiality.

American Psychoanalytic Association, *Principles of Ethics for Psychoanalysts and Provisions for Implementation of the Principles of Ethics for Psychoanalysts* § 6 (1983); accord American Psychological Association, *Ethical Principles of Psychologists and Code of Conduct* § 5 (1992);

American Psychiatric Association, *Principles of Medical Ethics With Annotations Especially Applicable to Psychiatry* § 4 (1995); National Federation of Societies for Clinical Social Work, *Code of Ethics* § 5 (1988).[12] In sum, the psychotherapist- patient relationship is a highly confidential one and each patient understands this at the commencement of treatment.

2. As discussed above, confidentiality is critical to the success of the psychotherapist-patient relationship in at least three ways. First, many individuals who could benefit from psychotherapy will be deterred from doing so in the absence of a privilege. Second, the therapist's demonstrated willingness to keep the patient's confidence is critical to the establishment of a sound "therapeutic alliance." A threat of disclosure such as that posed in the absence of a privilege will undermine this core precondition of successful treatment.

Finally, the threat of disclosure will interfere with a patient's ability to reveal fully what is on the patient's mind. If, as petitioner argues here, a psychotherapist could be required in a civil action to testify as to the contents of the treatment, patients would be unwilling or unable to engage in psychotherapy's most central technique. Few patients can be expected to lay bare their most private and potentially embarrassing thoughts, wishes and fantasies knowing they may someday be disclosed in civil judicial

---

12   Recognizing the threat to confidentiality posed by the one listed exception (i.e., disclosures required by a court of law), representatives of the various practitioners of psychoanalysis and psychotherapy have successfully lobbied on behalf of numerous State laws that extend a privilege to patient- therapist discussions. For example, a representative of the American Psychoanalytic Association participated in the drafting of the Illinois privilege statute under which Officer Redmond obtained protection from discovery with respect to the State law claims against her.

proceedings. This chilling effect would in turn deny psychoanalytic therapists the uncensored access to their patients' thoughts and feelings that is the *sine qua non* of their practice. The effect would be akin to stopping-up the general practitioner›s stethoscope or taking away the orthopedist›s X-ray machine. Psychotherapy, as a field, would suffer enormously in its ability to help people such as Officer Redmond better to resolve their inner difficulties and thereby become more productive members of society.

3. The confidential relationship between patient and therapist is one society should protect and foster. The past century of rapid economic and social change has subjected many Americans to "unprecedented psychic demands" at the same time as it has isolated them from the kinship, religious and other ties that might, in an earlier era, have offered them support. R. Bellah *et al., Habits of the Heart: Individualism and Commitment in American Life* 119-21 (1985). During this same period, the number of Americans utilizing the mental health professions has increased steadily, more than tripling between 1965 and 1985 alone. *Id*. at 121.

Individuals seek out psychoanalysis and psychoanalytic psychotherapy because these treatments offer important benefits. For example, psychoanalysis and psychoanalytic psychotherapy can help to improve marital relations, work performance and overall social adjustment. A. Bergin & S. Garfield, *Handbook of Psychotherapy and Behavior Change* 148 (4th ed. 1994). They can also help to alleviate specific symptoms such as sleep or eating disorders, anxiety, or depression. *Id*. Individuals who participate in these treatments also commonly experience a sense of liberation from internal inhibitions that results in increased creativity and productivity. 1 *Textbook of Psychiatry* at 473.

These benefits are particularly evident in the area of law enforcement, as this case illustrates. Police officers such as Officer Redmond confront violence, personal tragedy, and danger nearly every working day. This stressful environment may lead to various symptoms including emotional numbing and frustration that can interfere with the officer's interaction with community members. See S. Marans, *Community Violence and Children's Development: Collaborative Interventions, in* 11 *The Child in the Family* 109, 117 (C. Chiland & J.G. Young eds., 1994); *cf.* 1 *Textbook of Psychiatry* at 1231-32.

Through psychotherapy, officers such as Officer Redmond can learn to face and accept the strong feelings raised by unavoidable stressful and violent encounters rather than blocking these feelings out. *Id.* at 1235. This will, in turn, help such officers to remain empathetic and effective in their interactions with the community. Officer Redmond's decision to seek treatment in the aftermath of the shooting of Ricky Allen is exactly the sort of response society should encourage and support. Protecting the confidentiality of Officer Redmond's treatment through recognition of a psychotherapist-patient privilege will make it easier for her, and others like her, to seek treatment when they need it.[13] The privilege thereby promotes safer communities and more effective law enforcement, in addition to better adjusted and more productive individuals.

The benefits of psychoanalysis and psychoanalytic psychotherapy are well- documented. Rigorous studies of psychoanalytic treatments conducted by the Menninger Foundation, the Columbia Psychoanalytic Center, the Boston Psychoanalytic Institute and the New York Psychoanalytic Institute between 1954 and 1984 "confirm that patients suitable for psychoanalysis derive therapeutic benefit." H. Bachrach *et al., On the Efficacy of Psychoanalysis,* 39 J. *Am. Psychoanalytic Assn* 871, 911 (1991). Empirical studies of psychoanalytic psychotherapy have similarly concluded that "a

---

13   In the absence of a privilege, on the other hand, a prudent attorney might well advise law enforcement officer clients not to seek psychotherapeutic treatment where a wrongful death charge or other legal claim is pending or threatened. Law enforcement officers would face a Hobson's choice between seeking treatment which will increase their legal exposure, or foregoing the benefits of psychotherapy.

broad range of therapies, when offered by skillful, wise and stable therapists, are likely to result in appreciable gains for the client." A. Bergin & S. Garfield, *Handbook of Psychotherapy and Behavior Change* 180 (4th ed. 1994); see generally, N. Doidge, *Empirical Evidence for the Core Clinical Concepts and Efficacy of Psychoanalytic Psychotherapies: An Overview* (Jan. 1995) (unpublished manuscript). Moreover, a recent Consumer Reports survey of participants in psychotherapy concluded that «[t]he majority... were highly satisfied with the care they received. Most had made strides toward resolving the problems that led to treatment, and almost all said life had become more manageable.» 60 *Consumer Reports* No. 11 at 734 (Nov. 1995). Psychoanalysis and psychoanalytic psychotherapy thus provide substantial benefits to many Americans and these disciplines ought to be «fostered.» 8 Wigmore, *Evidence* § 2285 (McNaughton rev. 1961).

4. The societal benefits promoted by recognition of a psychotherapist-patient privilege outweigh any detriment to the truth-seeking function of civil litigation. Indeed, the balance of benefits to litigation harms is at least comparable to that justifying recognition of the attorney-client privilege. See *Upjohn Co.* v. *United States*, 449 U.S. 383, 389-90 (1981). In *Upjohn*, the Court extended the attorney-client privilege to the communications between a company's attorneys and its executives and managers, including those not in control positions, on the grounds that an attorney must "'know all that relates to the client's reasons for seeking representation if the professional mission is to be carried out." *Id.* at 389 (quoting *Trammel* v. *United States*, 445 U.S. 40, 51(1980)).

As described above, full disclosure is equally essential to the "professional mission" of the psychotherapist. Indeed, whereas an attorney has other avenues of fact-gathering (*e.g.* documents), the psychotherapist is limited to his or her patient›s full verbal disclosure upon which the entire success of the therapy relies. This therapy, in turn, helps patients, be they law enforcement officers such as Officer Redmond or others, to come to terms with problems that cause them much distress and that they deem too shameful or embarrassing to share with others. Successful therapy benefits not only the psychological and physical health of the patients themselves, but often their friends, families, co-workers and the communities in which they work and live. These benefits are at least as important to society as the promotion of the adversarial relationship.

Moreover, as in the case of the attorney-client relationship, the benefits of recognizing a psychotherapist-patient privilege far outweigh any detriment to the truth-seeking function. First, as this case illustrates, the psychotherapist-patient privilege generally does not preclude access to the only source of evidence. Officer Redmond testified at trial as to her recollections of the shooting and petitioner had an opportunity to cross-examine her. J.A. 122-67. Moreover, there were numerous eye witnesses to the shooting in addition to Officer Redmond, four of whom testified at trial. Thus, petitioner had ample means of obtaining evidence about the shooting and Officer Redmond's recollection of it, and the discovery she sought with respect to Officer Redmond's confidential communications to her psychotherapist was at best cumulative and duplicative. *Cf.* Fed. R. Civ. P. 26(b) (2).

Second, unlike attorney-client confidences, patient-therapist communications are not necessarily or even likely to be sources of objective evidence. In the attorney-client context, communications are generally aimed at discovering facts that are relevant to the legal issue of concern. Full disclosure in the psychotherapeutic context, by contrast, is not a process concerned with identifying and establishing objective facts but rather a technique designed to explore the patient's inner perceptions, concerns and difficulties. Patient-therapist confidences, therefore, are generally not reliable sources of "evidence" since they necessarily incorporate feelings and fantasies that, while they have great relevance to the patient's inner life, may bear very little correspondence to external reality.

In sum, the societal benefits that accrue from recognition of the psychotherapist-patient privilege far outweigh the litigation interest in disclosure. Accordingly, "reason and experience" support recognition of the psychotherapist- patient privilege.

C. Every State recognizes a psychotherapist-patient privilege by statute.

Principles of comity require that federal courts recognize the privileges established by State statute "where this can be accomplished at no substantial cost to federal substantive and procedural policy." *United States* v. *King*, 73 F.R.D. 103, 105 (E.D.N.Y. 1976); see also *United States* v. *Gillock*, 445 U.S. 360, 368 n.8 (1980). To do otherwise would create precisely the risk of inequitable administration of the laws and incentives for unseemly "forum shopping" that this Court condemned in *Erie R.R.* v. *Tompkins*, 304 U.S. 64 (1938). See *Hanna* v. *Plumer*, 380 U.S. 460, 467 (1965).

Every State has recognized a psychotherapist-patient privilege by statute. See Appendix A. Section 110 of the Illinois Civil Liabilities Code is illustrative. It states that, with a few listed exceptions, "in any civil, criminal, administrative or legislative proceeding... a recipient, and a therapist on behalf and in the interest of a recipient, has the privilege to refuse to disclose and to prevent the disclosure of the recipient's record or communications." Ill. Rev. Stat. ch. 740, para. 110/10(a) (1994).[14] Where State statutes universally embrace a privilege federal courts are generally persuaded to do the same. See, *e.g.*, *In re Doe*, 964 F.2d 1325, 1328 (2d Cir. 1992) (psychotherapist-patient privilege); *In re Grand Jury Investigation*, 918 F.2d 374, 381 & n.10

---

14   The Illinois statute defines "recipient" as "a person who is receiving or has received mental health or developmental disabilities services." Ill. Rev. Stat. ch. 740, para. 110/2 (1994). It defines "therapist" as "a psychiatrist, physician, psychologist, social worker, or nurse providing mental health or developmental disabilities services." *Id.*

(3d Cir. 1990) (clergy-communicant privilege). The unambiguous and widespread State statutory support for the psychotherapist-patient privilege weighs heavily in favor of this Court's recognition of such a privilege.[15]

D. This Court recognized the importance of a psychotherapist-patient privilege in proposed Rule 504.

In 1972, this Court promulgated and submitted to Congress twelve privilege rules, nine of which concerned specific privileges. While Congress substituted Rule 501 in place of these proposed rules, they nonetheless "provide a useful reference point and offer guidance in defining the existence and scope of evidentiary privileges in the federal courts." *In re Grand Jury Investigation*, 918 F.2d at 380.

Proposed Rule 504 provided for a psychotherapist-patient privilege. It stated that:

[a] Patient has a privilege to refuse to disclose and to prevent any other person from disclosing confidential communications, made for the purposes of diagnosis or treatment of his mental or emotional condition... among himself, his psychotherapist, or persons who

---

15   Federal regulatory authorities have also recognized the need for confidentiality with respect to treatments that carry with them social stigmas. For example, Department of Health and Human Service regulations strictly protect the confidentiality of alcohol and drug abuse patient records. See 42 C.F.R. 2.1 et seq. (1994). These regulations are intended to promote treatment by "insur[ing] that an alcohol or drug abuse patient in a federally assisted alcohol or drug abuse program is not made more vulnerable by reason of the availability of his or her patient record than an individual who has an alcohol or drug problem and who does not seek treatment." 42 C.F.R. 2.3(b)(2) (1994). As discussed above, these same concerns apply in the psychotherapeutic treatment context. These regulations illustrate that recognition of a psychotherapist-patient privilege is consistent with, and can therefore be accomplished at no substantial cost to, federal policy.

are participating in the diagnosis or treatment under the direction of the psychotherapist, including members of the patient's family.[16]

2 J. Weinstein, *Weinstein's Evidence*, 504-1. The Court's decision to promulgate this rule is "useful in furnishing guidance under Rule 501," *id.*, 504-3, and provides further support for the privilege.

E. Failure to recognize a psychotherapist-patient privilege would raise "difficult and sensitive" constitutional questions concerning patient privacy.

The Court has recognized that individuals possess a constitutional privacy interest in "avoiding disclosure of personal matters." *Whalen* v. *Roe*, 429 U.S. 589, 599 (1977); accord *Nixon* v. *Administrator of Gen. Servs.*, 433 U.S. 425, 457 (1977). For example, in *Whalen* the Court considered a State of New York policy that required physicians who prescribed Schedule II drugs (such as opium, cocaine or methadone) to provide to the State health department information regarding the drug prescribed and the patient›s identity. *Whalen*, 429 U.S. at 593. The Court held that this disclosure of personal medical information implicated the patients' right to privacy, *id.* at 599, although it upheld the program on the ground that the State had taken sufficient security precautions to safeguard this constitutional interest.

More recently the Second Circuit, applying *Whalen*, held that individuals possess a privacy right in "intensely personal matter[s]" such as their HIV status, and that an individual could accordingly maintain a Section 1983 action against a State agency that had disclosed his HIV-positive status without his consent. *Doe* v. *City of New York*, 15 F.3d 264, 265 (2d Cir. 1994).

---

16   Although Rule 504 defined "psychotherapist" as encompassing only psychiatrists and licensed and certified psychologists, this narrow definition is out-of-date. Many State privilege statutes currently include licensed clinical social workers such as Ms. Beyer. See Appendix B.

The Second Circuit stated that the privacy right to control the disclosure of one's personal matters "can be characterized as a right to 'confidentiality,'" *id.* at 267, and that "the right to confidentiality includes the right to protection regarding information about the state of one's health." *Id.*; accord *United States* v. *Westinghouse Elec. Corp.*, 638 F.2d 570, 577 (3d Cir. 1980).

Officer Redmond's privacy interest in the substance of her conversations with Ms. Beyer is stronger than that implicated in *Whalen* or *Doe, supra.* In standard privacy cases such as *Doe*, plaintiffs assert a privacy interest in information that they possess (*e.g.*, HIV status) but do not wish to share with others. Information of this nature is, of course, disclosed in psychotherapy as well. In addition, psychotherapy brings to light information about the unconscious that even the *patients themselves* were not aware of prior to the treatment. Such information emanates from the very core of the patient›s personality. «›The psychiatric patient confides more utterly than anyone else in the world. . . . [H]e lays bare his entire self, his dreams, his fantasies, his sins, and his shame.'" *Taylor* v. *United States*, 222 F.2d 398, 401 (D.C. Cir. 1955) (quoting M. Guttmacher & H. Weihofen, *Psychiatry and the Law* 272 (1952)). To disclose to third-parties personal information that the patient has uncovered through use of the powerful tool of psychotherapy would constitute a more profound invasion of personal privacy than that which implicated the privacy right in *Doe.*

In the absence of a clear expression by Congress, this Court has consistently construed acts of Congress to avoid raising "difficult and sensitive" constitutional questions. *NLRB* v. *Catholic Bishop*, 440 U.S. 490, 507 (1979). In the present case, allowing petitioner to discover the substance of Officer Redmond's communications with Ms. Beyer will profoundly implicate Officer Redmond's privacy rights. See *In re Doe*, 964 F.2d 1325, 1328-29 (2d Cir. 1992); *Caesar* v. *Mountanos*, 542 F.2d 1064, 1067 n.9 (9th Cir. 1976), *cert. denied*, 430 U.S. 954 (1977); *United States* v. *Layton*, 90 F.R.D. 520, 523 (N.D. Cal. 1981); *United States* v. *Brown*, 479 F. Supp. 1247, 1254

& n.8 (D. Md. 1979). This Court should accordingly construe Rule 501 to require recognition of a psychotherapist-patient privilege so as to avoid this intrusion into Officer Redmond's "zone of privacy."

In sum, all five factors to be considered under Rule 501 point strongly towards recognition of the psychotherapist-patient privilege as a matter of federal law.

CONCLUSION

The judgment of the United States Court of Appeals for the Seventh Circuit recognizing a psychotherapist-patient privilege as a matter of federal law should be affirmed.

Respectfully submitted,

Rex E. Lee

Carter G. Phillips*

Joseph R. Guerra

Dennis D. Hirsch

Sidley & Austin

1722 Eye Street, N.W.

Washington, D.C. 20006

(202)736-8000

Counsel for the Amici Curiae

January 2, 1996
*Counsel of Record

CHAPTER 23

The Ethical and Legal Implications of Jaffee v. Redmond and the HIPAA Medical Privacy Rule for Psychotherapy and General Psychiatry

by Peter P. Swire

INTRODUCTION:

I met Paul Mosher, my cousin, when our two professional passions intersected. Paul was the psychotherapist intent on ensuring patient confidentiality. I was finishing a two-year stint in the U.S. Office of Management and Budget, serving as Chief Counselor for Privacy. We both believed that mental health care would be far more effective if patients could trust telling their deepest secrets to their therapists.

More than two decades later, I can't remember precisely when Paul first reached out to me. Although we were second (third?) cousins, I don't believe we had previously met. I believe Paul contacted me in December 2000 or perhaps a month or two later. That December, we completed work on the HIPAA medical privacy rule. I had served as White House coordinator for the final rule, including review of over 50,000 public comments. We had faced many legal and policy challenges, but now the rule was on the books. It looked for a while that the new administration might cancel the rule, but President George W. Bush personally supported patient privacy, and the

HIPAA privacy protections are now a well-entrenched part of our nation's health care system.

When Paul and I got the chance to talk, he explained his interest in patient confidentiality and asked whether we might collaborate, bringing our two areas of experience together. I was glad to do so. The result was the article below, published in 2002 in the Psychiatrics Clinics of North America.

In re-reading the article today, I remember the dedication that Paul brought to the topic of psychotherapy and confidentiality. The article reflects his deeply-held views. Paul documented the "50-year effort to assure that that the law recognizes that especially strong confidentiality rules are needed for psychotherapeutic communications." He celebrated the history of states gradually recognizing the psychiatrist-patient privilege, and rejoiced when the Supreme Court in 1996 affirmed the strong privilege in *Jaffee v. Redmond*.

As a lawyer, I remember a couple of places that gave me a bit of trouble at the time, but I agreed to go with Paul's formulations. I can now reveal that Paul was the author for saying "ethical obligations typically exceed legal duties," and for concluding that "the actual decision that a psychotherapist arrives at in any situation, however, is subject first and foremost to the ethical precepts of the professions." My cautious legal approach might have added some qualifiers. I remember thinking, however, about unjust legal regimes such as medical experimentation under the Nazis. With that in mind, I agreed that ethics must come first.

The article reflects Paul's and my optimism about the special provisions in HIPAA for psychotherapy notes. In particular, the rule prohibits a third party, typically an insurance company, from requiring patient waiver of confidentiality as a condition for getting insurance coverage. The professional psychotherapist needs his or her notes to provide care. Fortunately, the HIPAA rule made clear that a bureaucratic insurance company should receive basic information about the number of sessions, but has no such need to see those intimate details of a person's heart.

Paul and I did not get the opportunity to work together after writing the article. I lived far from Albany, and our paths did not cross again. With that said, I took a special pleasure in writing this article with a co-author with such passion and conviction for the topic. The law actually improved for confidentiality with *Jaffee v. Redmond* and HIPAA. What Paul described as a "fifty-year effort" has actually resulted in a better world than it was before his work.

The Ethical and Legal Implications of Jaffee v Redmond and the HIPAA Medical Privacy Rule for Psychotherapy and General Psychiatry

By Paul W. Mosher. MD, and Peter P. Swire, JD

In Jaffee v Redmond [1], the US Supreme Court ruled in 1996 that communications between a psychotherapist and a patient are privileged in the federal courts [2—7]. In the new Health Insurance Portability and Accountability Act (HIPAA) medical privacy rule [8], the United States Department of Health and Human Services established confidentiality protections for medical records, in general, and for psychotherapy notes, in particular. This article examines the legal and ethical implications of these two developments. Together, they represent the culmination of a 50-year effort to assure that the law recognizes that especially strong confidentiality rules are needed for psychotherapeutic communications.

History

For confidentiality purposes, the distinction between general medical data and psychotherapeutic communications was articulated in the early 1950s and reinforced by events in the Cold War era. At that time, when the dominant form of psychotherapy was psychoanalytic in nature, courts and legislatures began to take notice of the fact that such treatment required a level of disclosure by the patient to the psychotherapist that went far beyond the disclosures most usually needed in typical medical encounters [9]. Long before psychoanalysis began the scientific study of the darker side of human nature, however, it was recognized that the inner life of the ordinary man could, if exposed, bring him into conflict with society. As Montaigne wrote in the sixteenth century:

> There is no man so good, who, were he to submit all his thoughts and actions to the laws, would not deserve hanging ten times in his life; and he may well be a man whom it would be a great injustice and great harm to punish and ruin. (Essays: Of Vanity)

Because most psychotherapy in the 1950s was conducted by psychiatrists, the early writing on the subject refers to psychiatrist—patient communications. The first legal decision creating a privileged status for psychiatrist—patient communications was Binder v Ruvell [10]. This 1952 case was considered so important that the entire text of the opinion was published in the Journal of the American Medical Association, a most unusual occurrence. In Binder v Ruvell, the court spelled out the rationale for special protection of psychotherapeutic communications, contrasting the necessity for such protection with the lack of a similar rationale for medical treatments in general:

The ordinary physician seeks from his patient disclosure of facts relating to a particular malady, insofar as the information might aid him in ascertaining the subjective symptoms; the psychiatrist seeks to ascertain the cause of mental or emotional disturbances of a maladjusted patient. His sphere of inquiry necessarily covers every experience of the patient. He may be interested in knowing the experiences of childhood. That may weigh very heavily with him in determining the cause of the disturbance. He may be interested in the experience of the patient during puberty, during adolescence. In fact, what he seeks to do is to bring back to the conscious memory of the patient things forgotten but which lied dormant in the subconscious mind. He probes deeply, and it is necessary for him to get that information out of the mouth of his patient.

From the 1950s to the 1990s, based on the reasoning first set forth in Binder v Ruvell, an extensive literature of legal case law and commentary developed both in support of stringent protection for psychotherapeutic communications and in support of the differentiation of such communications from those that typically occur in other medical treatments. The immorality of disclosing the former type of information obtained in a context that supposedly guarantees complete confidentiality was well expressed by a California jurist: ". . .there is obviously something revolting about the spectacle of a psychotherapist testifying to a patient's confidences in a criminal action in which the patient is a defendant" [11].

In the early 1970s, following a decade of study, a committee of the US Supreme Court first proposed a specific privilege rule providing a privilege for psychotherapist—patient communications [12].

By the 1990s, legislatures in all 50 states had established some form of privilege for psychotherapeutic communications, but the federal courts were divided on the issue. Jaffee v Redmond settled the question of a federal privilege and did so decisively. The privilege announced by the US Supreme Court in Jaffee v Redmond in 1996, like the attorney—client privilege, is an absolute privilege, meaning that it is not subject to case-by-case balancing by trial judges who might otherwise weigh the need for the evidence that the privilege excludes against the need of the justice system. By contrast, the executive privilege that protects confidential communications of the President of the United States is an example of a qualified privilege; that is, it is a privilege subject to case-by-case balancing by a judge. Thus, in Jaffee v Redmond, the US Supreme Court clearly signaled its intention that the psychotherapist—patient privilege must be as reliable and unequivocal as possible so as to promote an atmosphere of "confidence and trust" within the psychotherapeutic relationship.

Jaffee v Redmond also has symbolic significance that ultimately may overshadow its substantive implications. In an era when almost all observers agree that we have been facing a discouraging decline in our ability to maintain confidential treatment relationships, Jaffee v Redmond stands as a possible turning point in society's willingness to support confidential psychotherapy. This is so because in the federal courts where the pursuit of truth through the examination of all available evidence is ordinally a decisive value, privileges are generally looked upon with extreme disfavor. The fact that the US Supreme Court so strongly established the Jaffee v Redmond privilege therefore can be seen as an expression of a societal understanding that confidential psychotherapy is so important that other compelling considerations favoring disclosure should give way. Therefore, Jaffee v Redmond has ramifications beyond the Federal Rules of Evidence and the judicial proceedings in which Jaffee v Redmond now plays a concrete role.

To understand the significance of Jaffee v Redmond, it is important also to understand what it does not do [13]. For instance, Jaffee v Redmond does not have any direct legal effect on disclosures made under private arrangements, such as insurance contracts between insurers and patients, and Jaffee v Redmond does not directly affect disclosures that a psychotherapist makes pursuant to a patient's consent. This is not to say, however, that the symbolic meaning of Jaffee v Redmond is without effect in such situations; it has been recognized by legal scholars for decades that privilege rules in fact do affect the arrangements that citizens make for their interactions outside the judicial system, and so Jaffee v Redmond affects the way we view nongovernmental and contractual disclosures [141.

The ethics codes of the psychiatric and medical professions strongly support an obligation of practitioners to abide by the law; however, difficult situations arise where legal and ethical obligations can be in tension or even in direct conflict. Sometimes, the legal system requires disclosures that may be considered unethical. Sometimes, the legal system expects disclosures when ethical obligations point toward confidentiality [15]. Jaffee v Redmond and the HIPAA rule, to some extent, reduce the conflicts between law and ethics. They are based, in part, on the law's recognition of the ethical codes of professional groups. In turn, they now lend significant support to a psychotherapist who would resolve ethical conflicts in the direction of protecting a patient's confidentiality.

Difficult conflicts

In the real world at present, certain conflicts between the technical requirements for the conduct of psychotherapy and the ethical and legal obligations of practitioners have no clear path to a resolution [15, 16]. For example, some ethics codes urge the practitioner to disclose limits of confidentiality to the patient at the beginning of the treatment relationship, including, as an example, a legal obligation of the psychotherapist under state law to report credible evidence of child abuse. Ordinarily, a person given such a warning would then take the likelihood of a disclosure into consideration when deciding whether to disclose such incriminating information within the psychotherapeutic relationship. Taken literally, however, such a reporting requirement and the ethical obligation to abide by it could bring about a situation in which a patient who actually has been abused or has been an abuser cannot undertake psychotherapy for that problem without bringing into play the full force of the legal system intended to prevent or punish child abuse. Even more difficult to resolve is the situation of a patient in psychoanalysis—a treatment in which the basic technical rule states that the patient must not withhold any information from the analyst. How can such a treatment logically go forward after a patient has been handed a laundry list of matters, which if described to the analyst, will be reported to the authorities?

When a practitioner faces a situation in which a disclosure of confidential information is being requested or considered, a complicated set of legal, ethical, and practical considerations comes into play. To simplify the discussion here, we will consider separately those situations in which the patient agrees to a disclosure, and those situations in which a disclosure is sought or intended without the patient's consent. It is, of course, the latter situations in which Jaffee v Redmond and other privilege rules such as state statutes might come into play. The actual decision that a psychotherapist arrives at in any situation, however, is subject first and foremost to the ethical precepts of the professions.

When the patient consents

Patients frequently consent to disclosures of confidential information related to communications they have made to psychotherapists. Most notably, this situation arises in relation to third-party payment for the therapy itself. It may arise in other situations as well, such as in connection with applications for disability or life insurance, or for security clearances. Patients may also request (and hence consent to) the disclosure of information by a psychotherapist in a court proceeding in which they believe the therapist's testimony might assist their case. Because each of these instances of possible disclosure would not be taking place against the patient's wishes, none of them are affected directly by Jaffee v Redmond or other privilege rules. The HIPAA rule also generally allows a patient to authorize release to third parties.

Usually, in the context of third-party payment, the permission to disclose is referred to as a "consent" or "authorization," whereas in the context of privilege rules, the permission to disclose is called a waiver of the privilege. When the patient voluntarily waives the privilege, the therapist has no legal basis to assert a privilege on the patient's behalf. By analogy, when the patient has consented to the disclosure of confidential communications to third-party payers, the psychotherapist usually has no legal or ethical basis on which to decline to make such a disclosure. In some jurisdictions, such a disclosure may actually be required (to support the patient's insurance claim), but in the District of Columbia, such a disclosure might be illegal, even with the patient's consent. Where a consented-to disclosure is contemplated, a psychotherapist has an ethical obligation to disclose only the minimum amount of information needed to satisfy the purpose of the request. The HIPAA rule also generally expects only the "minimum necessary" disclosure that achieves the purpose of the disclosure.

An important principle of privilege law is that a waiver of the privilege must not be coerced; that is, for a waiver to be valid it must be freely given. Thus, the mere fact that the patient's waiver or consent exists is not sufficient in and of itself to justify a disclosure. Where doubt exists in the psychiatrist's mind as to the "voluntary" nature of the waiver, an ethical duty exists to resist disclosure until such a doubt can be resolved. A recent example of this issue was the waiver of the psychotherapist—patient privilege by Monica Lewinsky in the course of her interrogation by the Independent Counsel investigating President Clinton. At least one senior federal court judge has raised the question of whether her therapist should have, without an examination of the subpoena by a federal court, provided testimony regarding her treatment when the waiver on which a subpoena was based might have been extracted from Ms. Lewinsky as part of a deal to keep her out of prison [17]. By analogy, the fact that a patient has signed an authorization for disclosure of information to a third party such as a third-party payer is not in itself sufficient to remove all questions of ethics when a psychiatrist makes such a disclosure. In many instances, it is clear that the patient would have no choice but to sign a blanket consent in order to receive treatment when, in fact, the disclosure of only a very limited subset of information may be necessary and ethical.

Finally, even when a patient has given a voluntary consent to a disclosure or a voluntary waiver of a privilege, situations can exist where a psychiatrist is of the opinion that the disclosure is not in the patient's best interest. This might occur, for example, where a patient may have an incomplete understanding of the extent of the disclosures that might take place or of the possible consequences of such a disclosure. In such situations, an ethical psychiatrist should seek to avoid the disclosure and, in cases of doubt, should consult with professional colleagues and legal advisors prior to any release of confidential information.

In the context of psychotherapy, the issue of the validity of a general consent to disclosure signed in advance of the actual therapy is particularly troubling. Not only may a patient not understand what information would be disclosed as a result of the consent but it also may be that, at the time of the signing, the patient is not even aware of the nature of the information that could emerge during the psychotherapy. In ruling that such consents do not justify disclosure of all records of Medicaid patients to a state auditor, one well-known court ruling [18] put it this way:

It would be unreasonable to hold that an indigent patient who signs a form stating that a provider may release certain medical records to the State exercises a knowing waiver of his interest in not having his most personal confidences to the psychiatrist disclosed. It is far more likely that, if he reads the form at all, a patient would assume that the records would include only billing information and similar non-confidential matters.

When the patient does not consent

A disclosure of confidential information without the consent of a patient should be viewed as a most serious matter. In some instances, such a disclosure may be required by law, whereas in other situations, it may be motivated by an ethical duty or an attempt to avoid liability.

In the courts, information created as the result of a psychotherapeutic encounter is generally protected from compelled disclosure by state privilege statutes and, in the federal courts, by Jaffee v Redmond. In state courts, information that falls outside the specific protection of psychotherapist—patient privilege may be protected by physician—patient privilege statutes. HIPAA provides additional protections (discussed further below) against release in litigation of medical records. These safeguards, taken together, mean that subpoenas and other requests for information should not result in disclosure of confidential information unless the patient has affirmatively declined to exercise the Jaffee v Redmond or other applicable privilege. Furthermore, it is an ethical responsibility and, in some jurisdictions, a legal requirement that the psychiatrist assert the privilege on the patient's behalf in case of the patient's absence or incapacity.

Some disclosures are required by law without regard to the patient's wishes. For instance, physicians are required to report to authorities certain communicable diseases and gunshot wounds. In addition, every state now requires physicians and certain other professionals to report child abuse and, in some states, to report elder abuse. Failure to obey such laws can lead to legal action against the physician, including professional disciplinary proceedings. To the extent that such laws legitimately protect society, they are in consonance with ethical principles. On the other hand, there are situations in which a psychotherapist believes that the making of such a report, with the predictable consequences of intervention by the authorities, would do more harm than good. In such a situation, the law might be viewed as "unjust" if, in fact, it fails to take account of the particular circumstances. Although failure to make a report in such a case could involve a violation of the law, the psychotherapist might decide that withholding a report is the most ethical choice. Some professional groups have advised their members that professional judgment is the best guide in such circumstances even when the decision to violate the law might expose the professional to legal consequences. In the words of the Code of Ethics of the American Medical Association, "ethical values and legal principles are usually closely related, but ethical obligations typically exceed legal duties In exceptional circumstances of unjust laws, ethical responsibilities should supersede legal obligations" [19].

Similarly, the code of ethics of the American Psychiatric Association reads, "when the psychiatrist is in doubt, the right of the patient to confidentiality and, by extension, to unimpaired treatment, should be given priority" [20].

Finally, the ethical obligation to protect third parties from a patient's intent to harm them may arise in situations where the patient's threat is credible, specific, and imminent. Issuing such a warning without the patient's consent would constitute a violation of the confidential relationship but, at the same time, could be the most ethical course of action. In addition, although in many states the psychiatrist is not required by law to issue a warning, he may nevertheless be liable to an injured third party as the result of a failure to do so. In the best-known legal decision on this subject, the California Supreme Court held in the Tarasoff case that a duty to protect an endangered third party might exist under some circumstances, and the failure to carry out that duty could create a liability (i.e., exposure to being sued) [6].

Before such a warning is issued, professional ethics dictates that the therapist first seek to involve the patient in the process of protecting an intended victim rather than acting against the patient's wishes. If the patient's consent or cooperation cannot be obtained, then the psychiatrist who chooses to take protective steps should disclose only the minimum and specific information necessary to comply with the law. The patient's entire record should not be released.

Even following such a disclosure, in some states the patient's confidential communications to the psychiatrist may continue to be privileged; that is, information in the possession of the psychotherapist cannot be forced to be disclosed or used against the patient in a subsequent! legal proceeding simply because some or all of the information was disclosed earlier for a different purpose. Because the Jaffee v Redmond privilege is so recent, the question of the status of the privilege in a case after a "Tarasoff-type" warning is unsettled for the federal courts [21—23]. The new HIPAA rule suggests that disclosure, if it occurs, may be subject to a protective order. This order would prohibit the parties in state or federal court from using or disclosing the records for any purpose other than the litigation. It also requires the return or destruction of the records at the end of the litigation [Section 512(e)]. More generally, although the disclosure of confidential information may constitute a waiver of the privilege, the rules governing such situations (so called "waiver doctrine") vary within and among jurisdictions.

The HIPAA privacy rule

The HIPAA of 1996 recognized that stronger confidentiality protections are an essential part of the transition to electronic management of medical information. The medical privacy rule was announced by President Clinton in December 2000 [8]. President Bush reaffirmed in April 2001 that the rule would take effect, and compliance is now scheduled for April 2003, although some changes may occur before that time. The rule is notable for providing national standards for medical confidentiality for personal health information, with stricter protections for psychotherapy notes.

Explaining the details of the HIPAA privacy rule is beyond the scope of this article. For therapists, the general provisions apply to all electronic, written, and oral communications identified by patient. The ethical and legal restraints on disclosure of confidential information that existed before HIPAA remain in effect. The HIPAA rule adds a layer of protection by making certain disclosures illegal for the first time. In doing so, the rule provides a more complete legal basis for adherence to ethical principles by psychotherapists.

One notable feature of the rule is that it singles out "psychotherapy notes" for special stringent protection. As explained in the rule's preamble [8],

Generally, we have not treated sensitive information differently from other protected health information; however, we have provided additional protections for psychotherapy notes because of Jaffee v Redmond and the unique role of this type of information.

The definition of psychotherapy notes [8] provides

Psychotherapy notes means notes recorded (in any medium) by a health care provider who is a mental health professional documenting or analyzing the contents of conversation during a private counseling session or a group, joint, or family counseling session and that are separated from the rest of the individual's medical record.

Psychotherapy notes excludes medication prescription and monitoring, counseling session start and stop times, the modalities and frequencies of treatment furnished, results of clinical tests, and any summary of the following items: diagnosis, functional status, the treatment plan, symptoms, prognosis, and progress to date.

For information covered by this definition, especially strict rules apply. For instance, psychotherapy notes cannot legally be disclosed based on a general consent signed in advance of the psychotherapy. Instead, disclosure would require a more specific and limited authorization spelling out the information to be released, to whom, and for what purpose. Importantly, no third-party payer can condition enrollment in a health plan or payment of a claim on a patient's agreement to sign such an authorization. This limit for psychotherapy notes on release for payment is thus stricter than the general HIPAA rule, which permits disclosure without authorization for purposes of treatment, payment, or health care operations.

As HIPAA is implemented, therapists will need advice from their professional organization on how best to manage confidential information in this unfamiliar new world. Some topics will involve management and ethical issues. For instance, how will therapists assure that the correct records are separated from the rest of the medical record in order to qualify for the stricter psychotherapy-notes protections? How will demands from insurance companies to prevent these records from being kept separate be reconciled with the ethical requirement of confidentiality? Other topics may require legal clarification, perhaps from the Department of Health and Human Services or from legal counsel. For instance, when and how can therapists share information with others on a treatment team? What is the scope of the various terms that are excluded from the definition, so that the stricter protections do not apply?

It is not surprising to have uncertainty as a major new rule goes into effect. Despite uncertainty as to the details, however, the HIPAA privacy rule combined with the effect of Jaffee v Redmond provides an unprecedented set of legal protections to reinforce the ethical precepts underlying the protection of the confidentiality of psychotherapy communications.

REFERENCES

[l] *Jaffee v. Redmond,* 116 SCt 1923 (1996).

[2] Amann DM, Imwinkelreid EJ. The Supreme Court's decision to recognize a psychotherapist privilege in *Jaffee v. Redmond,* 116 SCt (1996): the meaning of "experience" and the role of "reason" under Federal Rule of Evidence 501, University of Cincinnati. Law Review 1997;65:1019–49. Available at: http://jaffee-redmond.org/articles/amimwink.htm. Accessed October 17, 2001.

[3] Ciccone JR. The United States Supreme Court and psychiatry in the 1990s. Psychiatr Clin North Am

[4] Lombardo PA. Newest federal privilege: Jaffee v. Redmond and the protection of psychotherapeutic confidentiality. Biolaw 1996;2(1 1):S201—9.

[5] Nelken M. The limits of privilege: the developing scope of federal psychotherapist-patient privilege law. Rev Litig 2000;20:1—43. Available at: http://jaffee-redmond.org/articles/ nelken.htm. Accessed October 17, 2001.

[6] Slovenko R. The case for psychotherapy. In: Psychotherapy and confidentiality: testimonial privileged communication, breach of confidentiality, and reporting duties. Springfield, IL: Thomas; 1998. p. 35–56.

[7] Weissenberger G. The psychotherapist privilege and the Supreme Court's misplaced reliance on state legislatures. Hastings Law J 1998;49:999—1007.

[8] United States Department of Health and Human Services. Standards for privacy of individually identifiable health information. 65 Federal Register (250) 82461—510 (2000). Available at: http://www.os.dhhs.gov/ocr/hipaa/. Accessed October 17, 2001.

[9] Mosher PW. Psychotherapist-patient privilege: the history and significance of the US Supreme Court's decision in the case of Jaffee v. Redmond, 1999. Available at: http://jaffeeredmond.org/articles/mosher.htm. Accessed October 17, 2001.

[10] Binder v. Ruvell (Civil Docket 52 C 25 35, Circuit Court of Cook County, Ill, June 24, 1952). JAMA 1952;150:1241—2. Available at: http://jaffee-redmond.org/cases/binder.htm. Accessed October 17, 2001.

[I1] Kaus OM. Concurring and dissenting, *People v. Stritzinger,* 34 Ca13d 505, 521 (1983).

[12] Imwinkelreid EJ. An Hegelian approach to privileges under Federal rule of Evidence 501: the restrictive thesis, the expansive antithesis, and the contextual synthesis. Nebr Law Rev 1994; 73:511–23.

[13] Slovenko R. The psychotherapist-patient privilege. Am J Psychoanal 1997: 57:63–73.

[14] Goldberg AJ. Proposed rules of evidence: hearings before the special subcommittee on reform of federal criminal laws of the House Committee on the Judiciary, 93rd Congress, 1st Session, 142–53, 1973.

[15] Wettstein RM. Confidentiality. In: Edwards R B, editor. Ethics of psychiatry: insanity, rational autonomy, and mental health care. Amherst (MA): Prometheu; 1997. p. 263—81.

[16]]Joseph DI, Onek J. Confidentiality in psychiatry. In: Bloch S, Chodoff P, Green SA, editors. Psychiatric ethics. 3rd edition. Oxford: Oxford University Press; 1999. p. 105–40. [17][17] Knapp W. Starr's legal tactics raise troubling questions. New York Times, Letter to the Editor. October 9, 1998.

[18] *Hawaii Psychiatric Society v. Ariyoshi,* 481 F Supp 1028—52 (October 22, 1979) United States District Court, D. Hawaii.

[19] American Medical Association. Code of medical ethics: current opinions with annotations. Chicago: AMA; 1997.

[20] Bloch S, Chodoff P, Green SA, editors. Psychiatric ethics. 3rd edition. Oxford: Oxford University Press; 1999 [Appendix].

[21] Harris GC. The dangerous patient exception to the psychotherapist-patient privilege: the Tarasoff duty and the Jaffee footnote. Wash Law Rev 1999;74:33.

[22] *United Slates v. Glass,* 133 F3d 1356 10th Cir. United States Court of Appeals (January 13, 1998).

[23] *United States v. Hayes,* 2000 WL 1289028 (6th Cir 2000).Chapter 22

CHAPTER 24

Paul Mosher and Psychoanalytic Electronic Publishing (PEP)

by Nadine Levinson and Peter Fonagy

P EP was devastated to be informed about the death of Dr. Paul Mosher September 13, 2021. It was a shock; PEP has been working with Paul through the last few months, unaware of his serious medical condition. Paul and his wife Paula have been an integral part of the PEP family. It was characteristic of Paul to place others ahead of himself and his own needs. He protected his colleagues in the PEP family; Paul never complained!

In this tribute to Paul, we will only focus on Paul's significant contributions to PEP. As this memorial book testifies, Paul made many other profoundly important, unique and on-going contributions to psychoanalysis, thereby providing us with the luxury of focusing on the immense technical and personal contributions he made to the PEP product, sufficient to justify a festschrift of its own. Paul brought his immense wide ranging experience to the PEP product, driving it constantly forward with his broader contributions to scholarship and writing; licensure activities; political activities to benefit the patient doctor relationship; legal issues and confidentiality, increased Medicare reimbursement for psychotherapy codes; the early establishment of the APsaA listservs, and what was perhaps most valuable for PEP, his pioneering vision of the dissemination of the psychoanalytic literature through computerization. His extraordinary set of skills, experiences and knowledge supported the concept of digitized psychoanalytic journals and books, and motivated the changes that enabled PEP to achieve an irreversible transformation that contributed greatly to psychoanalysis over the last half-century.

Paul's depth of knowledge and fervent interest in computers dates to the early 1960's. Paul was a passionate computer geek through and through, beginning in the pioneering days of personal computing. The potential of the democratization of the digital world was obvious to Paul, but to very few others. Making knowledge accessible to the widest possible group was Paul's leitmotif throughout his career. He was already a man on a mission, long before others could share his vision. He was able to create links and benefit from cutting edge insights of the field's greatest trendsetters – now we would call them influencers. He tells a story of going to a national computer meeting and hobnobbing with the likes of Steve Jobs and others also excited about the Internet, programming, and computers. He was determined to benefit psychoanalysis with the insights from this new world. He proudly proclaimed to Nadine Levinson that one of his first programs had been picked up in the early days by PEP's first search engine company, Folio Views. Paul loved programming, but especially programming that he envisioned would benefit his real love: psychoanalysis.

In 1980, and at his own expense, he created the hardcopy *Jourlit*, a precursor to PEP. It was a consolidated index of the psychoanalytic literature covering the journals and branching out to book reviews. By creating *Jourlit*, *Bookrev* and *Duallook*, using floppy discs and a special database code he created, Paul filled a giant gap in psychoanalytic scholarship at a time before the development of the Internet and when computers were not widely used by psychoanalysts for tasks other than word-processing. Peter Fonagy recalls talking with Paul about *Jourlit*. Paul's vision was a searchable free-text database with the fewest possible predefined fields and going beyond abstracts, which they agreed served the psychoanalytic journal literature poorly. Such a searchable free-text database would enable the entire

404

published article to be searched. In their discussion they touched on the benefit to Freud scholarship that would evolve from such a facility. What if *Jourlit* could track something like the use of Freud's Irma Dream across diverse psychoanalytic traditions and geographies? But of course, floppy disks were not up to the tasks, and hard disks were exorbitantly expensive.

The technological scene changed with the introduction of CDs. As early as 1991, with the advent of the "CD-ROM, the idea of having a consolidated and searchable CD of full text of the psychoanalytic journals was contemplated and first proposed by Paul Mosher to the APsaA Scientific Activities Committee. For those who knew Paul's thinking this was a small logical step to be made in the democratization of knowledge.

While the idea seems perfectly obvious to everyone now, it was anything but obvious in the early 90's when hardly anyone in the field of psychoanalysis conceptualized the power of a CD (let alone knew what a CD[17] was). In response to Mosher's 1991 proposal, APsaA members Vann Spruiell, Al Frank and Stan Goodman led an initial team called PACT in a first, but failed, attempt to produce a disc. Around the same time, similar ideas for a searchable text of the psychoanalytic journals were incubating in London with Peter Fonagy and David Tuckett. The difference between these initiatives was London's insistence that the project had to make commercial sense from the outset. PACT was relying on donations from the psychoanalytic community to sustain and develop the product. Ownership and copyright issues had not so far been addressed or resolved. The team of Tuckett (then Editor of the International Journal of Psychoanalysis) & Fonagy (Chair of the BPS Publications Committee) felt PACT was not viable even in the medium term. They created a business plan for what became PEP and one that would appeal to the Boards of both the American and British Psychoanalytic institutions.

---

17   One new user rang up customer service wanting to know where to put the CD. He thought the CD player was a platform for his glass of water.

Tuckett, Fonagy and Arnie Cooper, with Paul's assistance, were pivotal in convincing Judy Schachter, then President of the American Psychoanalytic Association to partner with the British Institute to finance this fledging enterprise and to digitize 6 premier psychoanalytic journals: *The International Journal of Psychoanalysis, the Journal of the American Psychoanalytic Association, Psychoanalytic Quarterly, Psychoanalytic Study of the Child, International Review of Psycho-Analysis and Contemporary Psychoanalysis*. Eventually, in 1995, Psychoanalytic Electronic Publishing was established, and Paul was one of the six founding Directors. The American Psychoanalytic Association and the Institute of Psychoanalysis (London) each approved funding (as a loan) of $300,000 each to jumpstart Psychoanalytic Electronic Publishing, Inc. The original six Directors were Nadine Levinson, Paul Mosher, and Judith S. Schachter from the US and Peter Fonagy, Martin Miller, and David Tuckett from the UK. Shortly after, Alice Brand Bartlett replaced Judith S. Schachter as a PEP Director.

CREATING PEP AND THE FIRST BETA CD

There were some tensions that arose when PEP was newly formed, with negative dialogue appearing on the APsaA and British websites. Some members asserted, that as they already were subscribed to all the journals on the CD, they therefore would not buy it, feeling the proposed price was too high. Others were upset by what was alleged as a bad process by APsaA in its due diligence and its eventual decision to not finance PACT, but instead to finance the PEP project with the British. A few proposed that the Journals should all be free and freely accessible, an open source. Several years later, some publishers complained that their Journals were not included.

But there was also considerable support for PEP. A posting by Drew Clemens stated, "I believe that the discussion about the CD-ROM project is now in danger of deteriorating into the kind of insinuations, suspicions of motives, moralistic claiming of the high ground, presumptions of bad faith, etc., that have been so incredibly damaging to many efforts of our Association in the recent decade. I hope we can stop, take a breath, and proceed on the assumption that we all truly want the CD-ROM project to be practical and successful. We also want the American to be a healthy organization economically, legally and interpersonally, and our elected leadership has a fiduciary responsibility to uphold that aim. Let's start with the expectation that our officers act responsibly and in good faith, and then constructively focus on reconciling honest differences about the means to achieve mutually desired ends."

Ellen Fertig, APsaA's Executive Secretary assisted in finding various legal resources in the US as well as organizing the initial Beta sales launch in Los Angeles in June 1996. Neil Shapiro[18], a technical consultant, together with Paul Mosher, Peter Fonagy, and David Tuckett designed the system structure and our special Document Type Definition (DTD). In it, the text of psychoanalytic journals would be categorized, so that the most sophisticated searches could be undertaken. Furthermore, the disc uniquely had the database categorized by name of journal, year of publication, and type of text (whether belonging in article, title, reference or author name). There were differences of opinion and no shortage of passion at each Board Meeting about indexing the PEP database (JTOC vs. ATOC); new Journals inclusion policy; what to do about the Mac CD platform; selecting Search Engines and developers; browsing vs. searching. JTOC prevailed as to how the content would be presented and, despite great expense the Mac CD platform was

---

18   Serendipitously Paul Mosher met Neil Shapiro in 1995 while on a train to the PC Expo Meeting. They discovered they had mutual computer interests. It became clear to PM how qualified NS was. The Board was consulted and after a thorough review, NS was asked to become our Technical Consultant. His function was to help make important technical decisions as well as the selection of the various vendors needed to produce the first CD.

supported. The PEP psychoanalytic journals contained were indexed and hyperlinked to each other.

Once the design for this complex structure was worked out and the contracts were being drawn up with the publishers, the PEP Board had to find a search engine that could be programmed to execute complex searches using the data structure that was defined. Neil Shapiro and Paul Mosher, after reviewing many software search engines, selected Folio Views. This search engine tested best when taking into consideration factors such as cost, speed, ease of use, dual Mac/PC platforms, and the way the result of searches was presented to the user. PEP also chose a digitizing firm that had solid credentials and offered the highest accuracy for the least expenditure.[19] All the text in the six PEP Journals to be digitized were coded and tagged according to a special design. Although we live in an electronic age it was (and still is) cheaper to have all the text retyped by hand onto the computer than to have it electronically scanned, and the tags then added afterwards. Throughout all these processes we had to ensure that our specifications and the accuracy of the text re-keying was no less than the guaranteed 99.9%.

The Journals selected for Archive 1 spanned over 70 years and contained the full content of six of the premier journals in psychoanalysis from 1920-1994 and included: *The International Journal of Psycho-Analysis, the International Review of Psycho-Analysis, the Journal of the American Psychoanalytic Association, the Psychoanalytic Quarterly, the Psychoanalytic Study of the Child, and Contemporary Psychoanalysis*. The contract negotiations were possible as PEP only asked for non-exclusive rights to publish and PEP guaranteed the publishers to maintain a three-year moving wall to protect the hard copy of the Journals.

The Directors worked pro bono and tirelessly to develop PEP; there was no management or secretarial infrastructure. Great distances separated the

---

19   The quotes to digitize ranged between $500,000 to $1 million dollars.

Board members. In those days, the only way the Board could function was to be in constant contact with each other by using e-mail. Although different tasks were delegated to different members of the Board, all correspondences were circulated to all members of the Board. Essential plans and decisions for the PEP project was carried out with consensus by email. Martin Miller estimated that PEP Board exchanged 100-300 emails per week. Paul worked closely with Neil Shapiro with the various technical implementations and the state-of-the-art search engine. PEP went through several painful transitions to produce the first few versions of the disc, which proved unexpectedly popular.

At the same time, David Tuckett and Nadine Levinson took over the complicated task of strategic planning and implementation of four phases of global sales and marketing. Paul, David and Nadine wrote the first early user documentation.

At the APsaA Meeting in June 1996 in Los Angeles, just after PEP came into existence, there were 300 individual and 20 Institutional sales of the PEP Beta. In July 1997, PEP brought the first physical Beta CD to the IPA meeting in Barcelona. At a vendor booth, Nadine Levinson, Peter Fonagy and David Tuckett took turns demonstrating the PEP CD to anyone who would come by and listen and watch.

Many more sales were occurring beyond anyone's wildest dreams and outstripping PEP's conservative business plan formulated by David Tuckett. Given the enormous success of individual sales, the clear result of PEP's academic product, and the knowledge that PEP proceeds would be taxed at the 75% corporate rate, the PEP Board revisited the legal question of shifting to a non-profit environment. Nadine Levinson investigated the feasibility of this difficult shift as well as taking PEP through the challenging process of implementation. PEP gross profits were substantial. But since all expenses were kept minimal, and there was no infrastructure as everyone worked pro bono, there were few expenses to offset the profits. In January 1999,

PEP slipped through a narrow window of time after which, such a change from profit to nonprofit structure would have been impossible. You might ask why this change had not been conceived of and implemented in the first incorporation. At the time, while we believed the PEP Project was a lovely and creative idea, we did not believe it would become financially successful, and thus, non-profit status was deemed neither warranted nor worth the time and expense.

On another front, the company selected to produce the final CD was continually not able to meet its production deadline of May 31, 1997. After several promises and further delays, Peter Fonagy, as Honorary Treasurer, and Nadine Levinson, with legal assistance, negotiated a settlement, which included receiving the PEP deliverables (the work completed up to that time). Paul's role throughout these challenging times was to keep engaged in the development and testing of the new Folio Search Engine and the development of a PEP Help File.

Sales continued to rise as soon as customers realized the PEP CD was a reality. Costs were kept low since the Directors did most of the work. Board members have worked on the PEP project on an average of two to three hours per day since 1996, which amounts to a total of at least 9,000 hours! During this time over 5,500 email messages passed between board members! Paul, like everyone on the PEP Board was dedicated to making PEP a success and to preserve and protect the psychoanalytic literature for generations to come.

PEP became an IRS Section 501C-3 Public Charity (a not-for-Profit Corporation) on January 20th, 1999. PEP's mission was to further the scholarship, research, and outreach of psychoanalytic literature. This change to non-profit status now meant that the two share-holding organizations, the American Psychoanalytic Association and the Institute of Psychoanalysis, became the sponsoring member organizations.

In May 2000, the first update Archive 1, was successfully published, covering the additional content of the six PEP Archive Journals from 1995 – 1997, and was shipped to 1016 customers. The initial loans from the Institute of Psychoanalysis (London) and the American Psychoanalytic Association were finally paid off in November 2000. The following December 2000, the PEP non-profit Charitable Foundation granted $20,000 each to the two supporting organizations.

After the release of the first CD, Paul Mosher and Nadine Levinson attended and personally demonstrated at a PEP Journals' Meeting in NYC at Mt. Sinai Hospital organized by Arnie Richards. Paul and Nadine "ran" a PEP booth in the book vendor area using their own computers loaded with the PEP CD-ROM. We were eager to show PEP off. It was pure joy watching Paul Mosher interface with various physicians from many specialties at Mt. Sinai who would come by and watch with amazement as Paul demonstrated the PEP CD-ROM and its unrivaled powerful Search Engine.

Soon after, the Internet emerged as a realistic alternative for data storage and retrieval. Paul was again one of the pioneers. With David Tuckett, he created a vision of the PEP Internet archive, which would ultimately eliminate the significant cost of CD reproduction, postage and updating and ensure access to PEP through any Internet browser. With the shift to the Internet, there were massive problems of user registration, limited knowledge, the connectivity options of many users, as well as copyright issues. In 2002, there were some further complicated contract negotiations involving IUP and *JAPA* to get permission to publish the PEP Archive on the Web. All of the other Journals and publishers were supportive. Paul Mosher had no shortage of professional family member contacts who were internationally known (Proskauer and Rose) and who worked to provided PEP and Nadine Levinson with legal assistance at a nominal rate because of Paul. PEP was finally able to redefine the correct *JAPA* rights as belonging to APsaA.

At a Board Meeting in Boston in 2003, PEP scheduled a meeting with one of the largest aggregators, EBSCO Publications. EBSCO sent a large stretch black limo to the APsaA hotel to pick up PEP Board members to take them to EBSCO's Ipswich corporate offices. Paul, always very reserved and unassuming, was quite abashed when the stretch limo pulled up. He joked that "some people" might get the wrong idea about PEP and our carryings on. He anxiously mused, "Will they think this is what we are doing with the money?"

With this shift to the Internet, Paul was particularly helpful in assessing the developer for the new PEP-Web interface. Global Village Publishing (GVPi) was selected after review of many different companies. Finally to honor Freud's 150th Birthday in May 2006, the new internet interface was available and included the Freud Standard Edition for free searching for anyone from anywhere in the world. The PEP Web Literature Search allowed a free search option of Archive and current content, a robust authentication system to protect copyright and facilitate subscriptions for the participating journals, and an open URL linking and other features to make it more attractive.

Each year PEP would add new content, but also new and improved features. Paul was especially interested in having features that would be user-friendly and work on small devices. He worked with Neil and GVPi to create the PEP Easy phone application that let PEP go anywhere on a mobile phone or tablet. A further contribution by Paul included the suggestion for PEP to develop the capacity to add bibliographic information and links for offsite publications not in the journals in the PEP Archive.

Concerned with PEP Board succession, Paul Mosher, in 2014, wrote the PEP Board Advisory Committee (BAC) proposal, further demonstrating his legal and writing skills. The BAC objective is to enable those serving on the Advisory Committee to learn about PEP and to be involved in special projects as they arise, so that they may decide if a more formal appointment as PEP Director is appropriate. Board members leaving the Board were invited to participate in the Advisory Committee if they wished. Having such a committee helped ease the inevitability of succession of current PEP Directors.

Each year, our General Annual Meetings rotate between the US and London. Most of the spouses attend (at the Board Members' expense). To keep costs down, some years we would meet consecutively in New York. At a very special meeting, belatedly celebrating PEP's 20-year Anniversary, the Board meeting was held in London during the renowned Wimbledon Championship. David Tuckett, a member of Wimbledon, secured tickets to one of the matches, as well as entry to the special Wimbledon Members' Friday evening cocktail party attended by royalty and previous Wimbledon champions. Both Paul and Paula loved being at Wimbledon. The PEP Board worked hard at our annual weekend Board Meetings, but cherished the evening dinners, where we all could relax and enjoy our spouses and each other's company.

Paul was by nature a cautious man. He often played the role of placing a stop on plans for change he considered too risky and potentially threatening to the program he was so pivotal in creating. In that caution there was often remarkable prescience. For example, he insisted that PEP should have reserves to deal with both the known and unknown. So, when Global Village Publishing (GVPi), the company that hosted PEP-Web, gave three-year notice that they were withdrawing as our developer and host (as of April 2021), PEP had the reserves to undertake a massive transposition onto a new platform and search engine. With support from Neil Shapiro, David Tuckett, and many others, PEP was able to make the transition in fall 2021, with a few glitches, but without incurring the kind of major financial penalty that unexpected radical changes can impose on small companies.

Paul was a man with strong views, which he would maintain despite opposition. This was core to his character and his massive achievements.

Paul was, at times, a challenge to PEP, but most generally a pleasure to work with. Above all he valued being a part of the PEP Team, which now includes Peter Fonagy, David Tuckett (CEO), Nasir Ilahi, Liz Allison, Andrew Gerber, Garrick Duckler and Nadine Levinson. Each of the PEP Directors with their own individual contributions has made PEP an extraordinary and creative psychoanalytic resource.

But another of Paul's more thoughtful contribution to PEP was to remind the PEP Board always to be sensitive and communicative about its charitable activities to the Member/Sponsor organizations and the PEP users. Many do not realize that the money PEP makes through subscriptions is used for website development and new content, for royalty paid to the Journals and Books, to support authors with Author Prizes, and to donate considerable sums to the Member/Supporting organizations for use with their own psychoanalytic programs.

Having our psychoanalytic Journals electronically digitized—Paul's original idea—is what will preserve and protect psychoanalysis and our literature and scholarship for future generations. PEP will continue to advance psychoanalytic scholarship and our psychoanalytic literature and its authors. For the implementation of these goals over many years, PEP received the 2019 Sigourney Award to the delight of all PEP Board Members. However, many of us feel Paul also should have received a solo award for all his other mammoth contributions to psychoanalysis.

Paul Mosher retired from the PEP Board in 2019, as a part of the Succession Plan rhat he designed with other members of the Board. He insisted that PEP have director rotations at different terms. It was strange having PEP meetings without Paul's unmistakable voice— sometimes of caution, sometimes of passion, but always of pragmatism and rationality influencing the many Board debates. Everyone recognized the massive contribution Paul made to PEP and through PEP to global psychoanalysis. The old and new directors held Paul in very special esteem. We knew and know that without Paul's vision and visionary insights into the world of electronic publishing we would not be here today. Paul Mosher, the founding PEP Director stayed involved with PEP until his death. During his last year, after leaving the Board, he served as a member of, and consultant to, the PEP Advisory Committee. We've noted that Paul's history and influence on PEP dates back many years, even before PEP and his role as Director. Paul, the true computer techie, and his ideas remain a pivotal force on the creation and development of PEP.

Acknowledgements

This book fulfills both its original mandate to honor the life of Paul Mosher, our esteemed colleague and friend, and also to recognize and include, in extenso, the history-making documents he created alone or with others. It provides access to unknown private writing as well as early relevant material. We owe our thanks to the Mosher family, who scoured files and provided photographs, and withheld nothing. Our varied contributors responded on deadline and expanded our reach and understanding by including personal memories and documents that elevate this volume into a repository accessible for further historical review. Ralph Fishkin steadfastly provided scrupulous care for details, the perspective of an intimate friend and colleague and both unflagging energy and a generous spirit, enabling the creation of a more readable volume. Jeffrey Berman provided his knowledge of book editing and production when we took our first steps into this project.

Throughout it all, supported by Arnold Richards and IPBooks, Tamar and Lawrence Schwartz dealt with my gaffes and lapses and fulfilled their promise, through Noel S. Morado, who patiently dealt with more changes than anticipated, while producing a document we could recognize as a book; one we learned on as we leaned on the professionals. Our cover designer, Kathy Kovacic, has mysteriously done her work by providing simple choices for the cover thus limiting our participation but not our appreciation.

Judith S. Schachter
June 12, 2022

www.ingramcontent.com/pod-product-compliance
Lightning Source LLC
Chambersburg PA
CBHW071036050426
42335CB00050B/1799